CW00467901

Peacemaker

Peacemaker

The life and work of Eric Gallagher

Dennis Cooke

Methodist
Publishing House

All rights reserved. No part of this publication may be reproduced, stored in a retrieval system, or transmitted, in any form or by any means, electronic, mechanical, photocopying or otherwise, without the prior permission of the publisher, Methodist Publishing House.

Copyright © Dennis Cooke 2005

British Library Cataloguing in Publication data

A catalogue record for this book is available from the British Library

ISBN 1 85852 263 3

First published by Methodist Publishing House
4 John Wesley Road
Werrington
Peterborough PE4 6ZP

Printed and bound in Great Britain by
Stanley L Hunt (Printers) Ltd, Rushden, Northants

Dedication

This book is dedicated to those working
to achieve peace throughout the world

Foreword

I feel honoured to have been asked to write a foreword to Dr Dennis Cooke's book, *Peacemaker*, being a biography of Dr Eric Gallagher. Eric was a man of God and a man of peace, a courageous worker for peace, at a time when all around in Northern Ireland – to use the words of W.B. Yeats – things were falling apart, the moderate centre seemed powerless, the blood-dimmed tide was loosed and the 'men of passionate intensity' on both sides of our religious and political divide were bringing us close to anarchy.

This book about the life and work of Eric Gallagher could, with equal appropriateness, be called a history of the Northern Ireland conflict, a study of inter-church relations in Ireland in the last half-century, a study of conflict-resolution and of reconciliation between divided communities, or a review of Methodist Church life and mission in Ireland in the last 50 years. This in itself is a testimony to the leading role which Eric Gallagher played in all of these aspects of life in Church and in society in his time.

Its publication is timely, coming as it does at a time when news bulletins have been dominated by peace talks between the two political parties which are at the extreme and opposite ends of the political spectrum in Northern Ireland. Whatever the outcome, Eric Gallagher's name will be inseparable from the search for peace. I believe that even more important to Eric would have been the title of Christian pastor and Methodist preacher.

Both because of his personality and because of his Christian faith, Eric was a friend whom one could trust; he was open, sincere and honest, he was one who spoke the truth as he saw it, but spoke it always in love. He was clear-eyed and straight-spoken, yet never spoke so as to wound. His assessment, for example, of Dr Ian K. Paisley, is a good example of his desire to be both realistic and lucid and fair.

I visited him in hospital not long before his death. Before leaving, I asked to read with him a passage from the Bible. I chose the concluding paragraphs of Romans 8. When I finished the reading with the words: 'Nothing can ever come between us and the love of God made visible in Christ Jesus our Lord', Eric remarked that this had always been his favourite Scripture passage. The words are the heart of all that Eric Gallagher lived for and worked for, all that he was and all that he did. May this book make his name better known and his witness and work for Christ and for peace more widely appreciated.

Cardinal Cahal B. Daly
Former Archbishop of Armagh

Acknowledgements

In the early 1990s I shared with Eric Gallagher my interest in writing his biography. However, at the time he was neither positive nor negative in his response. Then, when Eric fell seriously ill in May 1996, he asked me to visit him at the Lagan Valley Hospital and in our conversation together he said he would like me to write his biography.

It has been a great privilege to write the life of such a significant church leader. I have had access to all his documents: Autobiographical Notes, Jottings, Papers and Speeches, Prayer Notes, Poems, Sermons and, of course, his own publications. It is his extensive Autobiographical Notes which prompt me to suggest that he may have intended to follow his father's example and write his own autobiography. They certainly proved a very valuable resource and I have made frequent use of his comments recorded in these Notes.

The Gallagher family have been most helpful in the task of writing this biography. I thank them for all their support. Joan, my wife, read the script and made many useful suggestions. George Orr, one of the editors of the *Methodist Newsletter*, also read the text as it was being written and made many valuable suggestions to improve its presentation. I am indebted to both Joan and George.

The support of the Belfast Central Mission has been a key factor in this project. The Revd Donald Ker, Superintendent of the Mission, and his predecessor, the Revd David Kerr, made the necessary arrangements with the Methodist Publishing House which ensured the publication of this book. Indeed, BCM subsidised the print costs with a generous donation. My thanks also to Dr Natalie Watson, Commissioning Editor at Methodist Publishing House, and her predecessor, the Revd Gerald Burt, for their encouragement and guidance.

It is my hope that telling the story of Eric's life will be an inspiration to the generations which follow him.

Scripture Quotations are from the New Revised Standard Version of the Bible, (Anglicized Edition) © 1989, 1995 by the Division of Christian Education of the National Council of the Churches of Christ in the United States of America. Used by permission. All rights reserved.

Contents

1

Glimpses

Christ be with me, Christ within me,
Christ behind me, Christ before me,
Christ beside me, Christ to win me,
Christ to comfort and restore me,
Christ beneath me, Christ above me,
Christ in quiet, Christ in danger,
Christ in hearts of all that love me,
Christ in mouth of friend and stranger.

St Patrick's Breastplate

Eric Gallagher was essentially a practical man but his practicality was influenced and shaped by his hopes and dreams. While he saw his life as one of 'responses' to various circumstances and situations, or more specifically requests from others, the nature of his responses was inspired by his hopes and dreams, and these in turn by his Christian faith. In 'The Ulster I want to see', reminiscent of Martin Luther King's 'I Have a Dream' speech before the Lincoln Memorial in Washington on 28 August 1963, Eric outlined the hopes that he had for his native country:

> I want to see an Ulster to which all of us are proud to belong, an Ulster where you know and are happy I belong and I know and am happy you belong, an Ulster where we belong together. We may not see eye to eye or think in everything alike. Catholics were born here. Protestants were born here. This is our own native land and whether we like it or not we both belong.
>
> I want to see an Ulster where the word 'justice' means what it says and more than it seems to say, where it means more than the law-courts, where it means that everybody – no matter what his creed or race – has a fair chance and a good chance of work, of housing, promotion, community service, of everything that goes to

make the good life. I want to see an Ulster where Derry Protestants and Belfast Catholics will feel a common pride of belonging to the finest country in the world.

I want to see an Ulster throbbing with new industries in every county, an Ulster where every section will work together for the common good, where community development and co-operation will be the order of the day, where Protestants and Catholics West of the Bann, Catholics and Protestants in West Belfast, will join together in their efforts to bring a new sense of self-respect and purpose to their respective areas. I want to see an Ulster which has regained its confidence and self-respect.

I want to see an Ulster where Protestantism and Catholicism will spell out the economic and political implications of the Christian faith: where double-talk will disappear and everyone will have the courage to call a spade a spade, where we live out the logical consequences of the faith we possess and the gospel we preach. I want an Ulster where I can see before my eyes the outworking in the community of all that Old Testament righteousness and New Testament love imply.

I want to see an Ulster where Protestants and Catholics are prepared to talk about their political differences – an Ulster where everyone will recognize everybody else's right to his own political beliefs. I want still more to see an Ulster where political differences and emphases are based no longer on religious issues, where politics are 'for real' and where they deal with basic economic and political issues. I want to see an Ulster that is politically forward looking, where people are planning and working constantly for the future. The day should have long since passed of the political dinosaurs who want to burn Lundy or to resurrect McCracken. Their proper place is the political history museum.

I want to see an Ulster rid for ever of the bomber and the gunman, an Ulster where no one is afraid to allow the democratic processes to run their course. I want an Ulster where violence – physical and verbal – doesn't need to be outlawed simply because they are unknown – an Ulster where the obscenities about the Pope and the Police, and the rabble-rousing slogans have been defaced for ever from the gable walls.

I want to see an Ulster where boys and girls can grow up free from sectarian strife and bitterness, where they can understand something of each other's culture and background ....

I want to see an Ulster from which ghetto-housing and ghetto-thinking have disappeared ....

I want to see an Ulster that is worth working for. An Ulster like that would make us proud to be its citizens. It makes a vision infinitely more inspiring than all the nostalgic pictures put together of Catholic and Protestant folk-heroes of the past. That kind of Ulster is possible. It's possible if you and I – and others like us – are prepared to pray and pay for it. With that kind of Ulster the future can take care of itself.[1]

Eric had a world vision. His concern was not limited to the future of one of the four provinces of Ireland. He travelled widely, attended conferences and gave lectures in various parts of the world. But the issues that absorbed most of his attention were related to the community tensions and divisions in Northern Ireland. The Irish problem was known throughout the world and he was conscious not only of the suffering it was inflicting on the local population but also the damage it was causing to people's understanding of Christianity. 'The Ulster I want to see' summarizes this major concern of his life. He wanted to see justice established in Ireland, he wanted to see an end to the legacy of hatred which had characterized community relations in the country, and he wanted to see it replaced by a spirit of love and forgiveness.

This book examines how this awareness and vision developed. It looks at the influences which first alerted him to the problem of sectarianism in Ireland. It considers how this vision influenced his ministry and the various offices and responsibilities which he held in the Church.

People responded to his ministry in various ways. In the different Churches there were many who appreciated and valued his ministry, but there were exceptions, notably Free Presbyterianism. In March 1967 – when he was President-Designate of the Methodist Church in Ireland – he headed Ian Paisley's 'Black List', a list of Protestant clergymen who, he alleged, were guilty of apostasy. Paisley apart, in the wider community, Catholic and Protestant, Nationalist and Unionist, there were many who valued his stand against sectarianism. They may not have agreed with all of his opinions but they were convinced of his genuineness and knew that he was a tireless worker for a better and more just society for all. Sandy Scott, Chairman of the Steelworkers' Shop Stewards at Harland & Wolff shipyard in Belfast, is unstinting in his praise for Eric's contribution at a mass meeting of shipyard workers called in August 1969 in an effort to avert an outbreak of sectarian strife at the yard: 'We were very grateful to Eric and his contribution was very significant. Indeed, I am quite sure to a large extent we owe the success of the venture that we took on that particular day to the sterling work that Eric had done and the way that he identified himself with all that we stood for.'[2]

Many other tributes could be quoted, but a few will suffice at this introductory stage. Michael Hurley, S.J., founder of the Irish School of Ecumenics and the Columbanus Community, has highlighted Eric's contribution as a peacemaker: 'In my view, no one, this past century, in Church circles at least, did more to promote the cause of peace and reconciliation in Ireland.'[3] Cardinal Cahal Daly, Roman Catholic Primate in Armagh, 1988-96, who shared with Eric in many inter-church ventures, suggests: 'I believe that he was one of the great thinkers, one of the great church leaders in Ireland in his time. I think he more than anyone else transformed relations between his own Communion and the Roman Catholic Communion.'[4] Daly's statement is borne out by a confession from Kenneth Wilson, a recent President of the Methodist

Church in Ireland. Referring to his time in theological college when he was dubious of anything ecumenical, he acknowledges: 'Truth to tell, out of ignorance, I saw it as a threat to the truth of the gospel. As Eric was one of the leaders in the ecumenical world, I tended to regard him with suspicion. Why was he wasting his time cavorting with the enemy? Let him preach the gospel and lead souls to Christ. Of course he saw, clearer than many of us, that sectarianism and prejudice were the big sins of our land. Years later I confessed these things to him and thanked him for the true prophetic leadership he had given to the church. He laughed and said that we all have to mature sooner or later!'[5]

Politicians also were influenced by him, possibly by their meetings with him, their knowledge of his public statements, or through the letters which he frequently wrote to them. Lord Gerry Fitt, one of the founders of the Social Democratic and Labour Party in Northern Ireland in 1970, said of him: 'He stood out as a beacon of sense, tolerance and fairness among others whose hatred and bigotry they frequently did not even bother to conceal.'[6] Paddy Devlin, another former nationalist MP who served with Fitt in the ill-fated Power-Sharing Executive at Stormont in 1974, and one who described himself as a non-believer, commented: 'You could say I was spellbound at first sight by this Methodist hero. After that I must now confess to dropping his name whenever possible. People had to know I was important because I knew Eric Gallagher.'[7] On the Unionist side there was also recognition of his contribution. Lord James Molyneaux, leader of the Ulster Unionist Party for 16 years, 1979-95, is convinced that Eric's contribution was such that it must be seen as formative and distinctive in the history of the Northern province: 'When historians look back at the twentieth century they will certainly include Dr Eric Gallagher in the ranks of the few who made a distinctive and indelible imprint on the public life of Ulster.'[8]

Eric Gallagher drew inspiration from the love and support of a strong family circle. The home from which he came and the home which he and his wife Barbara created, each in their turn were firm bases from which he developed and exercised his ministry. How important a role these havens of understanding were and the sacrifices which Barbara and his children made in supporting him will probably never be fully known, but they should not be overlooked. In addition to the gifts and talents he possessed, readers may come to the conclusion that it was the influence of his home life more than anything else which enabled him to be the man he was and to work towards the fulfilment of the dreams which inspired him.

2

The early years

God takes a han' wherever He can find it
An' jist does what he likes wi'it.
Sometimes He takes a bishop's an',
Lays it on a child's head in benediction,
Then He takes the han' of a doctor t'relieve pain,
The han' of a mother to guide her child,
An' sometimes He takes the han' of a mild craither like me
to give a bit of comfort to a neighbour.
But they're all hands touch't by His Spirit,
An' His Spirit is everywhere lukin' fur han's to use.

Alexander Irvine, *My Lady of the Chimney Corner*

Ireland was in a state of high tension in 1913, the year Eric Gallagher was born. The near certainty that the Westminster Parliament was finally going to grant Home Rule to Ireland aroused opposition from almost the entire Unionist population of the country who feared it would lead to an increasing and dominant role for the Roman Catholic Church. 'Home Rule is Rome Rule' was the slogan which succinctly expressed the view of many Protestants and Unionists. Under the leadership of Sir Edward Carson, Solicitor-General in Arthur Balfour's Conservative administration in the first decade of the century, a provisional Ulster government had been set up, a volunteer army organized, and a series of large demonstrations held throughout the north, culminating at the City Hall, Belfast, on 28 September 1912, with the signing of the Ulster Covenant. Based on the seventeenth-century Scottish 'Solemn League and Covenant', it pledged the signatories 'to stand by one another in defending for ourselves and our children our cherished position of equal citizenship in the United Kingdom and in using all means which may be found necessary to defeat the present conspiracy to set up a Home Rule Parliament in Ireland'. Protestant Church leaders were committed to this course of action, as was illustrated by their signing of the Covenant immediately after the first two signatories, Edward Carson and Lord Londonderry. At various centres throughout the north 218,206 men signed the Covenant and 228,991 women signed a similar 'Ulster Women's Declaration'.

Up to this moment Unionists had pursued constitutional means of opposing Home Rule, a measure first proposed in 1886 by the Liberal Prime Minister, William Gladstone. Now they were openly declaring their willingness to resort to military measures if this was what was required to maintain the Union of the two islands. The use of physical force had a long tradition in Irish history and it was not surprising that Nationalist and Republican opinion in Ireland soon responded to the Unionist threat by the formation of the Irish Volunteers, which by June 1914 numbered around 130,000. Ireland was rapidly becoming an armed camp, but the outbreak of war in Europe on 4 August the same year effectively put 'on hold' the implementation of Home Rule which had secured final approval from the House of Commons on 25 May.

The home in Ballybay, County Monaghan, into which Eric was born on 24 August 1913 was not unaffected by this political turmoil. Robert Gallagher had been ordained at the Irish Methodist Conference in June 1912 and was married two months later to Helen McIlroy, a teacher seven years his junior. In his autobiography he writes that his bride 'was said to be one of the loveliest girls in the North of Ireland. I knew her to be one of the best'.[1]

Robert – 'RH' as he was sometimes known – appears to have had the friendliest of relationships with circuit officials throughout his ministry but that was not true of his first appointment as a married minister. Eric explained: 'There was difficulty with the circuit steward over the Home Rule Bill and they had to move in 1914. His refusal to sign the Ulster Covenant did not endear my father to those who thought differently.'[2]

Both parents came from a farming background. Robert's ancestry can be traced back to his great-grandfather, William Gallagher, who farmed at Syloran, near Moy, County Tyrone.

The McIlroys' known family history goes back further than the Gallaghers', indeed to Patrick McIlroy who was born about 1675. Records indicate that in 1710 he bought 112 acres of land in Tenpenroe, situated near Laghey Corner on the road from Dungannon to Portadown. Later the McIlroys moved a couple of miles to Moyroe, Killyman, where Helen was brought up.

Robert Gallagher always retained a sense of pride in the fact that he had worked on the farm when two of his older brothers had left to pursue careers in business. He claims he was regarded as 'a type of "cattle doctor", diagnosing their diseases and administering cures'.[3] On one occasion his grandmother had lost her spectacles and a careful search for them was unsuccessful. Later in a field where she had been walking, a cow was seen to be choking. 'Putting my hand down her throat', RH relates, 'I brought up the frame of my grandmother's glasses.' On another occasion he went to the help of a farmer who was being charged and tossed by an enraged bull: 'The bull tossed him, fortunately, in the direction of the fence where I got hold of him and dragged him to safety.' But the best story is of an encounter with a bull in the dark of the night:

> I was walking on a path that led across the fields to my home when in the darkness I heard a measured footstep meeting me. On its near approach I saw my danger. To turn and run was hopeless, so with an unearthly yell I charged the beast. He turned and fled, and which of us was the more frightened would be difficult to say.[4]

Both families had strong Methodist roots. The Gallaghers had been linked to the Primitive Wesleyan Methodists prior to the union of the Primitive Wesleyans and the Wesleyan Methodists in 1878.[5] During Robert's childhood they were members of Moy Methodist Church, part of the Charlemont Circuit.[6] A short distance away the McIlroys were members of Laghey Methodist Church, one of the churches on the Dungannon Circuit.

Eric was the eldest of five children: Evelyn was born in 1914, Herbert in 1917, Mabel in 1919 and Helen in 1924. Each of them speaks affectionately of their parents and of the happy atmosphere that existed in the home. Eric himself wrote: 'By any standards this was a successful marriage. More importantly it was a happy marriage even if the strains and stresses of circuit life and the ever-present struggle to make ends meet put inevitable pressures on it.' Family life appears to have been fairly structured and regulated but nevertheless very happy: they were all together at breakfast which was followed every morning by prayers, all kneeling by their chairs; and then they were off to school. Evelyn comments: 'It was a well disciplined household with my father very much in charge.'[7] Eric reflected on this aspect of discipline: 'Our childhood years were still dominated by the "spare the rod and spoil the child" philosophy', but he adds that his mother's wooden spoon and his father's belt were displayed more as threat than in practice. However, the father's strong personality did not overshadow the vital role played by their mother. Mabel affirms this clearly: 'My mother was the keypin as most mothers are, and she had a very gracious calming influence. My father was sterner, mother was softer.'[8]

Methodist ministers at this time were generally 'stationed' by the Conference to a different circuit every three years. This meant frequent changes of home for the family. In the first 20 years of Eric's life his father served on seven circuits: Ballybay, Portadown, Lurgan, Londonderry, Portadown (second term), Ballymacarrett (in East Belfast), and Ormeau Road (in South Belfast). 'RH' viewed his ministry as one which demanded his time right through the day: in the mornings he would generally be in his study, the afternoons he spent visiting, and he had meetings in the evenings. This was a demanding routine but he seemed to thrive on it, and possibly the improvements and growth he witnessed on the various circuits on which he served confirmed for him the lifestyle he had chosen. Herbert refers to the positive and optimistic approach his father took to circuit work and, indeed, every aspect of his life. 'Talk everything up, talk everything up', his father advised and practised. Consequently, anyone speaking with 'RH' got the impression that 'every circuit in which he travelled was the best circuit in Irish Methodism!'[9] The Ballymacarrett Circuit was said to be in poor condition when he went there in the late 1920s, but

Ballymacarrett also became 'the best circuit in Irish Methodism'.

This very positive attitude to church work and life in general must have had its beneficial effect on members of the family. Much was expected of them but it was expected within an atmosphere of positive encouragement. However, the father's optimistic approach is particularly significant in light of the almost constant turmoil which typified life in Ireland throughout this period. The period 1919-21 was particularly troublesome. Following the 1916 Easter Rising in Dublin and the subsequent execution of 15 of its leaders, which turned them instantly into 'martyrs' and provided an impetus to the republican movement, Sinn Fein became the most popular political party in the country. Events soon deteriorated and by 1920 full-scale guerrilla warfare had spread throughout the south and soon engulfed the northern counties. This was the period sometimes known by historians as the 'Anglo-Irish war' but more commonly known in Irish folklore as 'The Troubles'. J.C. Beckett has succinctly explained the tragic nature of the brutality that characterized this war:

> The struggle was not so much between two governments or two peoples as between two largely irresponsible armed forces. The British government found the greatest difficulty in exercising effective control over the auxiliary police and the 'Black-and-Tans' [a special force enlisted from among British ex-servicemen] on whom the bulk of the fighting fell, and the Dail [Eireann] had little choice but to leave 'The Irish Republican Army' to carry out operations in its own way and on its own responsibility.[10]

These were the conditions in which partition of the island took place, an option always preferred by Unionists should they fail in their opposition to Home Rule. In 1920 the Westminster Parliament passed the Government of Ireland Act, which provided for two Irish parliaments, one in the north and one in the south, and for a Council of Ireland to link them. While partition was unacceptable to Sinn Fein, after a period of difficult and protracted negotiations both sides eventually agreed to the treaty of December 1921, setting up an Irish Free State with dominion status and recognising the right of the six northern counties to opt out. In such conditions the Northern Ireland state was born, separate from the south, but always by law subservient to the Westminster Parliament.

'RH's ministry in a society inflamed by these ancient sectarian hatreds is significant, particularly his time in Lurgan, 1917-21, his first period as Superintendent. In 1920 tensions were running high in the town. In nearby Lisburn a District Inspector had been shot dead when leaving church and in retaliation houses not flying a Union Jack had been reduced to ashes. In these circumstances the Town Clerk of Lurgan called a public meeting in an effort to prevent the violence spreading. From the floor of the hall 'RH' supported the resolution which called on all sections of the community to avoid party expressions and to restrain any who might be intolerant. It was passed 'almost unanimously'. He writes: 'I was the only clergyman who attended the meeting and I have reason to believe that my presence and words helped to restrain tempers that might otherwise have become ungovernable.'[11]

The move from Lurgan to Londonderry in 1921 was particularly eventful. Due to the troubled state of the country all appointments had already been postponed for a year. Two brothers, W.J. and Edward Hylands, had undertaken to transport the Gallagher household possessions, including a piano, on a Model T Ford one-ton truck, basically a milk float, for a fee of £10. Though leaving Lurgan at five in the morning, they had only got as far as Killyman when a rear tyre burst. Edward walked into Dungannon and borrowed two solid-tyre rear wheels off a similar truck owned by a Mr Moore who was a Roman Catholic. They wheeled the tyres out to Killyman, fitted them, and the brothers proceeded on their journey. Jack Gilpin, our storyteller, continues:

> Somewhere about Sixmilecross they overtook five men on the road, four had bicycles and one was on foot. They asked for directions and the man walking volunteered to show them in exchange for a lift. As it

turned out it was a good exchange because some distance further on he advised them to take it easy when going down the hill, as round the corner a trench had been cut across the road. The trench was crossed by some means or other and the journey was resumed to Londonderry, arriving there at nine in the evening, sixteen hours after leaving Lurgan!

A wealthy gentleman had men standing by to unload the lorry and he took the Hyland brothers to a hotel for some food, but being so hungry they couldn't eat, so they started out for home.

They drove all night, sometimes without lights for fear of being mistaken for the Army or the Black and Tans. They were stopped twenty-one times by the security forces on the way home.

Gilpin concludes the story with a postcript that the Hyland brothers had to travel to Belfast to purchase a new tyre, ending up with a net loss of £2 on their contract![12]

'RH' was ably supported in church work by his wife. Mabel comments, 'Mother was a second minister in whatever circuit they were on. She did a lot of visiting and entertaining. The manse was always open.' Eric was very conscious of the fact that both parents were deeply involved in church work: 'Everywhere my parents served it was the same story: hard work, good order, meticulous administration of church discipline, a teaching ministry, leaving circuits healthier than they found them and, above all, the quite remarkably generous hospitality and graciousness of my greatly loved mother.' Members from the circuits on which they served confirm this analysis. Both parents were greatly appreciated by their congregations. But Robert was not only a hard worker and an able administrator, he was also regarded as a good preacher. It must have been in recognition of these various gifts that he was elected President of the Methodist Church in Ireland for the year 1946-47, an office he held while he was Superintendent of the Ballynafeigh (Belfast) circuit, 1945-50, the final circuit on which he served before his retirement. However, even in retirement he could not remain idle! He served for a period in the Falls Road and Ligoniel circuits, situated in West and North Belfast. He also used the time to indulge in his passion for Methodist church history, writing four books. After recording his own ministerial experiences in *My Web of Time*, he turned his attention to those he regarded as his heroes in the earlier days of Irish Methodism: *John Bredin*, *Adam Clarke* and *Pioneer Preachers of Irish Methodism*.[13]

Both parents kept a careful watch on the family finances. Apparently their mother had at some stage received a gift of a small number of Midland Bank shares from her father. They produced just about enough half-yearly dividend to buy a couple of articles of clothing for two of the most needy children. 'RH's main treasure was a golden sovereign given him by his mother when he had left home. On one occasion when financial pressures were particularly acute, Eric was sent to a nearby shop in Derry to have it changed: 'The shopkeeper clearly suspected why my father was parting with it and he said to me "Tell your father I will keep this for him until he has the money to get it back."'

On Monday mornings 'RH' generally played golf with some of his ministerial colleagues, including Dr William Northridge, then Senior Tutor in Edgehill Theological College, Belfast, the training college for Methodist ministers in Ireland. Family holidays were generally spent close to a golf course, which was possibly the reason why Portstewart was frequently chosen. The father played golf with both Eric and Herbert, but Eric seemed the only one who could occasionally beat him! The sons cherished these moments because, apart from holidays, their father was working and had no time to play cricket or football with them.

Christmas was always a happy time for the Gallagher family, not least due to the fact that the generosity of parishioners ensured that they had plenty to eat. They received various gifts: turkeys, geese, a shoulder of ham and other edible items. One Christmas in particular was etched in Eric's memory:

One year there was a gift of a couple of live poultry, what sex I don't know, though they were always spoken of as being on the male side. Anyway they came full of life with their legs tied together but with their wings intact. They were put into the pantry to await the time of their demise. In the meantime they were an attraction for small children. I made a routine call to see them once too often. They clearly had become tired of visitors. My approach was resented and with a croak and several flaps of its wings one of them soon had me retreating in considerable apprehension. That episode remained family folklore longer than I liked.

Parents ensured that letters to Santa Claus included suitably modest requests as 'Santa could not be expected to carry over-weighty burdens'. By six o'clock on Christmas morning they discovered the suggested gifts, and even more: 'The stocking was filled – he always contrived to make the most of a large orange and a large apple which seemed to fill the foot and push a bit up the leg of the stocking. Then there was always a largish net Christmas stocking as well with all sorts of trivia, a whistle, a balloon, a puzzle game, and at the top of the pile a small bag of sherbet to be sucked out through a liquorice tube. That was the very stuff of Christmas at its best.' At the foot of the bed they would find the present from their parents – a book or a toy and some item of clothing that was considered necessary.

Robert Gallagher always had an early Christmas morning service, so that the family could quickly depart for the train which would bring them to Trew and Moy station where two waiting ponies and traps, one from each sets of grandparents, would be waiting for them. Eventually the whole family circle would gather for Christmas dinner at Grange House, the house on the Gallagher farm, a little distance from the original family home at Syloran. Finally, after various games and entertainment, it was back to the traps, the station, and home. What an eventful day for young children!

Eric's early education began when the family was living in Lurgan. He attended a private school run by two sisters, the

Misses Fraser, one of whom was on his pastoral list years later when he was minister of University Road Church in Belfast. He is uncertain regarding the quality of the teaching which he received at this very early stage, because when the family moved to Derry in 1921 he was placed in 4th class where he found the work very difficult:

> In my first week the class teacher wrote on the blackboard 'Write a composition on a bicycle'. I duly wrote the words 'Write a composition on a bicycle' in my exercise book. I sat back troubled and mystified. I had never heard of a composition and I certainly knew absolutely nothing about how to write one. I would read and read intelligently but handwriting, sums and the mysteries of composition were not in my repertoire. I was well into Standard Five before I began to feel at home.

The time in Londonderry had a significant influence on Eric's growth in Christian faith. He and his mother attended a mission conducted by the evangelist, W.P. Nicholson, who was becoming known for his rather unusual methods of plain speaking which some regarded as verging on the uncouth at times. He was frequently critical of ministers and anyone he considered unorthodox in the faith. Nicholson's missions had been successful in the great number of people confessing conversion and also, it is suggested, in the dramatic change for the better in the way they lived. At one of these meetings, which Eric attended with his mother, the invitation to commitment was given and Eric's hand went up in response to a nudge from his mother. However, he notes, he felt no different the next morning. At some stage during this mission Nicholson was given hospitality in the manse and then later attacked 'RH' and Methodism in particular for using the book *What a Christian Believes and Why*, regarded by the evangelist as certainly heretical. Much more significant was Eric's experience as a member of the preparation class for membership led by his father. In retrospect, Eric wondered at his inclusion in the class as he was still quite young but his father evidently did not think so and was proved correct, because it was here that his son 'learned the reasonableness of the faith and developed a pride in Methodism'.

When the family moved to Portadown in 1924, Thomas Street School was just around the corner from the manse. After Christmas Eric was ill and missed school for some months. But there was a bonus: 'I was packed off every good day to the golf course where I quickly learned to love the game.' This relaxation had been suggested by Dr Hadden, the family doctor, but it also reflects an enlightened parental attitude!

Three months away from school during the previous year was not the best preparation for the scholarship exam for Methodist College, Belfast, which his parents had decided he should take at the end of August 1925. Despite this handicap he secured one of the two 'McArthur' scholarships available, although he modestly adds, 'I have no idea as to whether there were two, or more than two, entrants for that scholarship.'

'Methody', as the college is familiarly known, located on the Malone Road near Queen's University, had been opened in 1868 by the Methodist Church in Ireland with the two-fold purpose of educating the children of Methodist ministers and others, and training students for the Methodist ministry. At the beginning, and for some 50 years, the Principal of the Theological Department was the President of the College, and the Headmaster of the Educational Department was responsible to the Committee of Management through the President. This had been the situation when Eric's father had been a ministerial student, 1905-8, but it was a recipe for disaster as the administration of the school very much depended on good personal relations and communication between the Principal/President and the Headmaster, something which was not always guaranteed! However, in 1919 a new location for the Theological Department had been found nearby at Lennoxvale, and a happier situation existed when Eric started at the school in September 1925.

Because of the itinerant nature of the Methodist ministry the children of ministers were frequently sent to Methody as boarders. This was the situation for Eric and later on for his younger brother and sisters. He experienced considerable homesickness in his first year but then things seemed to improve. Reflecting retrospectively on his experience, he wrote, 'I have no regrets whatever at having been a boarder although I have always been thankful that my own children, when their time came, were day pupils. The first year was, I suppose, the hardest though by no means intolerable.'

For the first two years of boarding Eric was in Junior House, at that time under the supervision of Clarence Bailey, a Cambridge graduate who taught both chemistry and botany. Bailey apparently had high fitness expectations for his young recruits whom he wakened about 6.45 in the morning, had them change into their gym togs, sent them for a run around the neighbourhood, and then recommended a cold shower before breakfast! But Bailey had also a pastoral heart: 'He made a point of visiting the homes of the boys who did not live too far away. If the parents invited him for the weekend, he was the better pleased. A strange man in many ways but one who cared not only for his boys but also for the property.'

Before leaving home Eric had been worried how he would fare reading his Bible and saying his prayers in an open dormitory, the circumstances he would have found in his first few years at school. Fortunately, there were others of like mind who had started boarding at the same time and he was never conscious of any difficulty. In addition, he and his friends attended a weekly meeting run by some of the seniors, boys who were greatly respected in their own right. However, his growth in the Christian life was not always easy: 'As boyhood gave way to adolescence there were all sorts of questions and doubts to wrestle with. I kept them to myself and was amazed years later to find that there were others in the same dormitory wrestling for their faith.' He received help in various ways. Boarders were required to attend both morning and evening services at the nearby University Road Church and he found inspiration and reassurance in the preaching of its minister, the Revd Frederick E. Harte. Another who helped him was the Revd R. Ernest Ker, one of the tutors at the Edgehill Theological College, who was 'assistant chaplain' because there was no resident chaplain. Ernest Ker recruited three or four of the seniors to take Sunday school classes, and provided them with teaching notes for every lesson over the two years, 1930-32: 'They were a model of clarity: every week the aim and context were set out with precision. Difficulties, whether intellectual or textual, were faced and I learned and grew in the faith.'

In 1917 John W. Henderson had been appointed Headmaster. By all accounts he was quite a remarkable man, a good scholar and a successful educator who regarded education as 'essentially the art of encouragement'.[14] A brilliant student career in Glasgow University and success as a schoolmaster led to his appointment as Rector of Rothesay Academy in 1906, where he remained until taking up his post in Belfast. Eric had a high regard for his achievements:

> In many ways he was a kind of educational entrepreneur, full of new ideas – some of these ahead of his time – and he was ready to put them into practice. He created a kind of comprehensive system of education in the College, engineering and woodwork shops, a commercial section and a small agricultural experiment based on the farm at Quilly, Dromore, which he persuaded the Governors to acquire. Growing numbers required additional staff and this enabled him to recruit through a professional agency a generation of young ambitious and able teachers not only from the Irish universities but also from Great Britain, Oxford and Cambridge included.

Henderson's quite revolutionary ideas had their own particular significance for Eric! At one stage he had the dilemma of making a curriculum choice between Greek and other Arts' subjects or engineering, woodwork and science: 'I chose engineering and was thrilled with my first day in the machine shop. Little did I know that it would be my last. Dungarees were needed and that presented a problem. The only thing to do was to write home for the money to buy them. The reply did not take long and it was to the point. Latin and

Greek grammars were preferable to dungarees and a change of course was indicated.' He had mixed feelings about this advice but, in retrospect, he regretted that the timetable did not allow him to do science as well as languages.

Some less welcome aspects of the Henderson era related to his ideas on what constituted proper dress for members of staff and pupils. As one who was always himself immaculately dressed, he expected a similar standard from others, believing it would enhance the public image of the college. Ronald Marshall, in *Methodist College, Belfast. The First 100 Years, 1868-1968*, explains the consequences of this expectation as it affected the boarders: 'School uniform for day pupils came only in the nineteen-thirties but the dress of the boarders was regulated early in his regime. On Sundays the luckless boys were taken to church in bowler hats. The dress of the older ones, black jackets and dark striped trousers, was not too bad, but the younger ones had to suffer the conspicuity of Eton collars and jackets.'[15] Eric was well aware of the problems this created for his mother as she prepared and packed the required clothes, firstly for himself and then for the younger members of the family who followed after him.

Even Eric had his occasional brushes with authority! On one occasion he was punished for something he didn't do: 'I felt badly enough about it to seek my father's intervention for the first and only time. His response was not quite what I had hoped for. "Son", he said, "you must fight your own battles." It was good advice.' Generally, however, the lasting impression he made on both staff and fellow-pupils was very positive. He was known for his goodness and strength of character. This is illustrated by a story told by Winston Brownrigg, one of his contemporaries, relating to a time when a number of boarders were summoned to the Headmaster's office and one by one were questioned about the use of bad language among the boarders. Winston was in a line of suspected delinquents waiting outside the office. On the summons 'Send in the next liar!' he was ushered in:

'Do you use bad language, Brownrigg?'

'Well, sometimes, sir.'

'Where did you learn it?'

'From other boarders, sir.'

'Here is a sheet of paper. Write down the names of the boarders who use bad language.'

Winston thought hard, then said, 'Please sir, it would be easier to write down the names of all who don't use bad language.'

'Go on.'

Winston wrote: 'Edwin James. Eric Gallagher.'[16]

Although he gained second place in the Northern Ireland Junior Certificate examination in French 'the received opinion', otherwise known as his father's wish, was that he should concentrate on Classics in his final year. This meant that a lot of his classes were with the elderly and tiring R.J.F. Donald, his Greek teacher. Eric writes that he was affectionately known as 'Baps' and describes him as 'very much the Mr Chips of the college'. Apparently the small Greek class was held in the afternoon just after lunch in a classroom at the east end of the school: 'By that time Mr Donald was tired and more often than not would set us some work to do and then he dozed off to sleep. The temptation to watch the huge crane at work on the erection of the Ulster Museum across the road or to get on with some other work militated against the progress we might otherwise have made. When he woke up, his temper was not always predictable.' Is there a hint in these comments that Eric Gallagher was, on occasion, just like the rest of us, guilty of idling away precious moments when we should have been constructively employed? In later years, when addressing young people, he encouraged them to use their time well: 'One of my great regrets – I don't think I was the confirmed slacker – but I did not make the best use of my time. Sorry for it today. Easiest thing in the world is to get into the habit of wasting time – no one realises that better than I do.'[17] Whatever truth there was in this suggestion of his mismanagement of time, the fact is he set academic standards which his siblings sometimes found it hard to live up to.

Eric always retained happy memories of his schooldays at Methody. While he never excelled at sport he still enjoyed the excitement of Sports Day at the Balmoral Show Grounds just as much as the annual Prize Distribution held in the Ulster Hall. Even though his strength of character and qualities of leadership were acknowledged in his appointment as Senior Prefect in his final year, there were still areas of reserve and shyness which he found difficult to overcome: 'There were the school parties, "hoolies" they called them, when boys and girls could talk and dance together. Though the spirit was willing I was too shy to make the most of them.'

As his seven years at Methody were coming to an end he and his father had a difference of opinion over the choice of university he might attend. Eric had been encouraged by Adam Prentice Howat, one of Henderson's recruits who had been a student at St Andrew's, to sit for a St. Andrew's scholarship, providing him with information about set books and the quality of life at the university, including the knowledge that university students had free use of the golf links. Eric comments: 'I set my eyes on Scotland.' But it was not to be. While it would have been an adventurous choice, his father had other ideas, encouraging him to think instead of going to Trinity College, Dublin. Once again he was persuaded. 'My father was pleased: I later learned why. He feared that I might find the Calvinist influence in Scotland too strong. Evidently he thought I could stand up to the Anglican influence of Trinity more successfully.'

3

University and offering for the ministry
1932-36

If I proclaim the gospel, this gives me no ground for boasting, for an obligation is laid on me, and woe betide me if I do not proclaim the gospel!

1 Corinthians 9.16

Living in Dublin and being a student at Trinity College opened up a whole new experience of life for Eric Gallagher. Trinity had been established in 1592 by Elizabeth I in an attempt to stop students going to the continent and getting revolutionary ideas or being influenced by the Pope in Rome. For centuries it had been a bastion of Protestantism, particularly Anglicanism, and Catholics had not been admitted unless they accepted the Protestant faith. This in turn had made the Roman Catholic hierarchy suspicious of its influence, resulting in a rule that required Catholics to obtain special permission to attend the College or else face the possibility of excommunication. These were the conditions that prevailed when Eric was a student and, indeed, episcopal restrictions on Catholics attending were not lifted until 1970. The College was located in the centre of the city and in the 1930s its 40 acres served as a centre of Anglo-Irish culture and academic life, somewhat in contrast to the evolving Irish culture which existed outside its gates. As Eric commented, going through the front gates of the college was like entering 'a world that was light years away from the city bustle outside'.

Eric enjoyed the change of environment, the excitement attached to a new freedom, making choices, coming up against new ideas, living in a culture and country which was so different from the one which he had experienced in Northern Ireland. He revelled in the experience of exploring Dublin city, cycling and walking over the Wicklow Mountains or rambling in Phoenix Park. Moving to Dublin was to prove quite momentous in his life, a time when he learned more about himself and discovered something further of God's purpose for his life. It was a time full of mixed emotions, experiencing both fear and excitement, pain and joy, the former coming before the latter.

Throughout the summer of 1932 he had prepared himself for the Sizarship examination in Classics, a scholarship which would have given him both financial support during his undergraduate period and also certain privileges within the college. The examinations and vivas were held at the end of September prior to the opening of the seven-week term which started in October, the first of three in the academic year. During the examination period he stayed in rooms at Trinity with his cousin, Norman Gallagher, who had entered a year previously and had already distinguished himself by becoming a Scholar of the university – also in Classics – during his first year. The achievements of his cousin, however, do not appear to have inspired Eric: 'He was at his brilliant best and on top of the world. His success and brilliance instead of stimulating me had the opposite effect. I felt I was probably not good enough. The two-day examinations with their vivas almost demoralised me. I knew the result long before it was announced. My name was not on the award list.' As he suggests, the experience was traumatic for him, 'It was a long time after that before I was able to face any examination with equanimity. All too often I was to spend sleepless hours during the week or ten days prior to the next encounter with the examiners.'

During that first year he stayed at Wesley College, Methodism's counterpart in the south to Methody, located behind the Methodist Centenary Church at Stephen's Green, a short distance from Trinity; like Methody it provided residential accommodation for a limited number of university students. The student quarters consisted of a large room on the top floor overlooking the back quadrangle and a couple of smaller rooms. The large room held beds for six students, serving as a study and living room as well. Eric recalled his introduction to the other students: 'I had been allocated to this top floor room and was brought up to it as soon as I arrived.

The shock I experienced on entering the room is still vivid after all the years. In front of the coal stove a card school was in progress and the stakes were clearly considerable. I asked myself, "Am I to spend the next few years in the middle of this den of thieves?" Before many days had passed, I discovered that I had been the victim of a practical joke!'

The five others with whom he shared the living room-study-dormitory were enjoyable company and they all became good friends. He was the only Arts Faculty student among them, the others being enrolled for medicine, science or engineering. Despite missing out on the Sizarship he was able to pay for his accommodation out of the proceeds of scholarships he had won at Methody and which had been invested for him in Savings Certificates.

Each student had a tutor to whom he reported at least once a year. The tutor was chosen by the student rather than designated by the college, although a first choice was not always available. Norman had recommended Francis La Touche Godfrey as 'easily the best' but his list of students was full, so Eric had to look for another. Mr Godfrey suggested that he approach Professor Marks or Sir Robert Tate and that he toss a coin as to who should be asked first. Eric recalls the apprehension he had when he heard the name of Sir Robert: 'If there was any name that I did not want to hear, it was that of Sir Robert. He had already demoralised and demolished me in the oral exam in the Sizarship.' However, he went and asked Sir Robert to be his tutor: 'He listened and looked and then he said, "My dear fellow, you do me a great honour. I will be pleased to be your tutor".' Four years later when he was leaving Trinity he went to take his leave of the tutor whom he still feared but hardly knew: 'He greeted me as follows: "My dear fellow, this is very sad. Thank you for honouring me and I wish you well".'

Of the two main college societies, the Historical and Philosophical, he joined the latter, this again being Norman's recommendation. In retrospect he was sorry as he felt he would have found the debates in the 'Hist' much more interesting and congenial rather than 'the somewhat more pretentious meetings of the Phil'. Still, he had made his decision and he stuck with it! Those who later came to know his masterly impromptu contributions in public and church life will be surprised to learn 'It was two full years before I ventured to make my voice heard: all too late I found my feet.' It was not necessary for him to choose between the two religious societies: the Student Christian Movement and the Inter-Varsity Fellowship. He joined both and benefited from both.

As at Methody, Eric's Greek classes had an element of comedy about them. The lectures with Professor W.A. Goligher were held in the Registrar's office:

> They are chiefly memorable for the occasional telephone calls which interrupted him in full flow as he translated some moving piece of Homer or Euripides. He was a master of the short phone-call. It frequently went like this: 'Yes', pause, 'Yes', another pause and then 'No'. Down went the phone and before resuming the translation there would come the comment, 'Damn Fool'.

Sir Robert's lectures were completely different: 'He had in his day been, I believe, Officer-Commanding the Trinity O.T.C. [Officer Training Corps] and rumour had it that he had gained his knighthood for services rendered in 1916. Be that as it may, going to his lectures was like appearing before the Sergeant-Major on the parade ground.'

The spring and early summer of 1933 was a time of change and development in Eric's life. The Trinity system of examinations meant that students were assessed *after* the holiday period and not before it. Consequently, like many others, he took his books home at the end of the second term and used the period between the second and third terms to prepare for his exams. As the time approached his sense of fear returned: 'The prospect haunted me and by the time I got back to Dublin I was already sleeping badly and dreaming of disaster when I did sleep. When at last the day arrived, I was extremely nervous and in poor shape for it.' When the results came out he found he had achieved a Third Class Honours grade, not the disaster he had feared but far from the high standard he normally expected of himself.

Eric was now faced with some major decisions. From time to time he had thought hard and long about what he was to do with his life. He knew that his father and mother both hoped he would follow his father into the ordained ministry: 'I was often reminded that immediately after my birth my father held me in his arms and dedicated me to God, though let it be said that while my parents coveted me for the ministry they never allowed me to think that I was being pressurised in that direction.' It was always at the back of his mind that it would be as they wished but he had thought he would put the decision off until he had completed university. This plan no longer seemed possible: 'So here I was with no decision made and humanly speaking no prospect of a worthwhile university degree.' He shared the news of his disappointing exam results with his parents and also the dilemma he was facing: 'My father's advice was to the point but graciously made: "Make up your mind as soon as you can. If it is to be the ministry, get on with it. If not, then we had better talk about it".'

The method Eric followed in reaching his decision was in some ways unusual:

> And so there began some weeks of hard thinking and praying. I would willingly have put the idea of ministry out of my mind. But I couldn't. And yet to offer for it seemed an unworthy choice. I agonised and finally over some weeks with a sheet of paper ruled down the middle and headed on one side 'FOR' and on the other 'AGAINST' I wrote down the arguments as I saw them. At the end they about balanced but there was one that weighed heavily with me and it was really on neither side for it was a question, 'Can you live with yourself if you don't offer?' It was in the last analysis a repetition of the experience of the apostle Paul, 'Woe to me if I do not preach the gospel.' That decided it: I would offer and leave it to the Church to decide whether or not I was suitable and 'called'.

He knew his parents were pleased with his decision. His father advised him that he needed experience both in preaching and pastoral work. The best thing to do was to seek an appointment as Lay Evangelist,[1] offer as a candidate for the ordained ministry in 1934, and continue with an extern pass degree course. And so Eric applied for a vacancy that was advertised in the *Irish Christian Advocate,* then Irish Methodism's weekly paper. The vacancy was at Hydepark on the Ligoniel (Belfast) Circuit, the Revd John Glass the Superintendent. Having already qualified as a 'local preacher' he was eligible for the post. He preached before the circuit quarterly meeting, answered various questions, and was told that their decision would be forwarded to him in due course. He was a little surprised at this delay as he had been told beforehand that, if he did reasonably well, the appointment would be his. He later wrote, 'I believe the delay that I could not understand was providential. It was to determine the whole course of my future.'

On his return to Dublin there was a message that the Revd Wesley McKinney, Superintendent of the Abbey Street Circuit, wanted to see him. McKinney soon let him know why he had asked Eric to contact him: 'I have heard some cock and bull story,' he said, 'that you are proposing to leave Trinity. Is that true?' Eric told him what had happened. 'Are you mad?' he said. 'I have always thought that Bob Gallagher was a rock of common sense but now I doubt it.' When McKinney learned that the Ligoniel Circuit had not offered Eric the Hydepark appointment, he assured him that no offer meant no commitment on his part: 'He was as direct as my father. He left me in no doubt that I was throwing away a priceless opportunity of graduating from Trinity, an opportunity that many would give anything to have. He said that he would write to Mr Glass and to my father and at the same time offered me there and then an appointment at Lucan on his own circuit and where, he said, I could gain experience, pay my way and at the same time pursue my Trinity degree. I took him at his word. To this day I am grateful for his intervention. I never regretted it.'

With an assured prospect of being able to complete his degree in Trinity and earn a living at the same time – an assurance that was to prove unfounded – he started the summer term with some considerable concern regarding his prospects of obtaining a good degree in Classics. He reflected on his excellent grades in French and English in both the Junior and Senior Certificates and assessed the wisdom of changing to Modern Languages. While he had not opened a French book and read little English literature for almost two years he decided it was worth the risk and took it without consulting anyone else: 'It was probably the first really independent decision I had ever taken – after all, I had talked over the ministry decision with both of my parents and others. It was a turning point.'

Eric presented himself at the Honours French and English lectures and no questions were asked. Sir Robert Tate was informed of the changes but he did not seem much perturbed or interested. Thus the transition went smoothly and the change made him a much happier person. That summer term he enjoyed the English course under Professor W.F. Trench, which concentrated on Chaucer. French under Professor Rudmose Browne and Owen Sheehy-Skeffington, whose father had been tragically killed by a British army officer in 1916, gave little trouble, though he quickly realized that a great deal of effort would be needed. He noted that the women students in these lectures far outnumbered the men.

Albert McElroy, who later entered the ministry of the Non-Subscribing Presbyterian Church and eventually ended up as Chairman of the Northern Ireland Liberal Party, was a classmate who influenced him greatly. Eric describes him as 'Ulster born but Scottish bred, a fanatical Socialist and pacifist. He perhaps more than any other person awakened in me something more than the mild social conscience on which I prided myself.' McElroy brought into the lecture rooms every day his copy of the *Daily Herald* and, as opportunity offered, commented on the iniquities of the arms trade and the unfolding tragedy in Europe: 'I can still hear his vehement denunciation of Dolfuss, the Austrian Chancellor, as a "little

29

Fascist rat".' McElroy became a good friend and sometime later Eric was best man at his wedding.

Residence in France was a requirement for all Modern Language students taking French. Through the good offices of a Methodist minister in Parame, close to St Malo in Brittany, Eric was able to work for two summers on the farm of one of his members. Before he left on the first of these trips in late June 1935 'RH' felt it necessary to have a special word with him: 'He advised me to be on my guard as far as young French women were concerned: they had a seductive reputation.' To set his parents' fears at rest Eric wrote home that two of the farmer's daughters were of a similar age to Helen, his youngest sister, at that time not quite 11 years old, and the eldest daughter was working in Paris, so there was no need for them to worry! The sectarian riots that summer in Belfast in which 13 people were killed, many wounded, and over 2,000 driven from their homes, did not go unnoticed in Brittany, and Eric was asked what the violence was all about: 'I did my best to explain. Truth to tell at that stage of my career, like many another Protestant grammar school product, I did not know what I should have known then and what I know today. My explanations were halting and were probably put down to my lack of fluency rather than to ignorance or prejudice.'

Increasingly he was finding Trinity enjoyable but the conditions in Wesley frustrating. In January 1934 George Good, a first-year student who also had ideas of candidating for the ministry, suggested that they share rooms in college. The various costs were considered, reckoned manageable, and they moved into rooms on the ground floor of No.17, in an area known as 'Botany Bay'. It opened up still further a new and exciting world for him. There were increased opportunities for taking part in University life. He began to attend the meetings of the 'Phil' more regularly and going to whatever events caught his interest. There were public lectures and speeches by Eamonn de Valera, Sean Lemass, Lord Longford and British politicians like Harold Laski and John Strachey. Easily the most memorable event of all was the university mission conducted by William Temple, then Archbishop of York: 'The

Examination Hall was packed every night for a week. He offered no easy superficial gospel. The intellectual stature of the man challenged even the most cynical and sceptical. For an hour every evening he wrestled with us or more properly we wrestled with him. The impact was outstanding. He made the faith both credible and respectable.'

Evening dinner – known as 'Commons' – was served nightly in the College Dining Hall on the north side of the Front Square. It had, of course, to be paid for. Sizars, University Scholars and Fellows had theirs free of charge. It was obligatory for all other students to go on Commons at least twice per week – they were free to do as they pleased in vacation time. Eric was thankful for the requirement: 'You sat at any table [except the top table] and so you mixed with all sorts and students from any year. That was where friendships started and sometimes finished, where ideas were sharpened and minds extended.' Contemporaries whom he enjoyed meeting included: R.B. McDowell, perhaps TCD's most famous and eccentric Professor of History; his friend Donald Kennedy, later to be Bishop in the Church of North India; Eric Woodhouse, later Regius Professor of Divinity in the university; George Farley, killed in the King David Hotel bombing in Jerusalem; and C.A. Herbert, who went to the Indian Civil Service and came back to work in MI5.

In the spring of 1935 the Centenary Church was the venue for a week of special services addressed by the Revd Dr Leslie Weatherhead, the minister of City Temple in London, who was rapidly making his name as a pastoral psychologist. Eric notes:

Night after night huge crowds listened spell-bound. They came from all over the Free State and some from Northern Ireland. The church was crowded far beyond any safe capacity and Weatherhead did them proud. He made it all so easy. Depression and guilt complexes and senses of inferiority were understandable and treatable. There was no need to worry. Tragically before many years had passed he too was to have his own bouts of worry and depression and they would recur.

The duties at Lucan which Wesley McKinney expected of him were considerable. These included two services every other Sunday and three on the Sunday in between. There was duty in Abbey Street Church on one week night and a monthly 'cottage' or house meeting away out beyond Lucan, and, of course, there was the pastoral oversight of the Lucan and Cellbridge congregations. He was conscious he had received no training for the job, though the Revd John Bertenshaw, who had succeeded McKinney, was 'kindness personified'. One Sunday night he stumbled badly when using the Lord's Prayer and, as a result, for the rest of his ministry he always liked to have a copy open in front of him. Interestingly, he now found himself in a working pattern which, he suggests, became the pattern throughout most of his ministry: 'The Lucan appointment meant living in two worlds, the University and the Church [or more precisely the Methodist] world. With few and short exceptions it has been that way ever since – a divided interest between the Church and some other discipline or way of life.'

Serving in Lucan also brought him in contact with Sam Baxter and Willie Farrell, two probationers who had similar but heavier responsibilities on other parts of the Abbey Street Circuit. Both became his friends. Baxter, who was strongly convinced that above all else he was called to be a preacher and consequently spent a great deal of time on his sermon preparation, appeared to be concerned about Eric's ability in this area: 'He frequently came to see me in Trinity and would always ask to see my sermon book. He would look critically at my latest efforts and then with a sort of troubled resignation he would comment, "Well, at least you can manage to get a good title for them!"'

In his third and fourth years at Trinity, his assistance being no longer required at Lucan, Eric helped out in two other Dublin churches, Sandymount and Ringsend. In the last six months of his third year he offered as a candidate for the ministry and was guided through the process of examinations, interviews and 'trial' sermon by John Bertenshaw. At two of these stages some concerns were voiced! One of the requirements meant that he had to preach before a congregation which included at least three ministerial members of synod. The service was in the (former) Kingsland Church lecture hall in conditions that were far from inspiring: 'The hall was dark and the reading desk low. So that I could easily read my notes, I closed the Bible, placed the large hymn book on top of it and my own closed Bible on top of that again. I thought the service went well and was somewhat shattered later to learn that a lengthy discussion had taken place regarding my preaching from a closed Bible!' He prepared well for the next stage of candidating which included an interview along with the other five candidates before the Board of Examiners.[2] Knowing the enthusiasm which Methodist ministers had for John Wesley's sermons, he had learned large passages by heart and was able to quote passage after passage to the Board's evident pleasure! However, the mood soon changed:

> I was asked a question about Infant Baptism, a subject about which I had great reservations. My uncertainties quickly made themselves obvious and member after member began to probe more deeply. Eventually I was asked would I baptise an infant presented to me. After a moment of consideration I said 'Yes, I would.' But I still was not off the hook. The next question was 'Why?' and I replied that being baptised would not do the baby any harm. At last we were told that we could adjourn. After a long time a message reached us to the effect that all of us had been recommended to the Conference for acceptance. I later learned that as far I was concerned the hope was expressed that with maturity and the influence of Edgehill College I might see things differently.

All six candidates were accepted when the Methodist Conference met in Dublin in June and Eric's request to be placed on the 'List of Reserve' for one year so that he could complete his university course was approved.

In his final year Eric shared rooms with his cousin Norman. George Good had left university to take up an appointment as lay assistant in Sligo, his home circuit. Among the visitors to their rooms that year was a German professor who was engaged in research in Elizabethan English. Over supper they encouraged him to speak about what was happening in Germany under the Nazi regime. Initially he said that life in Germany was normal and that there was nothing to be over concerned about socially or academically. Norman and Eric were not convinced that he was telling the whole story: 'We pressed him and then Norman indicated anything he said was of course in confidence and that there was no possibility of his being overheard. He looked round the rooms and asked quietly if there were any "bugging devices". Assured at last that he was perfectly safe, he leaned forward and with a look of deep concern bordering on fear he said in what was little more than an audible whisper, "Life in Germany is Hell." ' This brief but firsthand insight into events in Germany was of particular interest to Eric. In late 1934 he had presented a major and masterly paper at the 'Phil' entitled 'Dictators and Dictatorship' in which he traced the history of democracies and dictatorships from the time of the Athenian ruler Pericles in the fifth century BC to the twentieth-century dictatorships of Mussolini and Hitler. He shared with his audience his special fascination with the personality of Hitler: 'In him I have an intense interest. Not that I altogether admire him – but about him to me there is a cloud of interest and of romance that makes me sit up and take notice of all his actions.'[3] While he acknowledged that Hitler had only been in power a very short time and that German propaganda and censorship made it difficult to come to an accurate assessment of the man, he did not hesitate to offer his own analysis: 'From all accounts Hitler is fired by an intense personal desire for power. In a short time he seems to have instituted a very effective reign of terror and so far his policy has been one of destruction rather than construction. Jews and Communists – we know his relations to them.' With prophetic insight he had this to say about Hitler's plans for the future: 'Saar troubles and Austrian problems may affect his destiny – but it might be truer to say that he will affect the destinies of Austria and the Saar.'

Eric was in his first term at Edgehill College when he returned to take his final exams at Trinity in October 1936. He was quite confident he had done well in his French papers and orals, and was hopeful of a similar performance in English. However, one paper created unexpected difficulty for all the examinees, their complaint being that the whole of the paper was practically given to one section of the course. They complained to the Professor who agreed with their judgement but apologized that he had not seen the paper beforehand and felt unable to interfere with a colleague's work. When the results came out Eric learned he had missed a First Class Honours by one mark: 'Of course I was disappointed, indeed bitterly disappointed.' His remorse is understandable but his achievement was considerable. He had not only changed course two-thirds of the way through his first year but he had spent the next three years as a part-time student working to pay his way through college.

4

Edgehill College
1936-38

Beware you be not swallowed up in books! An ounce of love is worth a pound of knowledge.

R. Southey, *Life of Wesley*, 1820. Ch.16

Moving from Trinity to Edgehill College meant some unwelcome changes for Eric. Students were expected to be in their studies every evening from Monday to Friday, only being allowed out with the permission of the Principal, Dr Alexander McCrea. Even with this permission they were expected to be back before the doors were closed at 10 or 10.30 p.m. What a stark contrast to life at Trinity! 'I had run my own life for four years and had learned what self-discipline means when it comes to regulating how I worked and studied. I was not the only one who found difficulty in accepting regulations.'

Edgehill Theological College stood in 3.5 acres of grounds at the end of Lennoxvale, off the Malone Road in Belfast, a short distance from the Methodist College where ministers had originally been trained. Purchased in 1919, the site included a large gentleman's residence and further ancillary buildings at the rear. Outhouses at the back had been turned into lecture and class rooms on the ground floor and single bedrooms large enough to hold a bed and a set of drawers upstairs. With additional bedrooms in the main house there was accommodation for about 20 to 25 students and a resident tutor, but this often meant cramped conditions, shared bedrooms and shared studies. A house for the Principal had been erected beside the building with connecting doors into it.

Lack of contact with other colleges created a feeling of insularity. As yet there was no link with the Queen's University of Belfast, even though the campus of the university was adjacent to the college. Nor was there any contact with Assembly's College, the theological college of the Presbyterian

Church in Ireland, also located nearby or, for that matter, with any other theological college. Closer links with these various institutions developed later but their absence contributed to a sense of isolation. 'All in all', as Eric notes, 'it was a grim prospect and a seemingly grim place.'

His initial disappointment with the college changed a little as he came to appreciate the quality of the teaching staff. Eric is unstinting in his appreciation of McCrea: 'He was more than a theologian: he was a first-rate preacher and communicator. He was a prophet voice in a generation that did not have too many prophets. To hear him speak on Amos was to be moved to the depths of one's being for he had a social conscience.' Dr William L. (Barney) Northridge, Senior Tutor, was an Old Testament and Hebrew scholar of repute, but his main contribution was in the area of pastoral psychology. His thesis on 'Modern theories of the unconscious' brought him the first Ph.D. awarded at the university and his publication of *Psychology and Pastoral Practice* in 1938 earned him a world reputation.[1] Eric suggests that Northridge's expertise in this area made the students a little wary of him: 'He was popular with the students and yet held in awe. They always worried as to what secrets of their lives and thinking he could identify from what they wrote and said and did.' He had ministered in various churches before taking up his teaching post in Edgehill. While on the staff of the Grosvenor Hall he decided to research conditions existing in Belfast's 'underworld': 'He dressed in the dungarees of a shipyard worker, drank dry ginger in public houses, slept in doss-houses, and kept his eyes and ears open. To help people, he always realised, it is first necessary to know people.'[2] Ernest Ker, Junior Tutor, a first class Honours graduate in Classics, had already helped Eric during his final year at Methody. He taught New Testament Greek and New Testament but was gifted in many other areas: 'He was infinitely more than a classicist. A gifted musician, an authority on the Wesley hymns, a Methodist historian in his own right, a lover of the arts, he was as near the complete scholar as could be and he was above all else a Christian gentleman.'

Conference had allocated 17 students to Edgehill in 1936, the year Eric started. Five were in their third year, four in second year, and seven in first year. Val Silcock was Senior Student. He was Belfast born and bred, small of stature but big of heart. He later served as a missionary in Burma (Myanmar) and on the outbreak of the Second World War joined the army as a chaplain and was posted to General Wingate's Chindits. Eric had two main friends, both in the first year group: Alan Booth, who later served the wider Christian Church in various capacities, most notably as Director of Christian Aid; and Edward (Ted) Lindsay, who served as Home Mission Secretary of the Irish Methodist Church for 18 years. His friendship with Booth was strong while they were in college – they shared a study – and that with Lindsay developed and grew stronger during their ministry in Ireland. Lindsay indicates that the students were not as submissive to the college regulations as their tutors thought! 'To beat the curfew regulations we climbed up the Library spouting and entered by a bedroom window. Later we got a skeleton key for the bathroom at the top of the spiral staircase [on the right of the main building], so we no longer had the hassle of climbing up the spouting.'[3]

Because they were graduates Eric and Alan were told they would be in college for only two years. Eric regretted this: 'I did not understand why it should be assumed that the possession of a university degree whether in law or anything else should be an indication that the graduate concerned needed less theological training than other students.' McCrea encouraged them to study externally for the Trinity Bachelor of Divinity degree and together they decided they would try to complete the degree while in college, a feat which both achieved. The question arose, however, as to what courses they would take in Edgehill. Eventually it was agreed that provided they kept up to date with the BD timetable of examinations they had planned, they would be excused lectures in Greek, Philosophy of Religion, Church History, Comparative Religion, and Psychology of Religion. Thus they were left with a core Edgehill curriculum of Old and New Testaments, Theology and Homiletics. Eric regretted missing the element of pastoral guidance which Northridge brought into his lectures on

Psychology of Religion, but he delighted in the opportunity to study the Bible in depth, particularly the whole field of biblical criticism: 'For me it was exciting. It introduced us to a new world. It never even in the slightest degree diminished my belief in the authority of Scripture or my acceptance of it as containing the essential Word of God.' His overall appreciation for the lectures he received is clear: 'Two years in Edgehill classes were a sharpening and developing stepping-stone to a fuller commitment to a proclamation of the gospel in a world where easy and superficial answers are unacceptable.'

Saturday mornings were unforgettable! Every Saturday morning staff and students assembled together in the main lecture hall which also served as the college library. Each week a different student was under obligation to produce and preach before the assembled group a sermon which it was expected he would be able to preach in any church or to any congregation. He also had to select and read suitable supporting Scripture passages. Having read his sermon as best he could, he then took his place in the lecture room and listened as each of the students and the staff, starting from the most junior student and progressing by seniority right up to the Principal, gave his criticism of the sermon and the manner in which it was delivered. Eric describes the ordeal: 'It was a harrowing experience to have one's masterpiece dissected, analysed, criticised and frequently almost pulverised!' He never forgot what happened on one of the two Saturdays he preached: 'I had already preached it in a number of churches and every time it had seemingly been very well received and appreciated. Not so when it came to my Saturday clinic. It took such a bashing that I don't think I ever preached it again.' Typical of his nature he still saw something good in the practice: 'The necessity to offer comments and criticisms was good for the critics as well as for the preacher.'

Much more beneficial was the opportunity for students to take services in churches around the country. There was always a demand from a number of circuits for this kind of student help. Each Tuesday the Senior Student would read out a list of places requiring a preacher the following Sunday with the name of the student required to take the service. Students were paid five shillings per service and also given a travelling allowance to cover transport by bus or train, whichever was the cheaper. Income from the services was divided equally at the end of each term but income for travelling expenses went directly to the student concerned. Eric saved the amount given for travelling expenses by cycling to all of his appointments, a practice which he copied from his father. Cycling in the rain to these churches sometimes led to unexpected problems, as happened when taking an appointment one Sunday evening in Newcastle, County Down, about 30 miles from Belfast: 'I arrived by bicycle sodden almost to the skin with feet squelching water in my shoes. A comfortable pulpit mat-rug seemed inviting so I pulled off my shoes and socks and conducted the service with my feet wrapped up in the mat. Everything went well until the stewards came forward with the offering. No one had told me that the preacher was expected to receive the offering plates at the communion rail!'

Academic pressure to complete the Trinity BD in two years did not keep him from enjoying the midweek hockey matches between the college and girls from the nearby Riddell Hall, the residential hall for Queen's women students. And along with Booth and Lindsay he also joined Collegians Rugby Club which had the enlightened attitude of regarding students as unemployed and therefore paid travelling expenses to the matches.[4] The Edgehill students were not always in the same team, Eric's scrummaging ability earning him a place in the 3rd XV.

Alan Booth's previous experience as SCM Secretary in Liverpool meant that he was very much in demand in SCM circles in Ireland. Both he and Eric were invited to attend the Movement's Quadrennial Conference held at the end of 1936 in Birmingham. Once again there was an opportunity to hear William Temple, and others including the Scottish theologian, Robert Mackie, and Visser't Hooft, the future outstanding first Secretary of the World Council of Churches. Eric describes the conference as a seminal experience for him. He was particularly moved by the session on the Overseas Church: 'It moved me deeply. As a candidate for the ministry I had indicated my readiness to serve at home or overseas as the Church wished. In 1936 the challenge to offer seemed strong and demanding. I hesitated and the moment passed. The issue came back ten years later and that time had to be faced.' Richard Crossman, the future Labour Party Cabinet Minister, was another who challenged him. He had been addressing an evening session of the Conference, analysing the international situation as he understood it, particularly the growing Nazi threat to the rest of Europe:

> We had been discussing the relevance of the faith in a threatening world and none of us were very hopeful. In fact we were afraid of what was seemingly going to happen. Crossman listened to us for a while and then he broke into the discussion. He told us he could not understand us. He made no claim to the faith, he said, but if our faith meant to us what we claimed it did we ought to be different people and we ought to show a different attitude to life and what was coming. That comment stuck.

On occasions some of the college community were involved in visits or projects within the Belfast area. Two such visits brought Eric into contact with a part of the city which he was soon to know very well. One was a visit to a linen mill on the Crumlin Road. Another was a survey of housing and living conditions on one of the city's new housing estates, Glenard, in the Ardoyne area. For those students involved in the survey it was a memorable experience: 'The hungry thirties had not disappeared and the conditions we found as we went from house to house left an indelible impression on some of us. But in a way what was far more memorable was the human dignity in both Protestant and Catholic homes the conditions had not succeeded in obliterating.' The survey had been masterminded by academics from the university and the returns were analysed by them. The eventual publication of a report on the survey attracted considerable newspaper attention. To Eric's surprise it also caused controversy in the church: 'What business had a crowd of irresponsible young people to be doing this kind of thing? It was an early lesson in what can happen to the best intentioned projects.'

5

Woodvale
1938-42

What I want you to remember is this – if you and I are going to be worth our salt, we must try to make the world a better place. Here is a world at war, a world where men and women and little children suffer because of selfishness and sin. You saw for yourselves a year ago what suffering really was. It is a world where often little ones are hungry because their fathers have no work. I ask you that as you grow up you will determine that as far as in you lies you will take that world seriously, and if you do, Belfast will have a better name than it has today because you lived in it and the world will be a happier place because of your influence.

Sermon, 'Taking Life Seriously', Luke 10:27,
preached at Woodvale, 5.8.1942

The 1938 Conference appointed Eric to serve as a probationer minister in Woodvale on the Agnes Street circuit in Belfast. Woodvale church – or 'Woodvale Hall' as it was then known – was a community church, drawing its congregation from the immediate area of the Upper Shankill, Woodvale, Ardoyne and Crumlin Road. It was a working-class area, its population employed in the local linen mills, Mackie's Foundry on the nearby Springfield Road, and the Harland & Wolff shipyards. Employment in the area had been badly hit by the depression of the early thirties but by 1938 the number back at work had risen and with that the spirit of the people. Eric's graphic picture of people returning from work provides an insight into life in the area: 'The hundreds of bicycles tearing down the Springfield Road at five o'clock in the afternoon when the Mackie's workers were rushing home was one of the sights of working Belfast: so too were the convoys of trams whining up the Shankill laden with their dunchered workers homeward bound from the shipyard and aircraft factory. And of course the female workers with scarves around their heads laughing, talking and shouting on their way to and from Ewart's and the other mills and factories.'[1] He quickly sensed the spirit of the people: 'I found myself among a people who had known what it was to be without work: now they had it and they were determined not to lose it, if at all possible. I made up my mind that I should work as hard as they did. In any case it was probably in my blood.'

Housing in the area provided the minimum of facilities. Some were fortunate to have two rooms upstairs and two downstairs but others were smaller: 'There were those where you could stand with arms outstretched in the main room downstairs and touch the chimney breast with one hand and the opposite wall with the other. The other room, if there was one, was just big enough to hold a bed with a chair beside it or a small table. And in all those smaller ones indoor toilet accommodation was totally unknown.' These limitations, whether the houses were small or not so small, he observed, did not affect 'the fierce self-respect evident among the people of the Shankill or Woodvale'. The great majority of the houses were clean and spotless. He soon discovered it was out of the question to arrange any social function for a Friday night if the women folk were expected to attend: 'Friday night was "bucket night" and nothing could alter that. Every week-end saw the scrubbed or washed semi-circle or crescent on the pavement outside the front door.'

Woodvale Hall had had a chequered early history. Built by the Belfast Central Mission the hall had originally seated over 1,000 persons. It had formerly served as the Belfast Exhibition Hall and had been erected near the Ormeau Bridge in the south of the city. Following a successful tent mission in Eastland Street led by the Revd George Thompson, it had been decided to seek a permanent site and to put a building on it. The opportunity to purchase part of the Exhibition Hall was taken in 1896 and 'Woodvale Hall' appeared on a site purchased from the Brookvale Flax Spinning Company in Cambrai Street with its back boundary wall separating it from the old Shankill

Graveyard. The work began successfully but by 1897 difficulties had arisen to such an extent that the Belfast Central Mission Committee considered that they had no option but to close it down. It lapsed for some months. However, the Sunday school was restarted and by the Conference of 1898 the hall was reopened. Eventually, in 1907, Woodvale became part of the Agnes Street Circuit, thus joining the congregations of Agnes Street, Shankill Road and Falls Road on a circuit whose total membership in 1938 was 1,112 senior and 807 junior members. With hundreds of additional 'adherents' it was at that time one of Irish Methodism's strongest circuits.

About 230 families were connected to the church. Youth and adult organisations were well attended: the Boys' Brigade, Girl Guides, Junior and Senior Christian Endeavour Societies, the Sunbeam Choir and a midweek meeting. Eric was impressed by the quality of the leaders and church officials: 'No congregation of its kind could have been more fortunate in its main officials. Each of them was completely committed to the work of the church. They were wise in their advice, generous with their time and discreet in every way. They led from the front and because they had the respect and confidence of the congregation they were never short of helpers.' Twenty-five years old when he arrived in Woodvale, he was conscious that a few thought 'he was far too young and would never do' but the events of the next four years were to prove them wrong, the same people being the first to acknowledge the great contribution he had made.

Despite his experience as a part-time lay evangelist while a student at Trinity he now found the pressures of sermon preparation 'almost terrifying'. He had to preach morning and evening for six Sundays out of seven to the same congregation – quite a demanding routine for anyone, not least a probationer minister! As the morning congregation was the smaller of the two and made up of 'the regulars and the faithful' he decided to use up his older sermons – with suitable improvements, if he could find them! – in the morning and put his main effort in sermonising into the evening service. He had not been trained in Edgehill to use a lectionary or, indeed, to follow the Christian year in sermon topics. After the first or second month he realized the risk in waiting until the end of the week before deciding on his sermon topic, so he developed a routine of preparation which he was to follow for the rest of his ministry:

> Each preacher finds his or her own solution. Mine was to lay awake on Sunday nights until I had more or less decided the text or topic for the following Sunday evening. That having been done, one could go to sleep. On Monday and Tuesday one could think and read around the subject for those were glorious years of freedom from the bane and ruination of pastoral life, the committee treadmill. On Wednesday it was possible to jot down notes and sketch an outline and think of illustrations that would light up the sermon for the congregation rather than, if one may use the word with particular impropriety, obfuscate it. On Thursday it was written and on Friday morning it could be preached two or three times to the walls of the room. Finally on Saturdays it was possible on occasions to preach it to an empty building. Over the years the timetable has had to be changed: life not of my making became far too complicated to allow the possibility of going through all the procedures which had been so helpful. But the basic criteria have remained to guide me all through my ministry.

Eric Gallagher regarded preaching as the supreme way of communicating a personal and challenging gospel. He believed that preachers need to avoid 'superficial sentimentality' and constantly seek to be relevant to the lives the congregation had to live: 'I have attempted to make the gospel speak to the situations in which people find themselves, whether personal, industrial, political or social. As a Methodist preacher I have been called to preach the gospel and to me the gospel is the good news of God to the world and those who live in it.'

He enjoyed visiting the homes of the congregation. His father's advice was to learn to listen: 'He was a great believer in letting people talk.' Eric very quickly came to appreciate the wisdom of this, observing that if the minister did not interrupt or insist in talking about himself, people would unburden themselves. He also adopted the advice of his uncle John, circuit steward on the neighbouring Crumlin Road circuit, who suggested that a minister should never leave a home after a pastoral visit without offering prayer. Finally, he remembered what Dr McCrea had said about hospital visiting: 'Men', he said, 'make it short.' It was advice which he followed down through the years. Sick people, he believed, do not need and do not appreciate interminable visits.

A short time after he was appointed to Woodvale he was made aware of a major problem which he knew had to be faced. While he was preaching one Sunday evening, he noticed that from time to time members of the congregation left their seats and moved into the centre of the building and nearer to the pulpit. At first he thought they were anxious not to miss any of the profound thoughts of the sermon! However, at the end of the service church officials alerted him to the real reason: 'They said that something must be done about the state of the building. Rain was pouring in through the roof and windows and the time had come to build a new church.' And in addition to the leaks and draughts there was a perennial problem with the heating system. Plumbers in the congregation had done all they could to provide a modicum of heat but with little success. 'Unquestionably the building for all its size was far from welcoming and satisfactory, even in summer. In winter it was a disaster.'

Eric learned that a Building Fund had been started as far back as 1929. It had had to struggle with Belfast's chronic unemployment and at the height of the depression in 1932-33 it had been discontinued. The Fund had been relaunched in February 1936 and through various fund-raising efforts – weekly collections, special efforts and having a refreshment stall at the Orange demonstration on 12 July 1937 – a total of £2,000 had been raised. Plans had been sought and produced but the proposals of the architect, while being very attractive, had been costed at a figure far above the £7,000 which the congregation considered was the amount beyond which they could not safely go.

This was the situation Eric found when he commenced his ministry in Woodvale. The people were somewhat dispirited because the task seemed beyond them. However, the new minister – albeit probationer minister – had an enthusiasm and determination which inspired others into renewed action: 'It was obvious that action was required straight away. The congregation had suffered enough.' Discussions with the Church authorities began immediately, deputations were received and listened to, new plans were considered by a meeting in February 1939 and by 22 May Messrs J. and R. Thompson, one of the most reputable firms in the building trade, had commenced work. Their contract was to erect a church and to use whatever material could be salvaged from the old building in the erection of a church hall at the rear of the new church – all for a price not to exceed £7,000 and with an undertaking to cost it at less than that price, if at all possible. Meanwhile the treasurers of the Building Fund, Mrs Madge McCutcheon and Mr T. Weir, had redoubled their efforts. More weekly collectors were recruited and throughout the war years in the winter blackout and in the summer, they did their rounds every Friday night. Eric comments: 'No tribute is too great as far as they were concerned and to Mrs McCutcheon in particular. She was the dynamo that kept the machine going.' He preached at both closing services in the old hall on 25 June and during the summer the congregation worshipped in St Matthew's Parochial Hall – conveniently located across the street – by kind permission of the rector, Archdeacon McDonald, and the Select Vestry.

The outbreak of war on 3 September was traumatic in many ways, not least because the changed circumstances meant it was necessary to review the wisdom of proceeding with the building project. Eric notes the questions that had to be addressed: 'Would the builders be allowed to carry on? Would they be able to secure the necessary timber and other materials required? Would air warfare make everything impossible and in any case would the costs soar and would the congregation be able to raise the necessary money?' Some now expressed doubts about the scheme, most notably the Trustees of the Methodist Church:

> For some reason that I did not understand then and have never understood the Trustees of the Methodist Church sent a deputation from Dublin to meet with the builders, the Superintendent [the Revd Albert Holland] and myself. They asked many questions and seemed altogether hesitant. They seemed desirous to have the scheme called off. Finally Mr Lance Thompson, the principal of the building firm, intervened and said pointedly his firm had struck up an eminently satisfactory relationship with Mr Holland and myself, that they had foreseen the likelihood of war and had actually in stock and earmarked for the scheme all the timber and other requisites. He believed if we were all left to get on with the operation nobody had any reason to worry.

And so the work proceeded and the new church was opened on 27 April 1940, eight months after the dedication of the new church hall. The completion of both premises proved to be a boost to the morale of the people and, despite blackout regulations and other limitations imposed during the war, attendances at the Sunday services and church organisations increased.

The threat of war in Europe in 1938 and the outbreak of war a year later forced Eric to rethink the near pacifist position which he had held at Trinity College. With crisis following crisis – Austria, Czechoslovakia, Poland – and his revulsion at the screaming and ranting of Hitler at his mass Nazi rallies, he re-examined his attitude to war: 'War to me was evil and it is evil still. But I had seen what was happening in Europe: I was convinced about the evil of Nazi domination. Reluctantly I had come to the conclusion that war was the lesser of two evils.'

This growing realization had one immediate though minor consequence for Eric. When Neville Chamberlain returned after signing the Munich Agreement with Hitler on 30

September 1938 and promising 'I believe it is peace for our time ... peace with honour', neither Alan Booth nor himself was convinced! 'A couple of weeks later, when we had time to think about what had happened, Alan and I made few friends when at a meeting we voted against a resolution of gratitude to the Prime Minister for the part he had played in reaching the so-called settlement.' But his change of mind had another far-reaching consequence. He had not arrived at the point where he could have easily volunteered as a combatant but he had no doubts whatever about the obligation of the Church to those who were combatants. They required pastoral care. In this context he felt called to offer his services as a chaplain to the Forces. He shared his thoughts with the Woodvale church leaders but promised them he would postpone taking any action until the church had been built and was operational. In the summer of 1940 he sent in his application to the War Services Committee to be considered for chaplaincy service.[2] The application was acknowledged and an accompanying letter indicated that, with the fall of France and the withdrawal from Norway, reorganisation of the fighting forces was taking place and no chaplaincy appointments would be made during the remainder of 1940. At the end of January the following year he received a letter from the Revd John England, Secretary of the War Services Committee, telling him that he had been nominated for a chaplaincy, and within ten days he received instructions from the War Office to report to Victoria Barracks in Belfast. A day or two later the Revd John Spence, President of the Church that year, asked him to come to his office at the Grosvenor Hall, Belfast. The conversation went something like this:

President: Mr Gallagher, you have a difficult choice to make!

Gallagher: What kind of choice, Mr President?

President: You have applied to become a chaplain to the Forces and, indeed, your application has been successful. However, the Governors of Methodist College would like you to be their next school chaplain. You will have to choose between these two positions.

Eric's demeanour indicates surprise at this news – the first he has heard of any suggestion of a post at Methody!

> Gallagher: Mr President, it is surely not for me to make that decision? When I offered as a candidate for the ministry I agreed to go wherever the Church wanted me to serve. I have asked to go as a chaplain to the Forces but if the Church wants me elsewhere it is for the Church to say so.

The President is somewhat nonplussed by Eric's statement and pauses to think before replying.

> President: Mr Gallagher, I do believe you are right! The Church has been very wrong in asking you to decide between these two positions. I need to consult with others immediately. I will contact you in a few days and inform you what you are to do. In the meantime do not contact the War Office.

By 19 February John England had written to tell Eric that his application to serve as a chaplain to the Forces had been withdrawn! The Church had intervened but it was not until he had reminded them that the responsibility of deciding his future lay with the Church and not with him. The sequence of events and the conversation with the President provides a valuable insight into Eric's understanding of authority in the Church and his perception of how he might best interpret God's will for his life. The Methodist Church in Ireland decided he should serve as Resident Chaplain at Methody but the appointment was not confirmed until the Conference of 1942.

Belfast was ill-prepared for the German air raids of April and May 1941 as the Northern Ireland Government and the Belfast Corporation do not appear to have thought that the city was in any real danger from the enemy.[3] Lord Craigavon had been head of government since the foundation of the state in

1921 and only his death in November 1940 brought a change of leadership, John Andrews, a few months his junior, taking over as Prime Minister.[4] Historians give Craigavon credit for preventing the province from sliding into anarchy in the 1921-22 period but thereafter suggest that a rather dilatory approach to government prevailed, coupled with, as Jonathan Bardon suggests, 'a fatal complacency and narrowness of vision in permitting the grievances of the nationalist minority to suppurate over two decades'.[5] Matters did not improve under Andrews and the general malaise was reflected in the lack of air defences for Belfast: 'When the Ministry of Home Affairs was informed by imperial defence experts that Belfast was a certain Luftwaffe target, nothing was done. The city had no fighter squadrons, no balloon barrage and only twenty anti-aircraft guns when the war began.'[6] As late as March 1941 John MacDermott, minister of public security, expressed his personal anxiety to Andrews that Belfast did not even have a single searchlight as the few it possessed had been sent back to England soon after the outbreak of war.

The German war machine had not been so careless, indeed, the reverse. On 30 November 1940 a single unobserved plane had flown high over Belfast taking photographs of suitable industrial targets and noting the almost total absence of any air defences. Such was the preparation by the Luftwaffe for the three night air raids on Belfast: 7-8 April, 15-16 April and 4-5 May. The second of these was the most horrific of the three and the one that most affected the Woodvale congregation. On the morning of Easter Tuesday, 15 April, Eric had taken part in a wedding in the Shankill church. Later that day he made a few pastoral calls before going along to the party planned by the young people of the church. He later wrote about one of these calls: 'While we talked little David walked up and down the room, my steel helmet on his head. It was a novel toy. Tom and his wife looked on and smiled. He was so innocent, so gay. And together they said as I left them for the night: "In this business the innocent suffer along with the guilty." Next day I saw the three of them taken dead from a pile of rubble, which was once a happy home.'[7] Noel Burnside, one of the older teenagers at the party in the church hall that evening, recalls how he helped Eric keep a vigil at the new church:

> When the party was over Mr Gallagher formed everyone into a circle and was just about to pronounce the benediction when the air raid sirens could be heard. He quickly arranged us into groups to be escorted home by the senior members. I left my party home and quickly returned to the church. We proceeded with the usual drill of opening all doors and windows and arranging the buckets of water, sand and stirrup pumps for handiness. Mr Gallagher was a very worried man because after a short time the whole of Belfast seemed to be ablaze with thousands of incendiary bombs and hundreds of high explosives being dropped on the city that night. He was really concerned about the church and we kept running from the front to the back because you didn't know the minute a fire bomb would come through the roof.[8]

While the new Woodvale church escaped serious damage, St Matthew's was less fortunate, an incendiary bomb being lodged in its roof. Eric, we are told, broke into the unprotected building and raised the alarm by ringing the church bells. In a goodwill gesture, almost unknown at the time, the rector invited the Methodist congregation to worship with the parish the following Sunday, Eric being the preacher.

Various theories have circulated attempting to explain why the north and north-west of the city suffered so much damage on that Easter Tuesday night. The most likely explanation is that a dense smokescreen released from the shipyards in an attempt to disguise their exact location might have been successful in confusing the German pilots who may have mistaken the Belfast Waterworks for the shipyards. Whatever the reason, many of the homes in the Woodvale area were destroyed. Within the space of one 24-hour period 14 of the congregation were laid to rest. Eric comments: 'It was a harrowing experience for an unordained probationer minister to have the responsibility to take those funerals: there was no representative of the Church at large or indeed of the remainder of the circuit present to support and share.'

Janet Devlin summarises the terrible consequences of the 'Belfast Blitz', as the three nights of air attacks are known: 'Inevitably it was the ordinary working family who suffered most in the attacks, with 100,000 made homeless and nearly 1,000 killed and 2500 injured over three nights. There was a heavy death-toll, and the material damaged involved works, stores, churches, halls, schools, shops, suburban villas, and humble homes.' Belfast had now experienced the same devastation and suffering inflicted on many other British towns and cities, but the thought remains that much of it might have been avoided if the authorities at the time had acted on the warnings they received.

The air raids, however, did have one good result: King George VI's calls for National Days of Prayer were now seen as a time for the various Protestant denominations to pray together. The day of ecumenical relationships in which both Catholics and Protestants prayed together had not yet arrived but mutual respect between the Protestant denominations developed and Eric appreciated this: 'As so often happens, non-theological factors came into play.' After Easter Tuesday the Protestant clergy in the Woodvale area met together and divided the streets into areas of responsibility with each of them undertaking to visit the air raid shelters in a given set of streets and to keep one another informed of matters affecting them.

Throughout his life Eric avoided identifying himself with any political party. This stance regarding the place of the Christian minister in party politics had its beginnings in Woodvale. He received an invitation to speak at a large political meeting: 'In many ways the invitation was tempting but I felt it obligatory to refuse. I came then to the conclusion that the Church's function is to encourage its members to be politically aware and active. It should however recognise that different members in good conscience will opt for differing methods and parties. The Church should support all of them and encourage them to recognise the integrity of each other.' He felt strongly that the minister joining a party, whether he wishes it or not, creates a psychological barrier between himself and members of his congregation who think differently. In his Autobiographical Notes he reflected: 'In my congregations I have had members of several parties. I have tried to encourage all of them and was able to do so more effectively, I believe, by not being a member of any party. That has never prevented me from having my own opinions and endeavouring to state the Christian criteria by which political and other decisions should be taken.'

He felt he had freedom to speak his mind on local and national issues while ministering in Woodvale. Quite unexpectedly, however, another opportunity to offer such comments opened up for him when Dr Northridge asked him to write 'Notes of the Week' in the *Irish Christian Advocate*. When he was a student at Trinity he had benefited financially by writing articles for the *Irish Times*, but this would be a more regular commitment even though its readership was smaller. The author remained anonymous but the 'Notes' were thought to have a semi-editorial status. The topics dealt with ranged from comment on the war, through local and national politics to domestic church issues. What was asked for was Christian comment on whatever subject was under discussion. His comments for the most part passed unnoticed but occasionally there were murmurings. On one occasion, however, his notes nearly landed both the editor and himself in the law courts. There had been trouble in Whiteabbey Hospital, at that time controlled by Belfast Corporation. A Corporation Committee of six had been appointed to enquire into civic affairs generally and Whiteabbey Hospital in particular. Its report was published in the summer of 1941 but rejected at a special meeting of the Corporation. Press and public reaction was critical in the extreme at the Corporation's treatment of the report. In the *Advocate* Eric wrote:

> Disgust, contempt and nausea are terms almost too mild to apply to the feelings of all decent citizens at the sorry farce enacted in the fair, but betrayed, name of democracy. With an irresponsibility that one would

hardly expect in a kindergarten, twenty-one members of Belfast Corporation deliberately sabotaged an honest and promising attempt to clean up the civic affairs of Belfast. The debate did little justice to democracy, the proceedings are a filthy blot on Belfast's already muddied appearance; the result shows how utterly bankrupt spiritually and morally we are.

He then went on to predict that the Government might well suspend the Corporation and appoint Commissioners, a prediction that was fulfilled. The note continued:

> The appointment of Commissioners may be a help towards efficiency, economy and purity, which last week's meeting would seem to prove impossible under the present regime. But this must be said, Commissioner rule is not democracy; but perhaps we are like the Germans – not ready for democratic rule.

Comment in the secular press led to litigation and writs for libel and Dr Northridge learned that the *Advocate* had escaped by a hair's breadth!

The demands of pastoral care following the Blitz did not allow much time to prepare for ordination in June 1941. His 'digs' in Oldpark Avenue had been half wrecked and he had been forced to make yet another change of accommodation, one of several during his time at Woodvale. His final written examinations in March had presented no difficulty but his 'trial' sermon at a public service had been planned for Monday 28 April, followed the next day by an oral examination in doctrine, church history and Methodist teaching, in front of ministers of the Belfast District. Dr McCrea, Chairman of the District, assured him that everyone knew how busy he had been in the aftermath of the Easter Tuesday air raid and that he could not possibly be expected to do any study in preparation for the oral exam. McCrea said he did not propose to carry out anything in the nature of a formal examination: all that would happen would be a couple of questions about his call to the ministry and the work he had been doing at Woodvale. He was not to worry about it. Eric felt reassured! However, when the time arrived for his oral exam – he was the only candidate for ordination on the District that year – McCrea seemed to have forgotten about their conversation the previous week: 'He proceeded to grill me with a most exhaustive and difficult set of questions on all sorts of subjects. I was completely nonplussed and annoyed as well and I fear I must have demonstrated my displeasure. The questions took me aback and I simply floundered or at times remained almost silent. I left the Synod abashed and troubled.' He later learned that the Synod had decided to recommend him for ordination as they felt 'he must be better than he sounded'.

The Ordination Service was held during the Conference in Dublin that year. He had spent the previous evening with his parents: 'They knelt on either side of me at the Communion rail following the ordination. It was for them the fulfilment of the prayers they had offered nearly twenty-eight years previously. For me it was a searching day and another step along a road that has never been without its difficulties and disappointments. And yet it was a road I know I had to travel.'

A year later the Methodist Conference met in Belfast and at its final stationing session on 10 June his appointment as Resident Chaplain to Methodist College was ratified. The experiences he had shared with the Woodvale congregation during the years of war had created a special bonding between himself and the congregation, beyond that which normally occurs between minister and people. He was grateful to God for the privilege he had had to minister in the area: 'I left Woodvale with a heavy heart but grateful to God for the opportunity to serve such an understanding and generous people. They had taught me much. We had come through much together and a bond had been created that has lasted down the years.'

6

Methodist College, Belfast
1942-50

The British Broadcasting Corporation
Broadcasting House, Ormeau Avenue, Belfast

Dear Mr Gallagher,

I have now heard from the Revd Kenneth Grayston in our Head Office about your address for the service on 12th December. Like myself he likes it very much but makes one comment. He feels that the end paragraph is not really as good as the rest of the script, for instance is there much point in asking people if they are Spivs? I know that you are aiming at everyday language, but perhaps this particular word comes with a bit of a shock. ...

Kind regards,
Yours sincerely,
Ursula Eason

Letter from the BBC, 23 November 1948

Eric Gallagher had left Methody in 1932 with the unpleasant memory of an incident which had occurred on the last night of the school term. It was customary for the wilder spirits – and often those not so wild! – to mark their departure by nocturnal farewell parties away from the attention of the resident staff. For the most part these affairs were innocuous enough. On occasion the more daring and amorous boy boarders were known to arrange rendezvous with McArthur Hall girls who were bold enough to make use of the Hall fire escape from the dormitory area. The 1932 ceremonies, however, were marked by something altogether out of the ordinary. Two or three of the teaching resident staff had been noted for their wide assortment of colourful ties. They had taken considerable delight in their choice of patterns in their attempts either to out-tie each other or to catch the attention of the pupils.

For whatever reason – possibly just a daredevil escapade – a small number of the departing seniors decided to mark the occasion by taking possession of as many as possible of the ties in question. Two or three days after everyone had left, Eric, as the head prefect in the Boarding Department, received a letter from the most senior of the staff affected: 'He told me in detail of the removal of the ties and the determination of his colleagues and himself to have them restored voluntarily, if possible, or otherwise by police intervention.' The letter disturbed him greatly. It was not hard for him to guess the identity of those concerned in the removal of the ties but he felt the resident staff had interpreted a harmless prank as a major 'crime', treating the matter more seriously than it deserved. However, he wrote to the culprits and passed on the information of possible police action if the ties were not returned. None of the persons concerned ever acknowledged his letter but he later learned that the missing property had been returned.

The whole episode upset him at the time: 'To me the affair was most unpleasant. I had a mixture of self-reproach for failure to satisfy myself and to take appropriate action over what had happened and also of some kind of guilt or shame at having to write as I did to my peers. The result of the whole experience was a reluctance to go back to school for a number of years afterwards.'

However, time is frequently a great healer and ten years later the incident did not appear to affect his enthusiasm for the new job. His sisters and brother had also been boarders in the school. Not much had changed since he had left! There was no change whatever in the layout or appearance of the buildings. The temporary huts of the 1920s were still temporary in 1942: colder in winter and no less hot in the summer. The main difference was in the living arrangements. McArthur Hall had been taken over by the Inland Revenue and was not available for girl boarders. Following the air raids of 1941 their numbers had decreased substantially and they were now housed in the main school building. Their quarters were in the east end of the school with a dividing door separating them from the male population on each of the two upper floors. The school dining hall on the main corridor had to cope with boys, girls and resident staff. This necessitated three long parallel tables running the whole length of the hall with a degree of crush and almost total immobility that was hard to tolerate during meals. The window sills served as shelves for the small receptacles in which each boy, girl and staff member treasured his or her infinitesimal ration portion of butter and jam. Appearance and hygiene meant little. The arrangement was untidy but practical. Amazingly there was little pilfering. Probably everyone was equally vulnerable and the game was not worth the risk. It also had its advantages. A little bartering system operated from time to time. For instance, Eric's youngest sister Helen, then a Junior Mistress while she was studying at Queen's University, had a mutually valuable understanding with the veteran Science master Alastair Clark whereby she exchanged her jam for his butter!

If there were few alterations in the buildings, the same could not be said for the personnel. Some of the teachers who had been there when Eric was a pupil had left, either by retirement or promotion elsewhere, or were away on war service, and new ones had taken their place. But there was still a strong nucleus of the old guard remaining with whom he was now to have the new relationship of colleague with colleague. Ronald Marshall, Alastair Clark, W.J. Bullick, J.A. Bown – all of them had taught him and all became close friends. Clark, one of the 'characters' in the school at the time, drew him aside and offered some advice: 'Sonny,' he said, 'don't look for trouble: there's a great deal of it around and it will find you.' Fred Jeffrey, whom he already knew, was among the staff who had recently come to the college.

In his first few years he found himself with the responsibility for the Religious Education curriculum right through the school, assisted only by a few students from Edgehill College who were needed to ensure each class had a teacher. In addition, he taught a number of 'secular' subjects: English, French, History and Current Affairs. His predecessor, Gerald Myles, had advised him that this wide range of subjects would gain him greater credibility throughout the school and particularly among the staff. But it was also necessary because until the 1947 Northern Ireland Education Act was introduced, Religious Education teachers were required to take a stated number of 'secular' subjects to ensure Government financial support.

Each Sunday morning there was the Sunday school to be held before the boarders went to their respective churches: University Road for Methodist boys and girls, Fitzroy for Presbyterian girls and the Crescent for boys, and finally St Thomas' for Church of Ireland boys and girls. It was always a problem to find sufficient teachers. Volunteers from University Road and some neighbouring churches were always welcome and some of the resident staff were willing to help. That Sunday school was compulsory did not make it popular with the pupils and Eric therefore resolved to make it as relevant and useful as possible, considering it as one of the most important of his obligations, declining invitations to preach which would necessitate absence from Sunday school.

Boarders were also expected to go to church in the evening. Evening congregations at the time were well attended, possibly more so than the morning services. The Revd Wesley Roddie, minister of the University Road church, a captivating preacher, had a reputation for inviting chaplains and choirs from the armed services stationed in Northern Ireland. Black American service choirs were always a special attraction. The church was filled to capacity every Sunday evening – on occasion some of the congregation would find themselves sitting on the pulpit steps. For the most part the boarders enjoyed the services although from the staff point of view there was always a problem of not losing contact with them in the crowded church and on the way back to the college in the blackout. Church officials frequently forgot to cordon off the seats at the back of the gallery, normally reserved at the morning and evening services for the Methody pupils. It was this problem which eventually led to the formation of a Boarders' evening service in the college.

On one Sunday evening in the Easter term of 1944 Eric had volunteered to take charge of the boarders. When he arrived at the church he was told that the seats in the gallery had been taken and that the best the stewards could do was to spread the boys all over the building in ones and twos and that some would be on the pulpit steps. Eric was aware that under these conditions he might well lose contact with some of the boys so he decided to take the group across the road to the Crescent Presbyterian Church. During the service he had time to consider the implications of what he had done and realized there could well be repercussions. He brought the boys back to the college at the conclusion of the service, discussed what had taken place with Ronald Marshall, the Senior Resident Master, and decided that he should immediately see Dr Northridge, then Secretary of the Board of Governors. Northridge was sympathetic and understanding about the situation and after several others were consulted Eric was asked if there was any solution to the problem. He indicated that his preference would be for a service in the college each Sunday evening for all the boarders, girls as well as boys. This short service soon became what he regarded as one of the week's highlights. He involved both staff and pupils in the reading of lessons and frequently had visiting preachers. The BBC often broadcast these services, providing he was the preacher.

Eric gradually took on further responsibilities within the college. When he arrived in 1942, he was asked to share in games duties and so on every Wednesday afternoon and Saturday morning he found himself refereeing some rugby match at Pirrie Park, the 15-acre site acquired cheaply during the height of the depression in the early 1930s. It had expansive playing fields and also accommodation which served as a preparatory school. Eventually he was asked to take responsibility for the 3rd XV, an added duty which he welcomed warmly. Then, at the start of the Easter term 1943, John W. Henderson, the Headmaster who had been in charge when he was a pupil, summoned a number of the staff – including Eric – to his office and announced that he wanted the college to have a Company of the Army Cadet Force in addition to the Air Training Corps which was under the command of another teacher, F.P. Rose. He believed it was a contribution the college ought to make since it was large enough to warrant both companies. Henderson announced that W.H. Mol would be the Commanding Officer and the other staff present would be his colleagues.

The Headmaster's announcement had taken all the staff by surprise, not least Eric. Once again, he reviewed his past feelings about military service and reviewed them in the light of his present position as a school chaplain:

> When I had time to reflect, I began to ask myself what I had let myself in for. For years I had been as nearly a pacifist as made no odds. Was I going back on all my principles? Like most other moral problems there were two sides to it. I had already had to face the challenge of service with the Forces and I had applied to be sent on active service as a chaplain. I had seen at first hand what the enemy had done to Belfast; war was a fact of life – there was no longer any argument about the rights and wrongs of military action. There was another side to the proposition as well – the war showed no signs of an early termination. Large numbers of MCB boys would unquestionably join up – was there not something to be said for giving them some idea about the elementary principles of army service? There was also my position as chaplain – would ACF membership help or hinder? On balance again I thought it might well help and be of no hindrance in my school responsibilities. So I let Mr Henderson's decision stand.

Throughout his time in Methody he never regretted this decision but occasionally in later life he often wondered if he had been wrong. It took up a lot of his time: on Tuesday afternoons they paraded up and down the school quadrangle, often to the amusement of others, and there were various exercises to complete on other afternoons; there were training courses to attend and every summer there was a training camp.

In 1944 with the apparent easing of the war situation, the college began to adjust itself to what should be done when peace came back. One change was to revive and develop the former House system for both boys and girls. Each pupil was allocated to a particular House and House Masters and Mistresses were appointed. Eric was appointed in charge of Bedell House and retained this responsibility until he left in 1950.

When he was appointed to the college he resolved that he would try as far as possible to keep in touch with the wider life of the Church. Consequently he accepted whatever invitations came his way to take services: the only qualification being that they did not affect his school duties. He was appointed as the Belfast District Youth Secretary and he was also elected to the Belfast Battalion Executive of the Boys' Brigade. In addition he was asked to act as leader of two or three harvest camps arranged by the YMCA for senior schoolboys. These were held near Clough in County Down and outside Lisburn. His duties were to find farmers who might be willing to have the boys as volunteer workers in the fields, to make a daily visit to the farms where they were working and to be responsible for the overseeing of the camp day and night.

The new Sunday evening Boarders' Service curtailed his ability to accept preaching invitations during term-time but it was possible during the vacations. One of his most frequent invitations came from the Moira Circuit and it was to prove the contact by which he met Barbara, his wife. Hospitality on the Moira Circuit was often in the Spence family home where there was traditionally an open door for Methodist preachers and, during the war years, for members of the serving Forces, whether British, American or Belgian. The house belonged to Mr Howard Spence. Also in the home were his sister May and their brother Edwin, whose wife had died many years previously and who had come to live with his brother and sister in Magheralin accompanied by his son George and daughters Emily and Barbara.

By this time the Gallagher family had come to regard the eldest son as − in Eric's own words − 'an almost hopeless bachelor'! His parents were becoming concerned that he showed no indication or inclination towards matrimony:

'Indeed, when the subject was broached I would say to my mother that if she were good enough to draw up a short list of possibilities, I would endeavour to make a final selection.' All this was to change as a result of his Moira preaching engagements:

> I found myself irresistibly and pleasantly drawn to Edwin's younger daughter Barbara. There was a charm and vivacity about her that made me immediately interested. And I tried to convince myself that the interest was reciprocated in spite of an almost ten-year difference in our ages. I did not need much convincing.

Yes, he soon discovered that his feelings were reciprocated and romance blossomed quickly! They had met in the summer of 1944 and before the holidays were over Barbara had been introduced to his parents: 'They were happy and so was I!' They were engaged at the beginning of December and married on 30 June 1945, the day after the summer term ended. His father officiated at the wedding assisted by Barbara's uncles, John N. Spence – who as President in 1940 had summoned Eric to the Grosvenor Hall to discuss the choice between chaplaincy to the Forces and chaplaincy at Methody – and R. Hull Spence, and the Moira minister, William S. Twinem. Eric remembered, 'Rain fell throughout the day: it had no effect whatever on our good spirits.' For their honeymoon they went cycling for two weeks around County Donegal and into County Sligo: 'To go cycling was not considered the natural thing to do but we did it and never regretted it.' The last few days were spent in Mullaghmore, County Sligo. Eric had promised to act as chaplain to a Boys' Brigade Officers' Training Course in Taunton in Somerset during the month of August and he completed his final preparations during those last days of the honeymoon: 'Barbara thus very early on discovered something of the kind of life she so uncomplainingly endured over the years.'

For a long time the Principal of Edgehill College had retained the title of 'Chaplain' at Methody, a piece of legislation that was not changed when the Theological College moved to separate premises at Lennoxvale. When Dr Northridge became Principal of Edgehill in 1943 he gave up the joint position in the school and Eric was officially named 'Chaplain'. He had been appointed 'Resident Chaplain' in 1942, a year later was officially Chaplain, and in 1944 was asked to be Senior Resident Master in the Boarding Department. Initially he was apprehensive that it would be difficult to combine responsibility for discipline with the work of chaplain: 'I felt and after all the years still feel that responsibility for discipline and the work of chaplain and spiritual adviser made uneasy bedfellows. It was difficult enough to be a class teacher and chaplain at the same time. The addition of full responsibility for the boarding department would, I felt, make the position intolerable.' He voiced his concern and reluctance to Mr Falconer, the new Headmaster, but to no avail.

His appointment as Senior Resident Master coincided with the beginning of married life. For the first three years they had a flat in College Gardens, which faced the school, but when the girl boarders were rehoused in their former premises in McArthur Hall at the beginning of the school year 1948-49, Eric and Barbara moved into a flat immediately above the central doorway of the main school building. Eric comments: 'It was to prove a very happy arrangement.' Just before this move their joy knew no bounds when a baby daughter, Ruth, was born on 21 May.

Barbara very quickly came to know the boarders – she agreed to take a Sunday school class on Sunday mornings and so began to make personal contact with them. Very soon she was inviting three or four boarders for tea every Sunday afternoon. In the relaxed atmosphere of the flat the pupils were very much at their ease. One Sunday afternoon remained in Eric's memory: 'Our guests included one of the most diminutive boys in the boarding establishment. His appetite was gargantuan, completely in inverse proportion to his size. He devoured every piece of bread offered to him and, ignoring the cake that was on the table, like Oliver Twist kept asking for more. When the last piece had disappeared Barbara asked him if he would like to have some cake. His reply was succinct: "No thank you, Mrs.Gallagher. Tea is not my big meal!" The same small boy [Charles 'Beamer' Maguire] like others before him grew tall: tragically he was killed when his jet aircraft crashed into a Scottish hillside when he was on manoeuvres.'

Boarders particularly became indebted to the Gallaghers for their love and hospitality. They were affectionately known as 'Mr and Mrs Fag', nicknamed after Northern Ireland's famous brand of cigarettes! Donald Hayes entered boarding at the age of ten and experienced the genuineness of their pastoral care: ' In an environment of food restrictions, inhuman initiation ceremonies, frequent corporal punishment and prevailing homesickness, Fag's sitting-room was an oasis of understanding, caring, compassion and pragmatic common-sense. I knew God cared, I knew my family cared, but it was nice to know someone else cared too.'[1]

At a special fiftieth boarders' reunion dinner in 1998 there was no hesitation regarding the choice of person to be the guest of honour – Eric Gallagher!

During Eric Gallagher's time as school chaplain there were signs that his ability was being recognized by others in the wider Church. One example relates to the situation which followed the death of the Headmaster, John Henderson, in May 1943. For whatever reason the Governors of the college were slow in appointing a successor. John Falconer, Vice-Principal, had been appointed acting Headmaster but seven months later no appointment had been made. Senior staff in the school – and others like Eric – were concerned that a further period of uncertainty would be damaging to the school and therefore drafted a letter to the Governors indicating their concern that an appointment should be made as soon as possible. There was need, they argued, for clear and authoritative direction at the top. In the circumstances they wished to assure the Governors that if, in their wisdom, they wished to appoint Mr Falconer, he would have the full and unquestioned support of the signatories and, they believed, the total staff. The document with a supporting letter was delivered to the Board of Governors a day or so before the end of the Christmas term.

Eric was spending that Christmas vacation with his parents in Portadown. To his surprise he had a visit from Dr Northridge who quizzed him about the letter from the staff and the motivation which lay behind such an unusual initiative. Eric did not regard himself as a spokesman for the staff but he tried to answer Northridge's questions, explaining the unease among staff members regarding the delay in appointing a successor to Mr Henderson. Northridge was particularly interested in learning about staff attitudes to Mr Falconer. The letter and the conversation must have had an effect because a few days later at the beginning of the second term the Chairman of the Board announced the appointment of Mr Falconer as Headmaster!

Another indication of a growing awareness of his ability is evident in his appointment in 1948 to an important Conference committee 'The Commission on the Condition of our Work'. The war had taken its toll and it was more and more evident that the Church could no longer afford to keep ministers in some of the isolated and very dependent appointments that had been such a marked feature of the pre-war Church. In any case numbers had decreased and there was a much smaller supply of candidates coming forward for the ministry. The Commission was composed of 41 ministers and lay persons. Two young ministers were included: 'To my surprise I was one of them.' The Commission presented an interim report in 1949 and again in 1950 when a small continuation group, of which he was a member, was directed to stay in being for one more year and report in 1951. This final report adopted by the Conference covered a wide spectrum:

> Matters on which the Conference made decisions included: the publication of a statement on the Faith and Worship of the Church; a revision of the boundaries of Methodist Districts and Circuits; an increase in ministerial stipends; a revised and lengthy statement on the conditions of membership of the Methodist Church in Ireland; the designation of a day to be known as Reformation Sunday; arrangements for the better promotion of interest in Overseas Work, a short term of ministerial service overseas and in Britain, and the care

of overseas students in Ireland; and the appointment of a 'Committee on Theological Thought'.

Eric appreciated the opportunity to serve on the Commission: 'This was my first introduction to the hard facts and inner working of the Church at large. It was a learning experience and one that helped me to know personally and come to respect some of the outstanding ministers and lay persons of Irish Methodism. The experience I gained from it were to stand me in good stead before many years were out.'

In 1948 his ministerial colleagues within the first ten years of 'travelling' in the Methodist Connexion elected him Chairman of the Junior Ministers' Convention and two years later he was asked to address the annual Conference on the subject of Infant Baptism, a request that he found a little ironic in light of the difficulties he had experienced as a candidate on the same subject at the Board of Examiners.

The late forties also mark Eric's initiation in the area of ecumenism. In 1945 the Methodist Conference had appointed him as one of their three representatives on the newly formed Youth Committee of the Irish Churches, whose immediate task was to prepare for Irish participation in the First World Conference of Christian Youth to be held in Oslo during the summer of 1947. Barbara accompanied him on this trip to Norway – a memorable experience for both of them. Spurred on by the enthusiasm for ecumenism he had witnessed in Norway he shared with Jim Boyd, a Presbyterian member of the Youth Committee, in organising an 'Irish Amsterdam' in the summer of 1949, basically a follow-up to the First Assembly of the World Council of Churches formed a year earlier in Amsterdam. Jim and Eric found it difficult to persuade the elderly members of the Irish Council of Churches about the usefulness of such a gathering in Ireland, concerned as they were about the amount of work that might be involved in arranging a residential conference – as they proposed – and also the financial implications. They agreed when the two of them volunteered to assume responsibility for the accommodation and financial arrangements. The venue was

Methodist College and the residential participants were housed and fed in McArthur Hall. Eric comments: 'The conference was a marked success. It was another milestone on my ecumenical journey.'

Sometime after they were married Eric and Barbara had discussed and prayed about the possibility of offering for overseas service. A visit to Belfast of the General Secretary of the Methodist Missionary Society brought matters to a head. He was to speak to a meeting of ministers in the Grosvenor Hall. Eric went to the meeting and at its conclusion spoke with the Secretary: 'The conversation was short. The Missionary Society was in greater need of money in the post-war situation than it was of missionaries. I put my offer "on hold" and it has been there ever since.' However, he was wary of staying too long in the school chaplaincy post: 'When I joined [the staff] in 1942 I had no thought of making a permanent career in education. At that time the mood of the Conference I thought unfavourable to ministers staying too long in what was called "a separated appointment". I had consequently made up my mind that I should leave before I outstayed my welcome.' During the year 1947-48 the Cregagh congregation in East Belfast issued him an invitation to become its minister after the Conference of 1950. Cregagh had a large congregation, at the time possibly one of the largest in British Methodism. He felt the invitation was both 'flattering and challenging'. The 1950 Conference decided it should be honoured and 'some days later with heavy hearts and yet with expectation we moved to Cregagh'.

7

Cregagh, Belfast
1950-54

So often people's reputations and characters are blackened and almost destroyed by hearsay gossip on the part of others who have never met or heard or talked to the person they are criticising.

Eric Gallagher, Autobiographical Notes

Only a last-minute change to the 'List of Stations' approved by the 1950 June Conference meant that Eric went to serve in Cregagh! Francis Kellett, minister of the Centenary Church in Dublin, had died near the end of 1949 and when the Stationing Committee met in May 1950 to begin its work on stationing, Eric's name was set alongside that of the Centenary Church and remained there until the first 'reading of stations' at the Ministerial Session of the Conference which met in Dublin in the second week of June.[1] The custom then was to have a reading on the first or second day of the Ministerial Session and then adjourn final decisions until the Ministerial Session met again at the conclusion of the Representative Session attended by lay representatives. Only at the final reading of the stations – and arising from a proposal by the Belfast District Stationer from the floor of the Conference – was his name changed to the Cregagh appointment and the name of Robert Livingstone set alongside that of the Centenary Church in Dublin.

In his Autobiographical Notes Eric reflected on the possible effect this late change in stationing had on his life: 'In the afterlight I am convinced that the sudden developments of those last few minutes of the Conference of 1950 changed the whole course of my life and ministry.' Itinerancy in Irish Methodism normally meant that most ministers served in appointments in various parts of Ireland. Eric had already served for 12 years in two Belfast appointments and it would have been quite understandable had the Church decided to appoint him to serve in Dublin or somewhere other than Northern Ireland. This late change of stationing – even though it was honouring an earlier invitation – meant that he would continue to serve in Belfast, possibly for another five years at least. He was clear in his own mind that at no time had he ever tried to influence the stationing process. The fact that at this point in his life – and, indeed, on later occasions – he found himself still serving in Belfast was due to circumstances entirely beyond his control and this gave him a peace of mind that remained with him throughout his ministry.

In 1950 Cregagh was part of the Mountpottinger Circuit which also included the congregations of Pitt Street, Mountpottinger and Bloomfield, the total senior membership being almost 1,300 hundred, making it the third largest circuit in Irish Methodism. Cregagh was by far the largest of the four congregations with 1,100 hundred families on the congregational roll. The church and halls had been built in the late 1920s and, like Woodvale, the congregation was drawn mainly from people living nearby – for the most part inside an area bounded by the Castlereagh, Beersbridge, Woodstock, Ravenhill, Rosetta and Hillfoot Roads. Many of the men were employed in the shipyard and aircraft factory. Most of them were skilled tradesmen, proud of their skills and proud of the work they turned out. A considerable minority were owner-occupiers with the remainder in houses rented privately or from the Housing Trust. There were a few self-employed business folk and a small number of teachers and bankers, and some in local or central government employment. Eric commented: 'It was sociologically "a good mix" and, as I came to realise, a reasonable "mix" also theologically with perhaps the emphasis in to-day's parlance veering towards the "conservative evangelical". Its Methodist roots were not pronounced and could hardly have been expected to be so, for the majority of those who attended the services or who claimed an allegiance to the congregation had joined it, as is the Belfast custom in a developing area, because the church was nearby and catered for the children and young people.'

The church seated about 600, equally divided between the gallery and the ground floor, with the majority of the young people in the upstairs area. On Sunday mornings the church was usually well filled and in the evenings extra seating was often required. Because of the large congregational roll Eric always had an assistant minister, three altogether during his four years on the circuit: Tom Crabbe, Ivan Biggs and Brian Cobbe. He found them to be hard workers and good colleagues. Church organizations for children, youth and adults were all well attended. Half-way through his ministry in Cregagh the Sunday school roll totalled 600 and there were altogether 60 Sunday school teachers. The Boys' Brigade, Girls' Brigade, and Youth Club all had large numbers and in addition to these a Youth Fellowship was started in February 1952, 60 to 70 attending each Sunday evening. It gave Eric great pleasure when one of the BB officers, Jim Brady, was selected to play for Ireland at rugby and even more when Brady was appointed BB captain at the age of 21: 'He did for the boys in his care what he told me Jack Kyle had done for the younger members of the Irish rugby team. He was a stabilising influence to whom all the boys looked up.' Both Eric and the assistant minister attended the BB camps and the young people's residential weekends.

Eric was particularly impressed by the evidence he witnessed of people caring for one another. When one of the men in the bowling club was diagnosed with tuberculosis – a rampant disease at the time – and discharged from hospital with the advice that his chances of survival depended on the amount of fresh air he could avail himself of, the men of the bowling club scanned the advertising columns of the newspapers and finally read of a second-hand revolving summer house that was for sale. A group went to inspect it and decided it would fit into the small back garden. They purchased it, had it dismantled and soon they had it erected where it was needed. 'It made a number of unexpected extra years of tolerable life possible for one who otherwise would not have had them.'

In Woodvale he had valued the weekly meeting for prayer and Bible study. It had its strengths and weaknesses but, adequately prepared for and organized, it had proved a great source of strength and encouragement. The Cregagh meeting took place on Wednesday evenings and was held in the minor hall with an attendance of something over 20. With a planned programme of Bible study aided by map and black board and with a period, not too tediously long, for prayer, the numbers grew steadily until the minor hall became too small. Eventually it was decided to move to the adjacent Smiley Hall where numbers well in excess of 100 attended regularly. One incident at the end of Eric's first year was memorable: 'One of the company in the prayer time moved me deeply when he prayed, "O Lord, we thank thee for thy servant whom thou hast sent among us. Thou knowest the work he is doing in this corner of thy vineyard. Thou knowest what we said about him before he came." I felt I had arrived.' The incident stayed in his memory down the years, not only for its amusing and pleasing side but also as an illustration of what he believed has been too common in Northern Ireland: 'So often people's reputations and characters are blackened and almost destroyed by hearsay gossip on the part of others who have never met or heard or talked to the person they are criticising.' Not long after this particular Wednesday evening Bible study another member of the congregation, a close friend of the person who had prayed for Eric, was crossing by boat to Glasgow. He was having supper in the ship's dining room. At the next table two other passengers were doing likewise. He could not help overhearing their conversation. Eric continues the story as it was later reported to him: 'They were discussing me and not to my advantage. Eventually the Cregagh member spoke to them. He could not help, he said, hearing what they were saying. He asked if they knew me personally and was told they knew all about me. He again asked if they had ever met me and he was eventually told they had not. He then told them that he belonged to the Cregagh congregation and had been inclined to hold the same views about me before my arrival because of the things he had been told. He went on to say that he had changed his mind and that he had determined never again to judge anyone without first hearing him and getting to know him.'

Both incidents were very important for Eric Gallagher: 'It is a great pity that many other Northern Ireland people have yet to learn that lesson. The lives of many of us would have been much easier if they had.'

Pastoral responsibility for the large number of families attached to the church led to two new initiatives. The first was a new system of indexing to simplify the visiting list for the two ministers. Eric quickly realized that the mobile society had arrived. Additions and deletions were the order of the day as some families moved to other areas and new families arrived. It was simply impossible to have unaltered pages. The normal visiting book which ministers used appeared inadequate as they tried to keep track of every member of each family. When they called at homes, they were anxious to be able to talk about each member of the family, where they worked or what school they attended. Some recall facility was needed.

An earlier conversation with Alan Buchanan when he was rector of St Mary's parish in Belfast, proved helpful in solving his problem:[2] 'He had let me see something of his card index system. I remembered enough of it to enable me to design my own loose-leaf system with a page for each family with all names, ages and useful information for every member and a column in which to enter the date of each visit. With a corresponding card for the index, it was possible to have all the family names filed alphabetically complete with details, and also to have them divided into district or area sections in the loose-leaf visiting holder.' When they went visiting they now had in front of them all the information they required and in addition to that each page carried the dates on which either minister had visited the home. There was also a section of green pages for insertion in the book. This contained the names and addresses of those who were ill, bereaved or elderly and who were in need of more frequent visits. From that time on, it was always possible to have visiting lists completely up to date. It was the simplest thing in the world to add or delete a page as and when a new family arrived or another moved to another district.

In such a large congregation there was a great deal of sick visiting to be done in the homes and the hospitals. Particularly in the winter months there were numerous funerals, and weddings also took up a great deal of time. Three funerals in one day were not unknown. In Woodvale Eric had been able to visit every home at least three times in the year, but in his four years in Cregagh he managed only two complete visitations of the congregation: 'That was a great regret to me for I am old-fashioned enough to believe that there is still no real substitute for meeting one's congregation in their own homes.'

The appointment of 'Congregational Visitors' was the second initiative which Eric introduced to improve the pastoral care of the congregation. In the 1950s ministers were still required once each quarter to write out and sign a 'Class Ticket' for every adult member. Under the traditional Methodist pastoral system these tickets were expected to be given by the 'Class Leaders' to the individual members. The problem was threefold. First of all some of those who received the tickets rarely, if ever, attended church, let alone presented themselves at Communion. There were, secondly, many others who had never formally been received into membership who, on every reasonable count, were well entitled to membership, even to the extent of communicating from time to time. And in the third place Class Leaders found themselves going to homes and distributing tickets to some members of the family and not to others. It all made for confusion and misunderstanding at best and for resentment at worst. It could further be made more unacceptable when the Class Leader was known to call at one home and not at another.

'This untidy and frequently misunderstood pastoral system coupled with the huge numbers for whom we were responsible,' Eric commented, 'led us to devise a scheme of Congregational Visitors. The complete pastoral roll was divided into a large number of small area sections and a Congregational Visitor was appointed for each section.' Regular meetings were held for the visitors at which they would be given a 'hand-out' of some kind, whether a bulletin or notice of a coming event, and in addition they were given oral information and answers to questions that might arise as they called at the houses on their lists. This meant that no homes were omitted and the ministers were quickly alerted to situations where specific attention was desirable. The visitors felt their work was useful and appreciated the fact that they had something to hand out in each home: they had not, as it were, to operate in a vacuum.

Soon after Eric arrived on the circuit he was aware of new opportunities for church planting in the Glenburn Estate which was bounded on its south side by the Montgomery Road and on the north side by the Hillfoot Road. Already Methodist families had purchased houses in it and others were negotiating with Messrs Stewart and Robb, the developers. Because Mr Robert Stewart was known to be a Methodist, Eric found himself approached again and again by Methodist would-be purchasers who were anxious that he should commend them to the developers. 'It was manifest', Eric declared, 'that there was going to be a sizeable Methodist community in Glenburn. Some initiative was called for if the newcomers were not to be lost to Methodism or indeed to any branch of the Christian Church.'

By September Eric had met Robert Stewart. He and his business partner had generously promised a site in the area for the building of a Methodist church. They had made the large house which was situated in the ground they were developing into site offices. 'I learned that he would be happy to place one of the rooms on its ground floor at our disposal for Sunday services, if we wished to make a start. The room measured twenty-one feet by twelve and we reckoned that we could place sixty chairs in it.' Eric discussed the proposition with Sam Johnston, Superintendent of the circuit, and Philip Hinds and Elijah Quincey, former and current circuit stewards respectively, and with their support brought the matter to the Cregagh Leaders' Meeting on 3 October. The leaders were enthusiastic and decided to ask the Church Extension Committee to provide 60 chairs. A month later a special Circuit Quarterly Meeting gave the final go-ahead and by December Sunday services and a Sunday school had started.

The project, however, was not without its cynics: 'Initially the commencement of services in Glenburn and the proposal to erect a building as soon as possible met with a measure of cynical comment on the part of some ministers and others. The suggestion was put around that the whole scheme could turn out to be my "white elephant". Today the Glenburn congregation and Sunday School are in the forefront of Irish Methodist work.' The new church soon grew quite rapidly. In 1950 they purchased two wooden halls – one a former Gospel hall and the other formerly used by the RAF – dismantled, transported and re-erected them on the site now available for the new church. By mid-October 1952 there were 14 teachers in the Sunday school which was making use of the two halls and the room in the estate Building Office.

With the expansion of the work at Glenburn it was soon evident that the existing accommodation was too small and that a large and permanent building was required. A building committee was formed in January 1953 and during May they decided that a 'two-way' hall was what they should try to build. This would provide a sanctuary recess at one end for Sunday worship purposes and a platform at the other end for weeknight meetings and events. The question, however, arose as to what should be the size and cost. Eric rightly decided that this decision was dependent on possible plans for expansion in the area by other Protestant denominations. The Church of Ireland had St Finian's parish church nearby at the top of the Cregagh Road and St John's on the Castlereagh Road just beside the Housing Trust estate. There was no likelihood of their putting another parish in the area for it would damage both existing churches. He had been appointed convenor of the Methodist Church Inter-Relations Committee in 1948 and had already established good relationships with his Presbyterian 'opposite numbers', so he had no hesitation in asking if there was any Presbyterian intention of starting a new church in the Glenburn estate: 'The answer was in the negative and on that assurance we decided to seek for a building that would accommodate approximately 400 people at what we hoped would be a cost not exceeding £20,000.' As often happens this ceiling figure had to be revised and in March 1954 the Circuit Quarterly Meeting accepted a tender of the sum of £25,470.

Building on the project started at the end of April and a stone-laying ceremony was held on the evening of Friday 18 June, one of the last important functions before Eric left the circuit. On that evening leaders and members of the growing Glenburn congregation marched from the temporary halls down the Cregagh Road and at Bell's Bridge roundabout they met members and leaders from Cregagh who had marched from the Cregagh church. Together as a united procession of witness they then marched back along Montgomery Road to the Glenburn site. Eight stones were laid that evening, one by Lady Kelly, widow of Sir Samuel Kelly, whose family had taken a keen interest in the old Castlereagh Road church which had existed prior to the Cregagh church. Another was laid in the name of the Joseph Rank Benevolent Trust by its secretary at the time, the Revd Bartlett Lang, a brother-in-law of Lord Rank.

Eric explains the background to the involvement of the Rank Benevolent Trust in the Glenburn venture and other church extension causes in Irish Methodism. In the spring of 1953 Philip Hinds had invited Eric to spend a weekend in London with him. They appear to have had a wonderful time: 'On the Saturday evening we had seen the famous Agatha Christie play "The Mouse Trap". On Sunday morning we had gone to hear Dr Leslie Weatherhead, in the afternoon we had listened to Donald Soper in Hyde Park and in the evening we had gone to hear Dr Martin Lloyd Jones in Westminster.'

On the Monday afternoon – without any appointment – they made their way to the home of the Revd Bartlett Lang in Reigate! 'We were not expected and it was some little time before we broke the ice with Mr and Mrs Lang. Philip engaged Mrs Lang in conversation while I talked with her husband. He was most interested in what I was able to tell him about church extension developments in Ireland. They insisted that we stay for afternoon tea and at the conclusion of a most memorable afternoon they motored us back to the station. Rank Trust interest in Irish Methodism increased dramatically after that visit. I look back on it with great gratitude. We had good reason to invite Mr Lang to lay one of the Glenburn foundation stones.'

The development of work at Glenburn was certainly a success story. The key factor, as Eric saw it, had been the early commitment to the venture given by Cregagh leaders and members living in the area of the new estate or adjacent to it. They provided the nucleus of a fellowship right from the start and undertook the responsibility of leadership in the Sunday school and other organisations that soon developed. They were a faithful and talented group of people and it was not surprising that the church grew so rapidly.

One of the unforeseen consequences of the church-planting at Glenburn was the revision of circuit boundaries which resulted in Cregagh and Glenburn being recognized as a new circuit as from the 1953 Conference. The rapid development of the work at Glenburn had meant that new decisions were being taken almost weekly and they needed to be taken quickly. It was time-consuming and almost irksome to have issues discussed at length among the folk at Glenburn and then again at the Cregagh Leaders' Meeting and finally to have them gone over again at the Circuit Quarterly Meeting in Mountpottinger. Most were agreed that in these circumstances new circuit arrangements were required and the necessary legislation was brought through the Mountpottinger Circuit Quarterly Meeting in December 1952, the Belfast District Synod in May 1953 and finally the Conference which met in Portadown a month later. The Mountpottinger Circuit now included Mountpottinger, Pitt Street and Bloomfield, while the new Cregagh Circuit included the Cregagh and Glenburn societies. It was a decision reached in the interest of improving administrative efficiency and it was carried through with the goodwill of the leaders in the various societies.

The Conference of the Methodist Church in Ireland had decided that 1953 should be regarded as a 'Year of Evangelism'. Eric brought the Conference directive to the Cregagh leaders and shared with them his concern that whatever was done should be well prepared and adequately carried out: 'I was anxious to avoid anything in the nature of what might be called a "tip and run" mission by an outsider who knew little of the local situation and who might come with little in the way of *ad hoc* preparation.'

The leaders decided on two major projects. The first was that a special series of services should be held in the autumn of 1953. These were to be carefully and prayerfully prepared for during the intervening months. The midweek meetings and the Sunday services would be used to remind the congregation of what was in mind. The Revd Edward Lindsay, a friend of Eric's from his Edgehill days and one who was already well known to some in the congregation, was invited to take the services. Lindsay was at that time stationed in Adare, County Limerick: 'I was convinced he had the qualities of heart and mind to meet the challenge of such a mission.'

When the time for the special services arrived Lindsay stayed with the Gallaghers in the manse at Ardenlee Avenue and this gave them the opportunity to discuss together the way things were going. Eric was pleased with the outcome of all the months of preparation: 'With great dignity and without anything in the way of cheap emotion he [Ted Lindsay] presented the claims of the gospel night by night to large congregations – the gallery was in use as well as the ground floor. The outcome far exceeded the expectations of minister and leaders alike.'

The second decision taken by the leaders was to do something unusual with the young people of the congregation – to engage them in the production of a play on the life and work of John Wesley! Again, Eric wanted everything well done and carefully prepared. He enlisted the services of Ted Hazelton, then on the staff of the Methodist College and a brilliant producer of school plays. For two or three months Hazelton kept a large cast busy at rehearsals. He wanted the play to have some local colour and persuaded Eric to write an Irish riot scene to replace an English scene in the original. The production took place over four nights in April 1953. It was reported in the *Irish Christian Advocate* of 24 April in very glowing terms and was so successful that in the following autumn it was on the stage again playing, as before, to crowded houses. Eric summed up the value of the production: 'The whole project did a great deal, as all amateur drama does, to bind together a large company of young people – actors, stage hands, back room folk, carpenters, electricians, stewards, ticket sellers and others. It was a huge success not only in teaching the young people and those who came to watch something about the beginnings of Methodism. It also helped greatly in building up the fellowship.'

The time in Cregagh was tinged with both joy and sadness for the Gallagher family circle. Joy came in the form of two new additional family members: Helen, born on 4 July 1951 and David on 22 June 1953. The family have always had a slight sense of amusement that Helen was born in the Ardenlee Nursing Home, close to the manse, as it later became the site of Dr Ian Paisley's Martyrs' Memorial Church.[3] Eric commented, 'She makes no claim to having been born again in the same place!' David was born just nine days after the death of Eric's mother, Helen. In the spring of that year she had not been feeling well and her doctor had referred her to the consultants in the Samaritan Hospital, Belfast. An exploratory operation was carried out: 'The news was brutal in its directness. My mother had six weeks before her at the most. For father, as for us all but for him especially, it was a devastating blow. We had always known him to be a person of strength and faith and those qualities did not fail him when the trial came.'

His mother had insisted on being told the prognosis: 'She faced the news with a calmness and Christian resignation which her children will never forget. She talked to us all about what lay ahead.' Her youngest daughter – also Helen by name – was in Kenya where her husband Jimmy was involved in veterinary research. She wrote a gentle and loving letter to Helen, insisting, 'Your place is with Jimmy and the children.'[4]

Involvement in the wider Church and society also continued during these years. In February 1951 Eric was appointed by the Ministry of Education to succeed Dr Northridge as a member of the Belfast Education Committee. The appointment introduced him to the inner workings of a Belfast Corporation Committee and to its membership which consisted largely of representatives from the different political parties. It provided an insight into the ways of local government. Membership of this committee meant automatic membership of the Board of Education in the Methodist Church. He was also elected to two other church committees: in 1951 to the Board of Examiners which has overall responsibility for the training of ministers both in college and on probation; and in 1953 to the General Committee which is basically the main policy-making committee of the Church.

His work on the Inter-Church Relations Committee witnessed some significant developments, especially in improved relationships between Presbyterians and Methodists. Both churches were concerned not to be seen to duplicate the work of the other, particularly in new housing areas. But they were also willing to go further and experiment in pilot projects – one on the Taughmonagh estate in South Belfast was identified – in which both churches might co-operate by the building of a church staffed by a minister from one of the denominations. Eric declared: 'Gradually as the Methodist Committee and its Presbyterian counterpart considered the challenge of the new areas they came to the conclusion that joint work was in the interests of the Kingdom of God.' As convenor of the Inter-Church Relations Committee it fell to Eric to recommend the following important resolutions to the 1953 Conference:

1. The Committee finds that there is cordial sympathy with the principle of the proposal that in the building of new Churches unnecessary duplication should be avoided. There is also agreement as to the desirability of the withdrawal of ministers by one or other of the two denominations in depleted areas by mutual consent.

2. That the Conference approve of the conferences which have been held with representatives of the Presbyterian Church, with a view to facilitating the supply of religious ordinances to small groups of our members in new housing areas, by members of both denominations using the same building for public worship and other activities on terms mutually agreed

upon ... and that Conference authorise their representatives to continue their efforts in co-operation with the Presbyterian Church to meet the needs of small groups of our people in ways which shall husband the resources of our Church and promote Christian fellowship.

3. The Conference approves the scheme submitted by the Committee for joint work and worship with the Presbyterian Church in Taughmonagh.

Similar resolutions were brought to the General Assembly that year. Both churches responded positively to the challenge and the opportunity. Eric was pleased: 'I look back to what was done that year with satisfaction.' But his delight was followed by a sense of regret at the change of heart he saw developing over the years: 'Regrettably both Churches have to some extent in recent years distanced themselves from the spirit of what we achieved. One lesson neither Church really learned was the necessity to staff the joint and co-operating causes with ministers wedded to the principle of working together no matter what the local difficulties might be.'

In this and in many other situations Eric was a pioneer working for the best interests of the kingdom of God.

8

University Road, Belfast
1954-57

One day last summer, boys and girls, something quite unusual happened to our family. A strange man stopped us on a lonely road in County Kerry. We were away out on the Dingle Peninsula on holidays, and my father, who was with us, wanted to catch the early train to Dublin. So we all got up, and were on the road in good time to do the twenty-mile journey to Tralee.

We were coming to the top of the mountain – near the Glen of the Madmen – when suddenly a man stepped out into the middle of the road. He put up his hand, and signed us to stop.

I should explain that because I was on holiday I was dressed – well, I needn't describe exactly – it certainly wasn't like a minister.

Anyway, he came over to the car. 'Would ye be goin' to Tralee?' he said.

'I am,' said I.

'Would ye be near the Bank?'

'What Bank?' I asked.

'The Munster and Leinster.'

'Yes, I'll be passing,' I replied.

'Would ye ever give this letter to the manager,' he said.

'Well,' said I, 'if it's all right with you.'

'Shure, it's all right,' said he, 'it's only a lump of cash. Just hand it in, ye don't need to ask for a receipt or anythin'.'

Well, you know, boys and girls, I looked at the man again. He seemed quite sensible. Then I looked at the writing on the envelope. And it looked quite sensible too – if you know what I mean. So off we went.

We reached Tralee long before the Bank opened, and, do you know, I was quite anxious until I handed the letter over the counter, and told my story. And right enough, the envelope did contain a roll of notes.

During the winter I've thought a good deal about this man. I'd never seen him before, and I've never seen him since, but he trusted me. And because he trusted me with money that must have been precious to him, I was anxious and uneasy until I had done what he wanted.

You see, life should always be like that. When people trust you, you don't want to let them down.

Have you ever thought that God trusted every one of you with something far more valuable than a lump of cash? He has trusted you with something very wonderful – your own life. You can squander it, or throw it away, just as I could have done with the money. On the other hand, you can hand it back to God again, well looked after, and good, and useful.

God has trusted you – don't let him down.

Children's talk in broadcast service
from University Road Church, 5.5.1957

Stationing decisions continued to bring surprises and changes for the Gallaghers, but none like the cliff-hanger that had brought him to Cregagh! In 1952 the Centenary Church, Dublin, had invited Eric to be their minister in 1955, when Robert Livingstone was due to leave. He was pleased with the invitation and accepted. However, the death of the Revd Wesley Roddie in October 1953 left a vacancy on the University Road Circuit which the Stationing Committee needed to fill. Articles in the *Irish Christian Advocate* at that time reveal a growing interest in student chaplaincy work at the Queen's University of Belfast so this may have prompted the Committee to search carefully for the right person to send to the circuit, as the superintendency also carried responsibility for the oversight of students. In these circumstances their choice fell on Eric Gallagher and so he left the Cregagh Circuit a year earlier than expected and took up the reins at University Road.

The congregation was not altogether unknown to him. He had worshipped there for seven years as a schoolboy and eight while on the resident staff of Methodist College. But he soon discovered that there is all the difference in the world between being a schoolboy having to go to the church or being an adult worshipper with no real roots in the congregation and being the appointed minister.

The church, situated in the South side of the city about half a mile from the centre, had been built in 1864 during a period of unparalleled church extension in Irish Methodism and in 1954, along with the Lisburn Road congregation, formed the University Road Circuit. With an adult membership of 832 and junior membership of 313 it ranked at the time as among the larger circuits in the Connexion. The morning service was well attended but Eric noticed that evening congregations were beginning to decrease, a trend that would soon affect other congregations in the city. He was also aware that younger members who married almost invariably moved away from the immediate South Belfast area. Already the houses in places like University Square and College Gardens were being taken over by the university or by architects, accountants and the like. A similar trend had commenced in Eglantine Avenue, Wellington Park and the lower part of the Malone Road. Substantial numbers of the former residents in all of these prestigious addresses had been University Road members.

Always interested in the social 'mix' of the congregations he served, Eric found that he was facing a new situation in University Road. He comments, 'The pastoral responsibility for eminent medical persons, for university professors and lecturers and for prominent business men was a new and rather daunting experience.' In addition to the lay members of the congregation he was also aware of 'an array of clerical collars to be concerned about', a reference to ministerial colleagues serving in 'separated' connexional appointments – Edgehill College Staff, the Chaplain at Methody and the Secretary of the Youth Department. He had always placed an emphasis on careful sermon preparation but possibly the composition of the congregation underlined this for him: 'The Sunday preaching preparation always demanded time and thought. The congregation was attentive and responsive and on occasion constructively critical.' His humility – or was it a lingering uncertainty regarding his own academic ability – made him add the comment: 'The preacher was always conscious that there were many present far better equipped intellectually than he was. The University Road pulpit was no place for shoddy preparation.' While he appears to have had these concerns about measuring up to the needs of the congregation, he eventually realized that human nature is basically the same everywhere as regards our need of the Christian gospel: 'I was soon to discover that they too were like the rest of us!'

He was not long in his new pastorate when he was faced with a rather delicate and controversial problem over 'pew rents' – a system whereby members of the congregation had the exclusive right to a particular pew in the church upon the payment of an annual rent. Eric was convinced that the system had long since outlived any credibility to which it might have been entitled. Nine years previously as chaplain at Methody he and Barbara had decided to sit downstairs in the church. They had had some difficulty in finding a pew on which no rent was being paid where they might sit. They had been invited to become pew holders but had declined because of their aversion to the system.

Two weeks after he arrived on the circuit, Norman Robb, at that time Lay Secretary of the Methodist Home Mission Fund, who was sometimes dubbed 'Mr University Road', called on Eric at the manse in Wellington Park. He wanted to question the new minister about his attitude to pew rents! Eric told him that he did not like them. 'Well I do and I don't want you to do anything to stop them,' Robb replied. Eric responded that he would not do anything to start a controversy over them but if one started he would not do anything to stop it. Eric later reflected: 'He felt my answer was fair enough.'

Eric soon discovered that the subject was a very live one in the congregation. It had been on the agenda of the Church Trustees for some time. The Trustees were responsible for keeping the property in good order and they depended on the income from the pew rents to keep them in business. However, he soon discovered that one or two of the Trustees – and some in the congregation – considered this method of financing to be 'unworthy'.

At his first meeting of the Trustees on 24 October the matter was on the agenda as 'business arising' from the minutes of the last meeting:

> With only one year's experience of superintendency behind me I was taken aback as to how to handle the situation. Feelings clearly ran deeply and it was obvious that the meeting was split, though I found it hard to assess which side was in the majority. Eventually after a long discussion I ventured to suggest that it might be wise to defer a decision until the next meeting and that in the meantime members might give some serious thought to the issues raised on each side of the argument. To my relief that suggestion met with unanimous approval.

When the Trustees met some weeks later it was soon clear that members had been giving a great deal of thought to the matter. Nonetheless it required a long discussion. Bit by bit Eric sensed that opinion was moving towards abolition. Eventually two members, James Smyth, a well-known dentist, and Robert Marshall, an eminent cardiologist, spoke in favour of doing away with the rents. Eric knew that both men had originally been in support of the system. 'Dr. Marshall spoke after Dr. Smyth and I asked him if he was prepared to propose accordingly. He was and so proposed. The motion was seconded and the vote resulted in a considerable majority in favour of abolition. It was all reasonably amicable and the meeting got down to the business of alternative financial arrangements.'

Eric went home that evening 'well satisfied with the night's work'. However, the next morning the phone rang at eight o'clock. It was Norman Robb. As always he came straight to the point. He wanted to talk to Eric and to meet him 'immediately'! Robb was then living in Sunningdale Park in the north of the city but within 20 minutes he was at the manse door. 'With some trepidation I brought him upstairs to the study. This time I thought it best to open the conversation. I said to him that the previous evening we had taken a decision of which I was sure he did not approve. I got no further. He broke in immediately and said that he certainly had not approved. Then he went on to say, however, now that the decision had been taken he was going to make it his business to see that it worked. And he did. That was typical of the man. He was one of the straightest men I have ever met, someone in whom you could safely confide your greatest secret.'

While pew rents was the business of the Trustees, student chaplaincy work was the responsibility of the Leaders' Meeting. Eric was already aware that the wider Church – or at least some within it! – were concerned about the pastoral care of students and that the possibility of residential accommodation for students had been suggested. The appointment of a Student Advisory and Support Committee in October was an important first step in involving members of the congregation in chaplaincy work. Eric initiated Sunday evening gatherings for the students, holding them sometimes in the manse and sometimes in the church premises. He valued the weekly lunches he had with the Church of Ireland, Presbyterian and Roman Catholic chaplains in the University Dining Hall as it provided an opportunity to swap information and ideas, to discuss whatever possibilities there might be of joint work, and to be seen together by both staff and students.

In May 1955 there was a most unexpected development. John McGregor, one of the Trustees, called one day at the manse on his way home from work to say that he had noticed that Fountainville Cottage at the corner of Fountainville Avenue – University Road church occupied the other side of Fountainville Avenue – was on the market. He suggested it could be a property the church should think of buying. The Trustees were consulted and were of the opinion that the property should be acquired, even though they were not altogether certain for what exact purpose! It was recognized that church courts move slowly. While committees were making up their mind, the opportunity could be lost. The Trustees were in a dilemma because connexional approval would also be required. In the event McGregor purchased the cottage in his own name on the understanding that his colleagues would 'see him right' – which they later did.

Two main suggestions emerged as the best use for the new site. Eric explains: 'I had no hesitation in suggesting student purposes while some others thought that the time had arrived when the Methodist Church should have a Headquarters building in the city and that the site was suitable for such a purpose. We decided that possibly both uses could be accommodated if thought desirable.'

It was one thing, however, to be clear as to the best use of the site. The way ahead was another matter. The Trustees were prepared to donate the site to the Methodist Church for student and other purposes but the Church was not so easily persuaded that it required either student or headquarters office accommodation. A considerable sum of money had been donated to the Methodist Church through the University Road Trustees by the late Dr Hugh Turtle, one-time principal of the major building firm, McLaughlin and Harvey, the money to be used for an agreed and specific purpose. The Trustees were of the opinion that the capital could well provide at least the nucleus of the cost of the kind of building they envisaged. Eric was asked to find out what uses any of the main Church departments might make of a building erected on the site. There is no disguising the disappointment he felt when he learned the responses of the personnel in these departments: 'With the exception of the Youth Department I found no takers. None of them could see any possibility of their wanting any such accommodation. The Statutory Trustees of the Methodist Church and the Home Mission Department were all convinced that they neither needed nor wished to have any accommodation in Belfast .... We were left without any likely

Church tenants of substance with the problem of "selling" the proposal on the basis of student usage.'

Despite this negativity the 1956 Conference agreed to the appointment of a committee to explore two possible avenues of development on the Fountainville site: firstly, a Community Centre for Methodist students and other young people and, secondly, facilities for connexional requirements. This second objective was included in the terms of reference to give the departments opportunity for further thought. Sir William Robinson, Managing Director of the Bank Buildings at Royal Avenue in the city centre, was appointed chairman of the committee. They decided 'Aldersgate House' would be an appropriate name for the new building and that part of the premises should be rented out to provide a source of income for its future maintenance. Eric declared, 'Sir William kept reminding us that he had no interest in supporting a scheme that was not financially viable.' This strong conviction of the chairman led to an embarrassing and, in retrospect, somewhat amusing problem for the Committee, and especially for Eric!

The problem originated in a request from the Wesley Historical Society (Irish Branch) that the WHS archives should be moved from its unsuitable location at the Carlisle Memorial Church, Belfast, to more desirable accommodation in the new building. Sir William was opposed to the suggestion on two grounds which to him were all-compelling. In the first place he had before him the ideal of a 'living building' erected for and used by young people. To put a museum into it would make it a 'dead building' and he would have none of it. Secondly, there was the necessity of making the whole project financially viable: 'He left us in no doubt about the duties and responsibilities of trustees. Our legal and moral duty was to secure the best possible return on our money and the paltry rent the Society could afford was in no way commensurate with what our responsibilities required.'

The embarrassment for Eric lay in the fact that his father was the one representing the case for the WHS! 'RH' was convinced that the new Aldersgate House would be the best place for the Society and its archives and he also thought that it merited a concession rent. Indeed, it was hard enough to persuade him that a rent of any kind was in order! The problem was not easily solved: 'The consequence of all this was that for a few months I found myself as the "piggy in the middle" carrying out a kind of shuttle diplomacy between two equally strong and determined protagonists. Things reached a climax when we were faced with the possibility of the resignation of our chairman, if the Society were to be given a tenancy.' Eventually, however, a solution was agreed: 'RH' conceded that the Society would pay a higher rent and Sir William accepted the Society as a tenant on the plea of the Committee!

Aldersgate House was eventually built at a cost in the region of £120,000 and opened on 29 April 1960 by Lady Robinson. Originally the committee had planned to have a four-storey building which would have included provision for student accommodation, but escalating costs limited the scheme to a three-storey building, thereby jettisoning their residential plans for students. Eric was moved to another circuit in 1957 but he stayed on as Secretary of the project until 1964. The 1960 Conference approved of a scheme of management which authorized the appointed committee *inter alia* to receive the rental income, reimburse University Road Church for out-of-pocket expenses incurred in student work, meet the charges of an assistant minister responsible for student work, maintain the property, liquidate the outstanding debt and establish a fund for the extension of work among students.

The scheme took up a lot of Eric's time, skill and energy. It has provided – as the 1960 Conference envisaged – the financial basis for continuing work among students and the committee's dream of a residential centre was eventually fulfilled, albeit on a different site in the nearby Elmwood Avenue.

Toward the end of his first year on the circuit Eric was pleasantly surprised to be the recipient of a very generous gift! Alfred Cotter called one evening at the manse on his way home from work. He shared with Eric his concern that his minister should have to visit the congregation on his bicycle in all kinds of weather. He had discussed the matter with church officials suggesting it was time they provided the superintendent with a car. They apparently were in agreement with Cotter's suggestion but indicated that the finances of the congregation could not sustain such an outlay. Cotter had then decided he would meet the necessary expense out of his own pocket! Eric cherished this magnificent act of generosity: 'He told me that he was determined that his minister should have a car and there and then produced a brochure for a Morris Oxford which would be ready for me the following day. All I had to do was to go and collect it and make full use of it. I was not to discuss the matter with him again.'

Eric had expected to serve the full term of five years at University Road but the Revd Sam Baxter's request to be moved from the superintendency of Belfast Central Mission after 22 months in this position – he enjoyed the evangelistic opportunities provided through Sunday preaching and the large audiences at the Saturday evening Film Services but not the administrative demands of the job – influenced the Stationing Committee to appoint Eric to the vacancy at the Mission. He had enjoyed his short ministry at University Road and – unknown to him at the time – moved to his final ministerial appointment, one that would last for 22 years!

9

Centre stage
1957-67

Whether I like it or not I am driven inexorably to the firm conclusion that God's will for the Church is that it should be one.

Eric Gallagher, Sermon on 'Church Unity', quoted in the *Northern Whig*, 16.1.1961.

Twelve months after Eric's appointment as Superintendent of Belfast Central Mission another major responsibility was placed on his shoulders: the position of Secretary of the Conference and Secretary of the Methodist Church in Ireland. The events which led to his election as Connexional Secretary in June 1958, three years after his election as Editorial Secretary of the Conference – a position which usually ranked last in the foursome of Conference Secretaries – could not have been anticipated by any of his colleagues.

In 1955 the Secretary of the Church, the Revd Joseph B. Jameson, had nominated Eric as Editorial Secretary of the Conference. Under normal circumstances Eric could not have expected any immediate elevation within the small group of Conference Secretaries, but events determined otherwise. Joe Jameson had been a sick man when leading the business of the 1955 Conference and died soon after on 20 August. The Revd Samuel E. McCaffrey, Senior Assistant Secretary, took over the responsibility of Secretary until the following Conference but had to relinquish it after one year because he had already been designated at the 1955 Conference as President of the Methodist Church in Ireland for the year 1956-57. So within a short space of time numbers three and four in the secretarial ladder had been elevated to numbers one and two! The Revd Richard [Dick] S. Morris was elected Secretary in 1956 and Eric was appointed his Senior Assistant Secretary.

Irish Methodists were shocked to learn on the eve of the 1958 Conference that Dick Morris had resigned from the Methodist Church and been accepted as a candidate for the ministry of the Church of Ireland. No one was more surprised than Eric Gallagher! He later acknowledged he should have recognized the signals which Dick gave him: 'On more than one occasion during the year [1957-58], he said to me that he was trying to work out ways by which he would divest himself of the Secretarial position and hand over to myself. There was each time the twinkle in his eye that persuaded me not to take him seriously. In the after-light, I am convinced that it was a *cri de coeur*.'

At the time of his appointment as Secretary of Conference Dick Morris was minister of the Sandymount Church in Dublin and he must have found it difficult making weekly trips to Belfast, the venue for most of the church committees. Consequently, a year later he was moved to University Road Church in Belfast as successor to Eric. It was Dick's second term in this appointment. Eric later reflected: 'Like many I thought at the time that it [University Road] was a good appointment. With the benefit of hindsight, I am convinced it was a major mistake. From the beginning the odds were stacked against him. He was back after a few years in a pulpit where good preaching was expected and appreciated. In his Sandymount years he would have had little opportunity to prepare sufficient new sermons to carry him through another term in University Road. Furthermore in the interval student work had taken on a new dimension.' In short, the move increased rather than relieved Dick's stress.

Dick's resignation on the Monday did not allow Eric much time to prepare for the business of the Ministerial Conference which started on the Tuesday. Wesley McKinney, the outgoing President, asked Eric to stand in as Secretary until the Representative Session met on the Wednesday. By the conclusion of the Ministerial Session all had gone well – far better than he could have anticipated. Some members congratulated him on the presentation of the business. Eric had expected the Representative Session on the Wednesday afternoon to appoint a special committee to consider the crisis and make recommendations on the Thursday morning regarding candidates for the post of Secretary. However, when Conference came to the business on the Wednesday it felt no need to reflect and give time to the matter! Eric explains what happened: 'Before I had concluded, [Revd] Henry Holloway, who was seated on the Press bench immediately below the platform, rose to his feet and interjected indicating that he saw no reason to pause. He wished to move the suspension of standing orders and propose that Eric Gallagher be appointed Secretary of the Conference. He clearly had the Conference with him. There was no other proposal. The appointment was made there and then.'

The election to the Secretaryship of the Conference entailed a dramatic change in lifestyle. From 1958 onwards there was, in addition to the work of the Belfast Central Mission, the ceaseless round of central Church committees, the responsibilities associated with a major role in the formation of Church policy and having to live with an inevitably increased attention on the part of the general public to anything he might say or do as reported in the media: 'In 1958 the Churches were still news and for better or worse my words and actions were increasingly reported as those of the Secretary of the Methodist Church even if the context was more often than not that of the Belfast Central Mission and the Grosvenor Hall in particular.' What Eric omits to say is that the media attention he increasingly attracted – especially over the next two decades – was largely due to the person he was and not solely due to the positions he held in Irish Methodism. Conference Secretaries before him or after him never drew the same measure of media interest. He knew possibly better than most the best methods of winning the attention of journalists but this skill alone was not the reason for their interest. His public statements and actions were seen as being relevant and meaningful to life in general and this was foundational to the interest and respect people had for him.

Eric was unaware at the time of the full implications of this dual role of responsibility in the Church, a complex role that was to remain with him after he relinquished the Secretaryship in 1967: 'For the remainder of my active ministry it was to be a kind of Dr Jekyll and Mr Hyde existence. Indeed as the years passed it was more of a Dr Jekyll on one hand and on the other a Mr Hyde wearing many hats.' He frequently found it hard to divide his time between his various responsibilities. At one stage Barbara's concern for Eric's health prompted her to enlist the support of the family doctor: 'When I arrived home one evening, I found our doctor waiting for me. Barbara unknown to me had asked him to see me. He put me through my paces and finally requested me to tell him exactly how many hours I worked each week. The total was a minimum of eighty-four.' Unfortunately Eric did not record the advice he received from his doctor but it possibly went unheeded.

Belfast Central Mission was born out of a clear sense of mission evident in Irish Methodism in the late 1880s. As the result of a house-to-house canvass indicating that thousands in Belfast had no church connection, the 1888 Conference appointed a Town Mission Committee and a 'general missioner' – the Revd Crawford Johnson – for the areas of counties Antrim and Down which were part of the Belfast Methodist District.[1] Johnson's work was mainly concentrated in Belfast itself and very soon it resulted in a proposal that a Methodist City Mission be formed. This was accepted by the 1889 Conference which appointed Johnson 'city missionary' within the 'Belfast City Mission' project, listed under the Knock Circuit. After a five-year period during which the new worshipping congregation moved from one location to another, a site between the Grosvenor Road and Glengall Street was purchased and by October 1894 the new premises had been built:

> The dimension thirty metres by twenty-seven metres. There was a gallery all round with tiered seating beneath and the hall seated twenty-five hundred people. There were five accesses to the gallery and five entrances to the building – four on the Grosvenor Road frontage and one on Glengall Street. The outside walls were of red brick

with moulded string courses. The structural work was of rolled steel and the roofing, galvanised corrugated iron.[2]

The mission project became known as the 'Belfast Central Mission' (BCM) and because the building fronted the Grosvenor Road the name 'The Grosvenor Hall' was also quickly adopted. In 1927 the Hall was rebuilt, the seating capacity slightly reduced, and a new internal wing 'The Ker Memorial Hall' included.[3]

Superintendency of the Mission, with its varied nature of congregational life and social witness, was a major task in itself, without any other additional connexional responsibilities. Conference normally appointed a second and third minister to assist in the work and this was further supplemented by the contribution made by two 'Mission Sisters'.[4] They all shared in the pastoral oversight of the over 800 families connected to the Mission, though Eric acknowledged that his own contribution in this aspect of the work had to be confined to emergency situations and to visiting the sick and bereaved. By the nature of the Mission's history members were scattered through all the Belfast postal districts – and beyond – thus making pastoral care more difficult. Youth work was the responsibility of the third minister but Eric continued the pattern he had followed in his other appointments by involving himself in the residential youth weekends. He took some pleasure from the fact that three candidates for the ministry – Robert Bradford,[5] Leslie Spence and Brian Chambers – came from the ranks of the Grosvenor Hall youth. Uniformed organisations like the Boys' Brigade, Girls' Brigade and a strong morning Sunday school also added to the wide dimension of youth work.

Eric's ministerial colleagues, whether second or third minister in the circuit rankings, appreciated the experience of serving with him. Bill Brown, who later emigrated to Canada, reflects the attitude of most who served in the Hall: 'I was very low on the totem pole but Eric showed me the most marked respect, affirmed my ministry generously, brought a sense of humour, humanity and warmth to every task, never asked me to do what he himself would not do, and embodied for me an intelligent, prophetic, insightful and courageous approach to ministry, whether pastoral or social.'[6]

The Hall boasted three different but equally important musical groups: the Church Choir, the Male Voice Choir and the Band, the last of which frequently won the annual Northern Ireland Military Band Championships. Each contributed to the congregational life of the Mission and to the more public occasions frequently held in the Hall.

The Saturday Night Film Service in the 1950s and 60s was a special feature of the Mission, attracting large attendances, anything up to 1,450 and more people. The congregation was quite mixed. Young people occupied the gallery and the older people sat downstairs. They came for different reasons: the youth generally wanted to meet other young people, some just came to pass the time, and there were those who disapproved of the cinema as such but felt no twinge of conscience about looking at a film in the Grosvenor Hall. There was always a brief message given by Eric or the second minister: 'Depending on the film on any given night or on something unusual in the local or national situation it was always possible to make a special plea for commitment or to refer to something of significance.'[7]

Prime Minister Terence O'Neill's invitation to Taoiseach Sean Lemass to visit Stormont on 14 January 1965 – an act of friendship after decades of verbal insults being exchanged between the leaders of the North and the South – provided the kind of situation which Eric felt worthy of comment at the next Film Service: 'I indicated that it could prove the start of happier relationships with the Republic. There was no demur. What was said was evidently acceptable. Clearly the emerging controversy over the visit was whipped up.' Later, when he wrote his autobiography, O'Neill expressed regret at the lack of support he had received from Church leaders for this initiative in reconciliation. On learning of his understandable feeling of disappointment Eric contacted O'Neill: 'I was glad to be able to tell him personally that at least one Churchman had spoken up for him.'

Open-air meetings at the Customs House Square on Sunday afternoons were Belfast's equivalent of Speakers' Corner at Hyde Park in London. Staff and laymen from both BCM and the North Belfast Mission (NBM) combined to provide the team of speakers which on occasions could address a group of up to 200. People of all persuasions, religious and political, formed the audience and often other speakers were in competition for the attention of the ever-changing crowd of listeners. Frequently Eric would meet people during the week who had seen him at the 'Custom House Steps' – as it was more popularly known. On attending the Belfast Education Committee on one occasion Gerry Fitt (later Lord Fitt), whom he had not previously met, came over to him. 'I heard you last Sunday at the Steps,' he said. 'If that is what the Methodists stand for, I like it.'

There were some who went to the Steps with the sole purpose of disrupting other speakers. Eric reports: 'There was frequent and from time to time orchestrated opposition. This for a period went as far as a young minister of a well-known "anti" denomination rigging up a loud speaker at my feet and attempting to drown anything I tried to say.' The BCM/NBM team anticipated trouble, especially if there had been anything controversial happening the previous week.

One Sunday Eric suspected that they could have a very difficult if not dangerous time: 'Barbara had read the signs of the times as well and suspected the same thing. In spite of my strong protests she insisted on coming with me. I was, however, able to persuade her to stay in the car parked away at the far end of the Square. Unexpectedly we got through that afternoon without trouble. The next Sunday I was down early. One of the regulars from Ballymurphy [West Belfast] said to me, "Was that your missus in the car at the far side of the Square last Sunday?" When he heard that it was he then went on "Did she think something would happen to you? Tell her there's not a man here but would break every bone in the body of anyone who laid a hand on you." I was not looking for that kind of support but it was good to know that I had so much good will!'

Major Ronald Bunting, a mathematics lecturer and former regular army officer who for a time in the 1960s identified himself with Ian Paisley's brand of loyalism, was one of those who turned up frequently at the Steps. He was an attentive listener who always made use of the time Eric gave for questions: 'He would put his hand in an inside pocket, produce a note book and then indicate he had some questions he would wish to put to me. Inevitably they had some bearing on the ecumenical movement and/or my theological belief. They were asked courteously and as I replied he would jot down in his note book the answers I gave. When the interrogation which included a number of supplementaries was complete, he returned the note book to his pocket and shortly after would leave the meeting. I always expected that the answers were relayed to his mentor for appropriate public comment as and when considered expedient.'

It is possible that Eric had an influence on Ronald Bunting. In 1970 Bunting dissociated himself from Paisley. He became quite friendly with Eric and phoned him from time to time. Indeed, on occasions he brought his mother with him to the evening service.

Sunday evening services in the large auditorium were very much a feature of the Hall. Even before his arrival as Superintendent journalists had taken a close interest in what was said from the Mission pulpit and this interest grew apace as the years passed and sectarian violence ravaged the province. Eric and the second minister took it in turns to preach. Richard (Dick) Greenwood shared with him from 1957-60, Tom Woods from 1960-62, and Joe McCrory in the years following 1962. Their sermons were always topical and biblical. One notable series focused on Protestant principles. The idea for the series was prompted by a widely publicized series on Catholicism which was attracting large numbers to Clonard Monastery, a church off the Falls Road in West Belfast which was staffed by the Redemptorist Order. On Sunday 12 October 1958 Eric spoke on the catholicity of Protestant belief, including some reference to how Protestants understood Apostolic Succession. It so happened that Pope Pius XII had died during the previous week and Eric judged it proper to make some reference to him at the beginning of the sermon: 'While Protestants cannot accept all the theories and dogmas connected with the Papacy, they nevertheless realise that the late Pope had by the quality of his life and influence borne a witness in the world that was beyond all computation. He has been a good man and the 20th century can ill afford the loss of such men.'[8] After the service some of the congregation thanked him for what he had said but when he reached his office the phone was already ringing: 'I answered the phone to be met with a torrent of abuse such as I had never before encountered for daring to say any word of appreciation or sympathy about any Roman Catholic, let alone the Pope.'

Sadly, this kind of phone call was to become a regular occurrence for him during the rest of his ministry. Some were spontaneous, some orchestrated, but there was no hour of the day or night when he was free from them. Most of the calls came in the evening. Eric comments: 'If both parents were out we endeavoured to ensure that any call would be answered by the person looking after the children. On only one occasion as far as I can recall did any of them hear or overhear the abuse. Ruth was beside me when the phone rang: that night she was terrified.' The small hours between two and five o'clock in the morning were a favourite time. Eric continues, 'I learned to lift the phone and then at the first sign of aggression to place it under the pillow until the abuse and the shouting had stopped.'

A few weeks after his reference to the death of the Pope Eric featured in the November edition of Ian Paisley's *Revivalist* magazine. Page one carried a major article entitled 'POPE PIUS XII – ANTICHRIST' and included a section – also in capital letters – headed 'ERIC GALLAGHER'S COLOSSAL EXAGGERATION'. Part of it read as follows:

> Preaching mark you on 'What Protestants believe', Rev. R.D.E. Gallagher could not find words to declare the goodness of Pope Pius XII. Influence for good 'beyond all computation' is what Mr Gallagher declares. The butchered bleeding burning Protestant Church of Colombia has another opinion and so has every true

PROTESTANT. Mr Gallagher is only preaching sermons on 'What Protestants believe', not because he is a convinced Protestant but because it furthers the interests of the Grosvenor Hall. Having exploited films he will exploit Protestantism for his own ends. He is but another pulpit opportunist and his true beliefs have now been declared.[9]

In relation to this particular article his hitherto private Autobiographical Notes include the quip, 'The criticism of pulpit opportunism was rich coming from such a source!' While Eric – with one exception[10] – never publicly responded to Paisley's attacks nor publicly criticized him by name, much of what he said and preached was intended to expose the fallacies and dangers of his message. On 4 January 1964 the *Belfast Telegraph* carried the banner headline: 'Minister denounces "religious fascists"' referring directly to Eric's sermon the previous day when he had spoken about 'the recrudescence of religious extremism which was showing itself in public abuse, in scurrilous and defamatory pamphlets, in political pressure groups and other types of coercion'. None could have misunderstood the target of the sermon, especially when it highlighted the religious separatism which is fundamental to Paisley's beliefs: 'The spiritual Pharisaism that outlaws and excommunicates everything and everybody it disapproves of has nothing to do with the Gospel of reconciliation set out in the New Testament.'[11]

Paisley's attacks on ecumenism did not deflect Eric from focusing on the importance of Christian unity, nor from preaching on it on a number of occasions. In January 1961 he enlisted the support on two successive Sundays of Dr James Haire, Principal of Assembly's College,[12] and Canon Anthony Hanson[13] – both good friends of long standing. Referring to the question of union with the Roman Catholic Church as only 'remotely academic' he added, 'that does not remove the obligation to remember that members of the Church of Rome are part of Christendom.'[14] In early July 1964 he once again returned to the nature of Protestant-Roman Catholic relationships: 'Let us remember that our adherence to our beliefs and doctrines must never mean a Pharisaic sense of superiority to our Roman Catholic fellow-countrymen. They are neighbours in the New Testament sense as well as in the civic sense.' He went on: 'In this province there is much for us to do together – there is the greatest evangelistic task this century on our door-step. I cannot believe that God is calling us to that task and asking us at every turn to maintain our religious guerrilla warfare.' Eric concluded, 'A gospel of reconciliation will never be preached effectively by those who have no desire for reconciliation among themselves.'

Eric continued to underline the need for reconciliation. At the Mission Anniversary meeting in 1965 he declared: 'I look out tonight upon a city that needs as it never needed before the gospel of reconciliation. What Ulster needs above all is a new soul, a new quality of life and a new understanding of all that the Christian gospel stands for.' Even as he spoke, the noise of martial music could be heard as marching men made their way to yet another protest meeting in the Ulster Hall. It was a time when Ian Paisley was accelerating his attempts to rouse public feeling against what he alleged was the betrayal of Protestantism by the Churches and the Government's surrender of Unionist principles to Nationalists and Republicans.

Not every topic on the Sunday evenings was controversial but they always sought to be relevant. On two succeeding Sundays in 1959 – these sermons were also widely reported in the public press – Dick Greenwood and Eric looked back on the significance and relevance of the 1859 Revival. On the first Dick spoke about what had happened in 1859. He reported that in the first year of the Revival Irish Methodism had gained 5,000 members, and went on to outline its social consequences as evinced by the work of Barnardo's Homes and the Salvation Army. The following Sunday, 11 January, Eric addressed the question, 'Could it happen again?': 'I commented that psychologists and psychiatrists were busy but that there was not so big a queue for ministers' consulting rooms. There was neither inside the Church nor outside it any sufficient conviction that the Church and Gospel were relevant. The

Christian pulpit was no longer the frontier of evangelism. The call in 1959 was not to emulate 1859. It was a call to faithfulness and obedience and a quality of life that would make its own appeal.'

Social work has always been an important aspect of work in a city mission. This has been expressed in various ways at BCM. There was the day-to-day contact with folk who called at the Mission in need of help, whether this meant food vouchers, clothing, financial assistance or the chance to share problems with a sympathetic listener. The responsibility for this routine social work was shared between Sister Mary Gihon – described by Eric as 'big-hearted and pragmatic'– and the second minister. In addition to this there was the Children's Home and also a Holiday Home at Childhaven, near Millisle, County Down. The latter was used mainly to provide short holidays for senior citizens during the summer months.

Then in the 1960s a home for the elderly was opened at Castle Rocklands, on the shores of Belfast Lough at Carrickfergus. The former owner of the house, Mrs Boyd, had bequeathed this large residence to another party with the intention that it should be used as a home for the elderly. However, the named beneficiaries had waived their right to the legacy and the executors had eventually approached Eric Gallagher and the Mission trustees to enquire if they were interested. Legal questions regarding the right of the executors to approach the Mission eventually confirmed the correctness of their offer and cleared the way for development plans – which included a new extension – to be implemented. Backed by generous Government funding the official opening of the home took place on 6 June 1964, a day which Eric remembered as being 'one of the wettest Saturdays that year'.[15] Not long after this another development was introduced on the 3.5-acre site: the building of bungalows financed partially or wholly by elderly residents who donated them to Castle Rocklands in return for life occupancy. Eric had first seen this arrangement during a lecture and preaching tour to the United States in 1963 which included visiting a number of homes for senior citizens run under the auspices of the American Methodist

Church. On returning home he found clear indications that the idea would be welcomed in Ireland. Soon a colony of 15 bungalows became part of the caring ministry of the Mission.

As Secretary of the Conference Eric had a number of issues to deal with but none more domestic, controversial or consequential than that surrounding the publication of the *Wesleyan* by a group of ministerial students and probationary ministers. A nucleus of about six were involved but some of their contemporaries were interested and sympathetic in varying degrees. An article, 'Why No Candidates?' in the October 1960 issue – it was circulated monthly – best illustrates the essential ethos of the magazine which sought to encourage a discussion of various activities in the life of the Church and in the process was frequently critical of its leadership:

> Younger men are feeling a desperate lack of confidence in the leadership of our Church. There is no vision! Some would say we are led by punch-drunk minds, hidebound by tradition, and with a neurotic fear of change, lest we make a mistake. Is this true? 'Is there a precedent?' is the policy-maker's slide-rule. Too often we are at the mercy of small men who generalise personal modes of adjustment into universal laws. Where is there a big man with a personal dynamic, who takes a long view of things, to whom we can look up? We cry out for leaders with creative minds and progressive attitudes who will not only produce but also tolerate original ideas and new insights.

> Perhaps most cursed of all is the current image of the 'good Methodist Minister'. The stereotype is a hand-shaking, tea-drinking, hard-working, totally innocuous CONFORMER. From Candidates to Ordination we aim to produce these newly-hatched and stamped, disciplined like-thinking CONFORMERS. Why do we fear the unconventional? Why do we superimpose the 'image' upon all individuality? Why do we fear the 'visions' only seen by younger men? Why do we sneer 'can any good thing come out of such immaturity and inexperience?'

Why must the heavy hand of officialdom so often crush to death the passionate enthusiasm usually found and so often resented, in younger men? Why did one lad sigh recently, 'Oh, I can't go into that fellowship. It's so stifling!'

In researching this topic I found conflicting opinions regarding the degree to which Eric was being targeted in this criticism of the leadership of the Church. Certainly Eric was involved in responding to the criticism: 'They were genuinely concerned about the future of the Church and had valid points of view to put forward. Sometimes I thought them rather negative in the way they went about things and occasionally their facts could be in dispute. For some time, along with others, I was concerned as to whether or not we should enter the lists of controversy. Good sense prevailed.' Eric's comments hint at the degree of concern felt by himself and others. Indeed, there is some suggestion that litigation to stop the publication of the magazine was considered. However, a sort of compromise was reached when the Editorial Committee of the *Irish Christian Advocate* agreed to provide space for some articles from the authors of the *Wesleyan*. This did not entirely resolve the matter for members of the Editorial Committee often resented the nature of the material presented and a form of unofficial censorship was introduced. Regrettably the problem was removed only when most of the authors decided to go abroad for further study or alternatively to look for opportunities of Christian service elsewhere.[16]

The controversy over the *Wesleyan* is possibly pivotal in explaining the exodus of about 10-15 newly ordained Methodist ministers to the United States and Canada in the early 1960s. There has always been a flow of talented professional people from Ireland to the USA but any graph of this migration as it affects Methodist ministers will show a distinct bulge at this period. Many of those who went did so because they felt they would not have a sufficient degree of freedom to express themselves within the Irish context. At the same time it must be added that much of the dissatisfaction and frustration arose because there simply were not sufficient openings in specialized ministries in a small Irish Church at that time.

Whatever the circumstances that prompted the increased emigration to North America it is sad to note that many who left – even though they went on to carve out distinguished professional careers in their new environment – experienced a sense of being 'cut off' from Irish Methodism in that few retained any interest in them. And whatever their evaluation of Eric Gallagher in the 1960s, their high regard for his contribution to the Church in Ireland in the decades that followed is unmistakable. Donald Williamson comments: 'Eric Gallagher was one of our great leaders and I am grateful to him and for him.'[17]

A special Manpower Committee set up by the Church in the 1960s also took up a lot of Eric's time. While this was chiefly the responsibility of the Secretaries of the Home Mission Department it was inevitable that the Secretary of the Conference would also be heavily involved. The title of the Committee reflected the age in which it met, one when the Church had still not got to grips with inclusive language or indeed the correctness of having women ordained to the ministry. That said, the work undertaken by the Committee was considerable. Every 20 years or so each denomination appears to engage in a major reassessment of its resources – financial and ministerial – and prayerfully considers how best they should be deployed. This particular in-depth study looked at every circuit and society in Ireland, the context in which they were serving the kingdom, and made recommendations for change and future development to the 1967 Conference. Nine of the 22 pages in the report were devoted to a careful analysis of the situation in the greater Belfast area, reflecting both the high number of Methodists in the region and also a commendable awareness of proposed radical changes for the city, particularly those relating to the introduction of new motorways, something which would necessitate considerable population relocation.[18]

The 1950s, and particularly the 1960s, were a time of growing ecumenical awareness among the leadership of the mainstream Churches in Ireland. The formation of the World

Council of Churches at Amsterdam in 1948 and the subsequent WCC Assemblies at Evanston, 1954, and New Delhi, 1961, heralded a sense of excitement and anticipation among many of the leaders of the Presbyterian Church in Ireland (PCI), the Church of Ireland (COI) and the Methodist Church in Ireland. Representatives of these Churches who attended the WCC Assemblies returned to Ireland enthused and eager to pass on the message of the themes considered and adopted. Professor James L. Haire, later appointed Principal of Assembly's College and Moderator of the General Assembly, wanted his home church to grasp the significance of what had happened at the first Council at Amsterdam: 'While there were deep divisions, which were not concealed, there was also a real unity which showed itself in one great forward step, when all the Churches officially recognised one another as Christian and voted unanimously to form a World Council of Churches.' He was convinced that a new day had dawned which would affect future relationships between the Churches: 'The Body of Christ is a unity which makes it impossible for us either to forget one another, or to be content with agreements on isolated parts of our belief.'[19]

As Secretary of the Conference Eric frequently had contact with these ecumenically-minded Presbyterian and Anglican Church leaders. Indeed, as Convenor of the Inter-Church Relations Committee since 1948, he had already established good relationships, enjoying the experience of working with like-minded colleagues.[20] This was particularly true of his contact with Haire and the Revd (later Professor) Jim Boyd, PCI Convenors for Inter-Church Relations: 'They were easy to work with and all of us shared the same convictions. There was a degree of trust and confidence between us that could not have been greater had we all belonged to the same denomination. With complete loyalty to our respective Churches we were able to work together in the greatest possible harmony and see each other's point of view.' The fruit of this good working relationship can be seen in the joint schemes and united congregations which were started at Taughmonagh, (South Belfast) in 1953, Braniel (East Belfast) in 1960, and in 1959 a federation scheme in the North Connaught area. In relation to the shared Belfast schemes Eric reflected: 'The philosophy behind them was that it was both foolish and wrong in relatively small housing areas for both Churches as it were to be seen to be in rivalry with each other.'

Other joint ventures soon followed. In 1962 united worship with the Church of Ireland and Presbyterian Church at Shannon Airport commenced. A year later separate bipartite conversations were launched, one with the Presbyterians and the other with the Church of Ireland. The remit given by Conference which defined the purpose of these conversations was succinctly expressed: 'with a view to closer unity'.[21] The wisdom of uniting these separate arrangements was soon evident so the Tripartite Conversations were created in 1968. Further shared congregational schemes were created while these unity conversations were being held. By 1970 a joint venture with the PCI at Knockbreda (South-East Belfast) had started and there were joint schemes with the COI at Monkstown and Glengormley – both new housing areas in the greater Belfast area – Glencairn (West Belfast) and Strathfoyle (Londonderry).

The difficulties involved in operating these joint schemes were never overlooked and problems arose from time to time. However, with the advantage of hindsight Eric later highlighted some of the key factors involved in ensuring a successful partnership scheme:

> You can draw up the best of all possible plans for co-operation and shared buildings but you are in for trouble if the respective congregations are not convinced of the rightness and need of the scheme. They simply must learn the need to understand and compromise. And that applies still more to the ministers and clergy appointed to serve in those congregations. If he/she is one of 'the awkward squad' there will be trouble as sure as night follows day.

Ecumenism in the 1960s was not limited to improved relationships between the Protestant Churches. It was also a time when small unofficial steps were being taken to create friendship across the Roman Catholic-Protestant divide. While there were voices warning against any forms of contact, political or religious, there were also those who were active in promoting better understanding and growing tolerance. Eric was one of these. From the end of the 1950s and throughout the 60s he was one of a small group of Roman Catholic and Protestant clergy and laity who met monthly in Belfast. Robert Murphy, a curate in St Paul's parish on the Falls Road at the time, appears to have taken the initiative in drawing the group together: 'We would meet every month or so; start with a Scripture reading, followed by prayer; then discuss the [political] situation and see in what way we could do anything that would be helpful.'[22] Eric's involvement in this group illustrates his belief in the usefulness of wider Christian contacts and also possibly prepared him for the cross-community initiatives in which he would soon take a central role.

The first Protestant-Roman Catholic 'official and public' initiative was a response to the unrest and turmoil which developed in connection with the flying of a tricolour from the Sinn Fein offices in Divis Street, West Belfast, in the early autumn of 1964. Elections for the Westminster Parliament were pending and this in itself guaranteed increased excitement and tension. The flying of the tricolour in itself was not illegal, but it could be banned if the police considered that it could lead to a breach of the peace. On other occasions the police had been content to take no action; Paisley, however, was determined that the flag should be removed! At an Ulster Hall rally on Sunday 27 September, he threatened to march on Divis Street and remove the offending flag if the police did not take action. This threat appeared to influence the police who sledgehammered their way into the premises and seized the flag.

The riots that followed have been described as the worst that the city had experienced for 30 years. Because the police had acted, Paisley had called off his march to Divis Street and held a victory rally instead at the City Hall. But the threat to take action himself had set in train a sequence of events which did nothing to improve relationships between the two communities, Catholic and Protestant, nationalist and loyalist. Representatives of the three mainstream Protestant Churches had arranged to meet on the Friday morning to consider if there was anything positive the three Churches could say or do. Shortly before nine o'clock Jack Sayers, editor of the *Belfast Telegraph*, phoned Eric at his office:

> He wanted to know what the Churches were doing. I told him and he asked if the Roman Catholic Church was involved or if it had been mentioned. The reply was as could be expected at that time in the negative. That was not good enough for an editor who was far ahead of his time. 'If Mullaly [Monsignor P.J. Mullaly, Vicar-General of the Down and Connor Diocese and acting for Bishop Philbin currently in Rome] was prepared to join you would you meet with him?' I said 'Yes as far as I am concerned but I don't know about the others.'

Sayers agreed to get in touch with Monsignor Mullaly and phone back. The answer was positive. The Monsignor would be happy, if invited, to meet with the Protestant representatives and would await an invitation. Armed with this information Eric went to the scheduled meeting with the Protestant clergy.

> We met at noon in Church House and talked about a joint appeal for an end to violence. At an appropriate point I asked if we should not ask the Roman Catholics to join. They were not too sure and someone said 'They would not be prepared to join with us and in any case Bishop Philbin is away.' 'Well, why not give them the chance. Why not phone Monsignor Mullaly?'

Eric reports that the phone call was made and very soon Mullaly was in Church House. 'We talked the situation over and it was common cause that an appeal should be made. The question was asked "Should it be a joint appeal or two separate ones?" "I will settle for a joint one or nothing" said the Monsignor and history was made.'

In April 1965 there was another significant but less public cross-community initiative. Representatives of the same three Protestant Churches met to consider the nature of the charter being prepared for the new university about to be launched – the location still undecided at that time.[23] They wanted the charter to make adequate provision for chaplaincy work and possibly also allow for the creation of a Faculty of Divinity. The group discussed an approach to the Prime Minister, Terence O'Neill. As they reflected on the best tactics to employ they were unanimous that a joint approach with the Catholic Church was likely to be more effective than going it alone. Eric, the Methodist representative in the group, was asked to contact Cardinal Conway, who agreed to discuss the matter with them in Armagh:

> Thus some days later three of us, Dr. John Greer, the Revd Andrew Adams and I made our way to Armagh. The Cardinal received us graciously but with circumspection. We seemed to be weighing each other up. Eventually he said we had made our case. He was favourably disposed but would have to carry out some consultation. He noticed our surprise and then remarked, 'You know, I have not all the power you people think I have.' He would let us know before too long.

The answer was in the affirmative and soon a small committee met in the Grosvenor Hall premises. 'It was the first time in my ministry that any Roman Catholic cleric had crossed the door. His arrival was noted.' The group soon reached agreement that a letter be sent to the Prime Minister asking him to receive a deputation led by the Archbishop of Armagh (COI), the Cardinal, the Presbyterian Moderator and the Methodist President. Eric was deputed to send the letter.

> Before mid-day on the morning of its delivery to Stormont Castle I was called to the phone. It was the Secretary of the Cabinet, the late Sir Herbert Black. He enquired if the letter was authentic. On being so assured he said that its receipt had caused something near to consternation in the corridors of power and he had been

instructed to talk with me about it. I asked him if he wished me to go up to Stormont. He replied that he would come to see me at the Hall. He did and he was left in no doubt about the seriousness of the request.

On 28 April a delegation representing the four Churches met with Captain O'Neill at Stormont. Arrangements were put in hand that led to satisfactory negotiations with the emerging university's representatives. Eric later wrote in his Notes: 'I have no doubt but that the contact made at that time with Cardinal Conway had a great effect on developments that were tragically not too far distant.'

In 1966 Eric, like many others, was deeply concerned about the deteriorating Northern Ireland situation. He believed it was imperative for the Methodist Church to speak out publicly on how it understood Christian principles should be applied in civil and community life. Accordingly he prepared a lengthy resolution based on the insights of biblical teaching for the Conference that year. Four pages in length, after a preamble it set out with biblical support five obligations on the Methodist people, namely:

1.   The necessity to safeguard and witness to the faith;

2.   The obligation to maintain and live out the Christian doctrine of love and reconciliation;

3.   The call to promote the just society;

4.   The onus on the civil powers to uphold justice and righteousness;

5.   The requirement for everyone to obey the civil powers and duly constituted authorities in all proper regulations.

In its conclusion the resolution stated *inter alia*:

The obligation to love demands that we demonstrate to our neighbours of whatever faith, to our opponents as well as to our friends, those qualities of love which were found in Christ. This demands renewed and ceaseless effort until bitterness is made to disappear from every part of Irish life.

Any form of injustice, inequality or discrimination based on creed, race or colour is contrary to God's will. The Conference consequently calls on all sections of the community and in particular those in positions of influence and authority to work by word and deed for the removal of all injustice from our land.[24]

The Conference recognized the appropriateness and necessity of the resolution and authorized its publication under the title A *Call to the Methodist People and a Statement of what the Methodist Church Believes.* In retrospect the *Call* stands out as an indication of the awareness of Conference – prompted by Eric Gallagher – regarding the existence of injustice in the Northern Ireland community and the necessity to correct it.

In the latter part of Eric's period as Secretary of Conference he experienced a major bereavement in the death of his father on 22 January 1965. 'RH' had been a considerable influence on his life and Eric always recognized this. The esteem in which he held his father is very evident: 'I am grateful to God to be the son of one whose integrity, devotion to his God and service to the Church and his love and sacrifice for his family I never for one moment in my life had reason to question.'

Each year the Irish Methodist Conference designates a year in advance one of its ministers to be President of the Church. In June 1966 it designated Eric to be President for the year 1967-68. As Secretary of the Conference he had worked with nine Presidents: R.J. Good, R. Ernest Ker, Robert W. McVeigh, Charles W. Ranson, James Wisheart, Frederick E. Hill, Samuel H. Baxter, Robert A. Nelson and Samuel J. Johnston. Eric reflected: 'I had the most cordial and harmonious relationships with each of them. Some sought more secretarial advice than others and I cannot recall any instance where it was ignored when it was asked for.' In June 1967, as tensions in Northern Ireland continued to rise, he became President of a Church which served the whole of Ireland. Apart from his student days in Dublin his main life experience had been in the North, and Belfast in particular. However, his year as President meant that his services would be required throughout the island and, indeed, further afield.

10

President
1967-68

Insist on the necessity for individual commitment to Christ.

Sermon, (The Church's Supreme Task),
Dungannon Methodist Church, 31.3.1968.

The 198th Conference of the Methodist Church in Ireland which met in Belfast from the 9-15 June 1967, coincided with the tail-end of the third Arab-Israeli War, or 'six-day war' as it is sometimes known. Eric Gallagher was very conscious of this conflict as he rose to give his inaugural address at the Installation Service in the Grosvenor Hall on Monday evening 12 June: 'Tonight I speak against a background of international fear and tension. The events of the last seven days have shaken our complacency and reminded us that we in Ireland are as much involved in the affairs of the nations as any other part of the world.'[1]

Eric used the occasion to set out his priorities for the Church: 'Against a background of chaos and destruction abroad and of the secular society at home I suggest we have three main things to do. The first is to fight the right battle. The second is to fight it in the right place. The third is to fight it in the right way.'

He was convinced that the Church was asking the wrong questions and fighting the wrong battles: 'We can never justify the time and the energies we have put into the futile puerile and irrelevant controversies of the last decade.' The basic question the Church should have been asking was 'whether or not there is a God and what kind of God He is and what importance He has'. He declared: 'We have the inescapable obligation to proclaim God to our contemporaries in language they can understand, to proclaim Him with such informed conviction that they will see Him as the divine contemporary, always relevant and Sovereign; to proclaim God and Jesus Christ His Son as Saviour and Lord, our only ultimate standard for every situation.'

Secondly, the Church must fight the battle in the right place and this is in the world outside! Consequently 'the Church must say "Go" to its members before it says "Come" to those who are not its members. The Church is and must be always a missionary body or else it is simply NOT the Church.' To this end the laity needed to be enlisted, awakened, and educated that this was their God-given task: 'God calls us in Methodism to re-capture that neglected doctrine of the Priesthood of all Believers. Mission is the task of ALL the Church: ministers, local preachers, everybody.' Eric drove home his message in terms that left no room for misunderstanding: 'Mission means the penetration of every part of life – the housing estates and the suburbs, the factories and the schools, the Universities and the political world by Christians who "know their stuff and will do their stuff".'

Thirdly, he concluded that it was important to fight the battle in the right way and this was by being the Servant Church. The opposite had often been the case: 'The right battles can never be fought in the bitterness and rancour of religious guerrilla warfare. Christian strategy must never be one of hatred.' He underlined the need for a loving and caring ministry: 'The New Testament Church was a Servant Church and a Missionary Church and it carried out its mission by the sheer quality of the lives of its members.'

These were themes which he repeated again and again during his Presidential year when he visited congregations in every corner of the island, whether it was to lay a foundation stone, dedicate a new building or simply pay a Presidential visit which of itself was a special occasion. He wanted folk to be asking the right questions, focused on the real task of mission in the secular world, a task in which every member would be enlisted, and a ministry which would be characterized by Christian love.

As author of the Pastoral Address to the Conference and members of the Methodist Church in Ireland Eric made a further contribution to this particular Conference. By custom the writer was always anonymous but in 1967 it was common knowledge who had written it. The Address dealt with three closely related topics: the involvement of the Methodist Church in Ireland in Church Union negotiations with the Church of Ireland and the Presbyterian Church in Ireland; its membership of the World Council of Churches; and its attitude to Roman Catholicism. He had been asked by the Pastoral Efficiency Committee – the body responsible for suggesting the subject of each Pastoral Address – to write on these topics mainly because the Church had been criticized for its stance in these areas by a group of laity who campaigned under the title 'The Irish Methodist Revival Movement'. Their literature was circulated in a magazine type publication *Whither Methodism?* The group argued that the ecumenical stance of the Church and some of its ministers in particular was in danger of betraying Reformation and Wesleyan principles. By far their main criticism was directed at the WCC and the Roman Catholic Church.

Convinced of the importance of the Address, Conference decided to publish it under the title *Where Methodism stands Regarding Church Union, the World Council of Churches and Roman Catholicism* and make it available to congregations and others who might care to read it. The document underlined the biblical basis of the quest for unity in the Church: 'The quest for Church Union does not spring from any kind of Church politics or from the expediency of finance or shortage of ministers. The basis is a sincere desire to know fully and to make evident the implications of Bible teaching regarding the People of God in both the Old and New Testaments.' It referred to John 17: 'If all the world is to believe, we must take our Lord's petition "that all may be one" more seriously than we have so far done. A spiritual unity already exists between believers. It is not of our creation but we must seek to acknowledge and express it adequately.' A careful explanation of the developments which led to the various Bipartite Conversations was given and an assurance that the MCI was 'not seeking unity based on any compromise of truth'.

Chapters 2 and 3 of the 15 page document set out the missionary origins of the World Council of Churches and the implications of membership. It sought to remove misunderstandings of the organisation, circulating in Methodism and elsewhere, particularly regarding its supposed authority: 'It is not a World Church. It cannot be a World Church and it has never sought or pretended to be a World Church.' And again, 'Membership of the Council has never entailed acceptance of all that the Council says. Any statement of the Council is of weight precisely as it commands the support and agreement of its members.'

The final chapter dealing with the nature of the Roman Catholic Church and relationships with Roman Catholics was perhaps the most controversial subject of all. An affirmation of minority rights – whoever that minority might be – was significant particularly in view of the formation of the Northern Ireland Civil Rights Association (NICRA) five months earlier. Many of its aims related directly or indirectly to the question of minority rights.[2] *Where Methodism stands* declared: 'If we take the teaching of the Bible as our all sufficient rule of practice we are obliged – not to concede but – to recognise that every member of any minority group in Ireland has full rights – whether to housing, votes, education, civil liberty or work. It is also essential for us to make every possible constructive attempt to maintain and live out the Christian doctrine of love and reconciliation.'

Critics were suggesting that Church union with the RCC was underlying the ecumenical agenda but this was firmly dismissed: 'Any Church union negotiations with the Roman Catholics are out of the question and will remain out of the question as long as the Roman Catholic Church maintains, as essential, doctrines which we hold to be false.' While being fairly blunt in this statement the document still defended discussions between Protestants and Catholics on various subjects, including 'the Vatican Council and its decrees, the structure of the Church, community relationships, marriage and other topics of deep interest'.

The publication of *Where Methodism stands* must have helped in some measure to pave the way for two significant developments during Eric's Presidential year: one related to relationships between the three mainstream Protestant Churches and the other to Catholic-Protestant relationships. In March 1968 the COI, PCI and MCI, now engaged in Tripartite Negotiations, published a *Declaration of Intent* regarding the purpose of their discussions which they indicated would be brought for approval to their respective governing bodies. The *Declaration* (quoted in part) declared:

> We the duly appointed representatives of the Church of Ireland, the Methodist Church in Ireland and the Presbyterian Church in Ireland, acknowledging our several Churches as being within the Church of God, and seeking to preserve the truths in our several traditions, affirm our intention to seek together that unity which is both God's will and His Gift to His Church.
>
> We make no claim to know the exact form which unity should take, or whether we shall attain to it: we are seeking no unity apart from the Will of God: and we solemnly undertake to submit ourselves to what God will say to us together through the witness of our several Churches.
>
> We recognise that in so submitting ourselves that any such unity between our Churches will involve change for us all.

In May 1968 the COI General Synod approved the Declaration, and the following month both the PCI General Assembly and the MCI Conference gave their agreement. There was considerable optimism in all three Churches that a significant step had been taken. The first few months of the Tripartite Conversations had been very positive. Back in October 1967 Eric had publicly described the new arrangement as 'the greatest single challenge and opportunity the Protestant

Churches in Ireland had had since the Reformation'. In retrospect some might conclude that the challenge was rejected or hopefully just postponed.

The development on the Protestant-Catholic front possibly had its origins in Pope Paul VI's call for a Day of Peace on the 1 January 1968. The Pontiff's message, sent from the Vatican on 8 December 1967, is carefully included in the large book which records Eric's journeys, correspondence and addresses during his Presidential year. The Revd Dr Alfred Martin, PCI Moderator 1966-67, drew Eric's attention to the document and suggested he write to Cardinal Conway proposing a joint call by the four Church leaders to pray for peace in the world. Though initially hesitant Eric thought well of the idea and contacted the Cardinal to see if he might take the initiative in inviting the COI Primate, the PCI Moderator and himself (MCI President) to jointly sign a call to prayer for peace. The Cardinal's handwritten letter to Eric on 23 December confirms his role in this venture:

My dear President

Thank you so much for your kind letter and the copies of the agreed statements which you enclosed. ... I do feel that it will do a great deal of good and I must thank you again for your initiative in suggesting that I might write to you and to the Primate and to the Moderator in this sense. I hope I shall have the pleasure of meeting you before long. I feel we could all have a very enjoyable and useful conversation together which would do us all a great deal of good. May I renew my good wishes for Christmas and the New Year as I remain

Yours very sincerely

+ W Cardinal Conway

Both James McCann, the COI Primate, and William Boyd, PCI Moderator, agreed to sign the joint call to pray for peace. The four Church leaders made the following appeal:

At the beginning of a new year we gladly join in calling upon all our people to renew their prayers to Almighty God for the peace of the world.

The conflicts which are raging at present are tragic in the toll of human suffering which they entail and the danger of a third world war preoccupies the minds of men of goodwill everywhere.

Without wishing in any way to pass judgment on the merits of particular conflicts, we appeal to all our members to cultivate in their own hearts that spirit of peace which our Lord Jesus Christ wished to reign in the hearts of his followers and to intensify their prayers that God will give to us all that peace which the world cannot give.

Remembering that prayer and action are demanded continually if peace is to be built and if it is to endure, let us seek to bring the hope of peace to those who have no hope and strive for the healing of those ills and evils which destroy peace between man and man.

This was the first ever joint appeal or message given by the leaders of the four mainstream Churches in Ireland. It was an example which has been followed ever since.[3] Slowly but surely the lines of communication between the Church leaders were being put in place. It would not be long before the value of these links would become clear.

In December 1967 Jack Lynch, Sean Lemass' successor as Taoiseach in the Republic, made an official visit to Captain O'Neill at Stormont. Some of the emotions witnessed on the occasion of Lemass' visit in January 1965 were again in evidence but it is worth recording that on this occasion Sir George Clark, the Master of the Orange Order, and his successor-in-waiting, Mr John Bryans, both openly supported the visit. Eric, as MCI President, issued a public statement welcoming the meeting of the two Prime Ministers: 'I am confident that not only Methodists but all people of goodwill North and South will equally welcome the meeting between

Captain O'Neill and Mr. Lynch. The action of the two Prime Ministers can only make for the maturity and successful development of both countries.' He sent the full text of his statement to both Lynch and O'Neill and received personal letters of thanks in return. In O'Neill's Christmas card to Eric that year he once again expressed his gratitude for the public statement of support: 'Thank-you very much for welcoming my meeting with Jack Lynch. I wish some of the other Church Leaders had your courage – including my own!'

Heads of Churches always receive invitations to garden parties at Buckingham Palace, Hillsborough Castle (County Down), and Aras an Uachtarain, the official residence of the President of the Republic. Eric accepted all such invitations and Barbara went with him. Indeed, she accompanied him on most of his official engagements during his 12 months as President.

Immediately following his presidency – and undoubtedly because he had held this office – Eric made two significant overseas trips: he was a delegate at the Fourth WCC Assembly at Uppsala, Sweden, from the 4-20 July; and in November he travelled with Barbara to the Ivory Coast and Nigeria.

The main theme of the WCC Assembly, 'Behold, I Make All Things New', focusing on the needs of the hungry and dispossessed, was a topic close to his heart. The reality, that the rich were becoming richer and the poor poorer, dominated Uppsala's socio-political and economic discussions. The main report declared: 'To be complacent in the face of the world's need is to be guilty of practical heresy.' Within this context the issue of racism developed as a major concern for the Assembly. Eric later reflected, 'Its major significance was the emphasis laid on the scourge of racism. It was no accident that the Central Committee in 1969 gave authority for the setting up of the controversial Programme to Combat Racism which was to make a major impact on Irish ecumenical developments.'[4]

He enjoyed the companionship of other representatives from Ireland: the Revds Robert Brown and Carlisle Patterson (PCI), and Archbishop George Simms; also the experience of meeting again some of the leading ecumenical figures:

Dr Philip Potter, Dr Visser't Hooft, and Archbishop Michael Ramsey.

Eric was delighted that Barbara was able to travel with him to West Africa. The main purpose of his visit to the Ivory Coast was to share in the opening and dedication of a new hospital at Dabou. The hospital was apparently a considerable contribution to the medical provisions in the Ivory Coast, a fact underlined by the presence at the ceremony of the President of the State. Eric's knowledge of French – which he had taught at MCB in the 1940s – enabled him to bring greetings from both the British and Irish Methodist Conferences and to preach the following Sunday in a village church to 'a large and expressive congregation'. In Nigeria Eric and Barbara visited Irish ministerial and lay missionary personnel and saw something of the work they were doing: the Revd Paul Kingston, Robin and Florence McIlderry in Oturkpo, Osmond and Sylvia Mulligan at the Ilesha hospital, and the Revd Tom Johnston at Kaduna in the north. In Ibadan they were thrilled to meet Soyode Franklin, a friend and contemporary of Eric's who had studied medicine at TCD. He had often stayed with the Gallagher family when 'RH' was minister at Knock in the 1930s and Yemi, his son, had received similar hospitality from Eric and Barbara. Soyode, now Director of Medical Services for the Western Region, introduced his Irish guests to many of his Nigerian friends, making this part of their Nigerian trip the one that gave them 'outstanding pleasure'.

11

Peacemaker
1968-71

*We know that people have been talking about us all
over the world. We have not liked it but it's only recently
that Christian people have begun to realise their own
share of guilt. We didn't really think that we either could
or should do anything about what was happening. True
enough over the years a few Christian prophet voices
had reminded us that we were living in a fool's
paradise. They told us what we should be doing but we
didn't listen. We said nothing, we did nothing to put
things right. We evaded our responsibilities and we did
not want to be counted when the agitators and
reactionaries were calling the tune. We simply failed to
love the highest when we saw it.*

Broadcast Service from BCM, 5 January 1969

Community tension increased during 1968 as marches and
demonstrations arranged by NICRA were often met with
counter-demonstrations. These were planned by Ian Paisley,
backed up by support he received from the Ulster Constitution
Defence Committee (UCDC) and the Ulster Protestant
Volunteers (UPV), organisations which he had created for the
purpose of acting as a counter-demonstration force.[1] The very
suggestion of a counter-demonstration often prompted the
police to ban the original demonstration, as was the case in
August when a loyalist threat of counter-demonstration led to
the ban on a NICRA demonstration in Dungannon, planned to
follow a march from Coalisland to Dungannon.

Events on 5 October in Derry brought the Northern Ireland
problem to the attention of a world audience. Civil Rights
campaigners had planned a march in the city for that day to
protest against discrimination in housing and employment but
it was banned by William Craig, the Northern Ireland Minister

for Home Affairs. Television coverage of police batoning the marchers who ignored the ban was transmitted across the world within hours. The presence of Nationalist leaders and Westminster MPs at the front of the march added to the importance of the event. The Cameron Commission, appointed in 1969, later described the unrestrained police batoning as 'without justification or excuse'.

Some days after the Derry march a group of Protestant Church leaders went to see Terence O'Neill at Stormont to express their concern at the worsening situation and to enquire in what way the Churches might help. O'Neill immediately suggested that a message from the Church leaders, including Cardinal Conway, would be significant. Eric relates the difficulty they had in preparing a statement: 'We attempted to compose what might be regarded as a suitable appeal but made little headway. There was an evident amount of indecision regarding precise wording.' Faced with this impasse O'Neill suggested he would withdraw and attempt something on his own. 'He returned in a few minutes with a draft which we were pleased to accept with a minimum of alteration. It indicated an ability on the part of the Prime Minister that many of his detractors have been all too ready to deny.'

After the statement had been agreed – regrettably the Cardinal when contacted felt he could not sign but expressed his support for the action – the Church leaders continued to talk with O'Neill about the developing violence and counter-violence. The conversation turned to the situation in Derry. 'You know,' said the Prime Minister, 'it should be governed by a Catholic or Nationalist Council. I know that and I long to see the day when they control it for they are by far the majority. But Derry is a sacred cow to the Unionists and they will never ever, if they can prevent it, allow Derry to be ruled by anyone but themselves.'[2]

The idea of a broader Church platform, possibly a Community Relations Committee, in which representatives of the Irish Council of Churches (ICC) could share with representatives of the Roman Catholic Church (RCC), was now being considered by some within the Executive of the ICC. On

21 October the Executive prepared a resolution for the Council which called for 'consultation with members of the Roman Catholic Church with a view to discovering how the Churches together can make an effective contribution towards improving community relations in Ireland'.[3] However, when the full Council met on 7 November – Eric Gallagher was in Nigeria at the time – they appeared to hesitate in mentioning the RCC specifically and adopted a resolution to 'consult with responsible church leaders on what practical steps might be taken to advance the work of reconciliation'.

On 7 December Eric met with two other members of the ICC Executive in Armagh: Jack Weir, Clerk of the PCI General Assembly, and Archbishop James McCann, COI Primate. They decided to write confidentially to the British Prime Minister, Harold Wilson, warning him of the increasing polarisation of opinion that was developing and expressing a fear that there could soon be 'an explosion of real violence if confrontation is continued'. They affirmed their total support for O'Neill's efforts in introducing reform and improving community relations but hinted at an erosion of moderate opinion: 'With this loss of confidence, both in the aims of the Civil Rights movement and of our political minority, we are aware of a most distressing dissipation of moderate opinion.' They indicated their intention to seek a joint approach with Cardinal Conway to the whole situation. If this joint approach could not be obtained they saw 'no alternative to a further escalation of bitterness, polarising of loyalties and all too probable violence'.

Suspicions had been mounting that the IRA was using the Civil Rights movement as a political means of furthering its aims. It was not known for certain at the time but history has confirmed that this was the case. Cathal Goulding, then IRA chief of staff, later claimed that it was the IRA who created NICRA: 'The IRA set up NICRA. The Army Council of the IRA set up NICRA, it and the Communist Party together.'[4] With hindsight, therefore, we can see that there was some justification for indicating a 'loss of confidence' in NICRA but it might also be true that the letter indirectly reveals the gulf in understanding which existed between the Protestant and

Catholic communities. It was a gulf which Eric and others were determined to bridge.

Two days later Terence O'Neill made his famous 'Crossroads' speech on radio and television, warning his listeners that Ulster stood at the crossroads: they could live happily together in the Province by attending to the interests of each section of the community or choose disaster by ignoring this. He received a massive surge of support from moderates in both communities but the election which he called the following February did not produce any substantial strengthening of his political support in Stormont.[5]

In mid-December 1968 Eric met Cardinal Conway at a private supper party in the home of Dr Alfred Martin. He had what he describes as an 'adequate conversation' with Conway during which he shared with him the current thinking within the ICC Executive regarding the possibility of setting up some form of cross-community group. They agreed to discuss the matter further in early January. A letter from the Cardinal a few days later suggested Friday 3 January as a possible date.

The meeting on 3 January appears to have been a one-to-one with the Cardinal. Eric possibly did most of the talking as he had to explain both the workings of the ICC and the purpose of their proposed Advisory Group on Community Relations. The ICC Executive, he suggested, envisaged it having a two-fold responsibility:

> The first would be that of being a group in existence which would be speedily and easily called in the event of emergency or crisis in the community.

> The second term of reference would be that of a long-term consideration of Community problems. We thought of a group which would be able to represent different points of view to each other and thus create better understanding and indeed, where possible, make suggestions for joint action by the Leaders of the Churches or unilateral action if such action might seem best in the interests of all.

The Cardinal's first reaction was one of caution, suggesting that the group could be regarded as an attempt to put a safety valve on legitimate protest and a suppression of reasonable demands. Eric was quite surprised at this and assured the Cardinal they had not envisaged the group acting in this manner. He explained further:

> On our side we recognised that there were legitimate requests and demands to be met, and we had no intention or wish to see them being suppressed. Indeed I said that we have all been living in our own gardens with the walls around us. If this crisis goes over quickly the walls will go up again and we will be unaware of how the other feels or lives. The tendency may well be for us on our side whose consciences have been stirred to relapse, not because we want to, but because events force us into a state of complacency. I said, 'You must not allow us to let our consciences go to sleep'.

This explanation with its added personal reflection apparently had a considerable effect on the Cardinal, who now seemed convinced of the desirability of setting up the Advisory group and agreed to bring the business before his fellow-bishops. Eric promised to furnish him with a formal letter from the Protestant Church leaders setting out the proposal.

On the day following this meeting with the Cardinal there was a vicious attack on the People's Democracy marchers at Burntollet Bridge near Derry. NICRA had not supported the plans by this radical left-wing group who intended to mirror the 1966 Selma to Montgomery Civil Rights march in Alabama by marching from Belfast to Derry. Leaving Belfast on 1 January they encountered opposition by loyalists along the route. At Burntollet Bridge on 4 January they were attacked by demonstrators using stones, bottles, sticks and iron bars, and as a result 13 marchers later received hospital treatment. What added to the gravity of the situation was the allegation that the police – who had monitored the progress of the march at every stage and had warned the marchers that there was a threat of violent opposition ahead in the area of Burntollet Bridge – had not offered them protection from the counter-demonstrators.

Condemnation of the incident by Protestant Church leaders and by the ICC Executive at its meeting in Belfast on 8 January was widely reported in the Press. The *Belfast Telegraph* carried the headline 'Clergy berate Orange attack on marchers' and included much of the statement in its report: 'We place on record our profound disquiet at, and disapproval of, the events of last Saturday. Whatever may be said about the wisdom and motivation of the Civil Rights march, it took place with the consent and recognition of the Government. We are convinced that there is no justification whatever for people, either individually or in groups, taking the law into their own hands and we unreservedly condemn such action.' The statement went on to declare that the attacks were 'in flagrant contradiction of the accepted principles of true Protestantism'.[6]

That same day the ICC Executive also drafted and agreed the text of a confidential letter to Cardinal Conway – later signed by the Protestant Church leaders – outlining proposals for an Advisory Group on Community Relations. The Revd Dr Norman Taggart, ICC Secretary at the time, explains the reasons for avoiding publicity: 'It was felt that this was the most effective and appropriate way of proceeding in the circumstances, on account of the suspicion in which ecumenism was held.'[7] The letter was friendly and positive:

Your Eminence

We write as persons holding positions of major responsibility in our Churches and we greet you in the name of our Lord Jesus Christ.

Although we are, and have long been, concerned for the establishment of justice and mutual respect in our Northern Ireland community, recent events have underlined for us the need for urgent action in this respect. We believe that the achievement of this may be advanced by a better understanding of each other's position and concerns and, where possible and if desirable, joint action towards that end, whether publicly or otherwise.

We accordingly wish to suggest there may be advantage to be gained from some type of joint consultative body from our respective Churches. Such a body might well enable all of us to understand and, where considered possible and advisable, to further the ends of each.

We earnestly and urgently offer this suggestion to the consideration of your Eminence. We believe that in normal circumstances such a suggestion has much to commend it, but at this present time in the history of our province we are particularly anxious for bridges to be built and to be kept open.

Should Your Eminence consider consultation advisable before coming to a decision on this suggestion, we should be ready for an appropriate number of representatives on our side to meet with you and/or any representatives you may care to appoint to meet us.

In deep concern for the well-being of our province and its Christian heritage,

We are, yours sincerely,

James McCann, Jack Withers, Gerald Myles, Albert McElroy, Joseph Cooper, George Snell, Norah Douglas.[8]

The third item of ICC business that day was also highly significant. Eric proposed that the Executive should write to the Prime Minister, Terence O'Neill, requesting the Government to set up a judicial and public enquiry into the circumstances and causes underlying much of the recent controversy and unrest. It read:

We earnestly call upon the Government to institute a judicial and public enquiry into all the events and decisions which surround the present controversy. We particularly request that such an inquiry would address itself to the following points:

a. the composition and aims of the Civil Rights Movement

b. the constitution and aims of the Ulster Constitution Defence Committee, the Loyal Citizens of Ulster and other similar organisations

c. the events in Londonderry leading up to and on 30th November 1968 and again in Londonderry leading up to and on the 4th January 1969

d. Government decisions connected with these events and

e. instructions given to and actions taken by the police connected therewith.

This call for an enquiry was welcomed by the Prime Minister and while his Government disagreed that it should take the form of a judicial and public enquiry – supposedly for legal reasons – its other recommendations formed the basis of the Cameron Commission appointed later that month.

Eric Gallagher had had a vital role in all three items of the ICC Executive business. As Chairman he had prepared for the meeting well in advance, arriving with draft statements/letters for all three matters which were accepted with minimum alteration. The idea of calling for an enquiry was his but one is tempted to surmise that his meetings with the Cardinal may have influenced him to some degree in this direction. The proposal for an enquiry certainly met with the Cardinal's approval! Writing to Eric in mid-January he indicated he would 'lose no time' in putting the idea of the Advisory Group before his fellow bishops and he was 'confident of a sympathetic response'. Referring to the letter to the Prime Minister which called for an enquiry the Cardinal wrote: 'May I say that I have been deeply moved by the letter published in today's press. I heard it on the wireless when I was in Manchester this morning, from where I have just returned, and it gave me great heart. I must express again my appreciation of the genuine spirit of Christianity shown by the Protestant Churches in these difficult days.'

Jack Withers, Eric Gallagher and Archbishop McCann met with Cardinal Conway on 5 February and agreed that the Ad Hoc Committee – as it came to be called – should consist of six members: two Roman Catholics and four Protestants. The three mainstream Protestant Churches would each have a member and the smaller Churches on the ICC were to be represented by John Radcliffe who was a Non-Subscribing Presbyterian. The six appointed by the end of March were all clergy: Denis Faul and Patrick Walsh (Roman Catholic), Eric Elliott (COI), Harold Allen (PCI), John Radcliffe (Non-Subscribing Presbyterian) and Eric, who became its Convenor. The RCC bishops suggested there should be no publicity attached to the meetings of the group and this advice was followed throughout its existence.

On 18 April there was a series of terrorist attacks on public buildings and utilities, including attacks on the Silent Valley reservoir and electricity installations at Castlereagh. That evening Eric, McCann and Withers met for business with the Cardinal at Ara Coeli, his official residence. Then a further meeting took place ten days later on 28 April, again at Ara Coeli. At one point the conversation turned to the recent explosions which were being attributed to the work of the IRA. Eric later recalled some of the conversation: 'The Cardinal said he did not believe they were the work of the IRA – they would not be so mad as to carry out the Castlereagh bombing for it was a strong Protestant area. He said it was more likely to have been the work of loyalists trying to bring O'Neill down. And then he asked if we had heard the report that the PM had resigned.'[9]

The next day Eric wrote to O'Neill and wished him well. He commended him for his perseverance in introducing reform: 'Your programme of reform must now go ahead no matter who succeeds you. This you can look upon with satisfaction as an indication of success.' O'Neill replied immediately: 'You have been a brick in the New Ulster building but unfortunately we have not been allowed to complete it. I do so hope that we are not going to be in serious trouble.' In Eric's Autobiographical Notes he comments: 'That trouble was not long in coming.'

Eric had had several meetings with Terence O'Neill and was well placed to make an assessment of his period as Northern Ireland Prime Minister. His analysis is perceptive and interesting:

> It is difficult to come to a clear and unambiguous judgment about Terence O'Neill. Like many of the rest of us prior to 1967 or thereabouts he just did not realise how deeply the minority felt. He had had little contact with the other side and indeed I suspect little enough contact with the grass roots of his own. He was essentially a patrician who did not mix easily with other people. Again and again I noticed how in company he seemed ill at ease until he gravitated to someone whom he knew and then he could and would talk easily enough. When he did realise the score he embarked on his reform programme because he was convinced it was both necessary and right. Behind his time in one sense and yet ahead of it in others. Had he taken his colleagues with him at the time of the Lemass meeting he could well have been unassailable. He did not and paid the price.

April had been a particularly demanding month for Eric. The terrorist attacks on the vital electricity and water supplies had heightened tension in the province, especially as most people had regarded them as the work of the IRA. On 21 April 1,500 troops from 39 Brigade had been sent in to take responsibility for guarding vital installations. That evening Eric was in Primitive Street Methodist Church – located in the Sandy Row area of the city not far from the Belfast Central Mission – to hear 'trial sermons' by probationary ministers.[10] During the last hymn Eric noticed Paddy Scott of Ulster Television (UTV) moving about at the back of the church. Scott indicated that he wanted to speak to him and passed on the message that he was wanted immediately at the television studios. Eric replied that he could not leave before 9.45 at the earliest as he had to preside over the discussion on the sermons.

He reached Havelock House shortly after 9.45 and was met by Brum Henderson, the Managing Director of Ulster

Television, Paddy Scott and the Revd Horace Uprichard, one of UTV's Religious Advisers. 'They said the province was in turmoil. People wanted someone to give a lead. The Prime Minister and Cabinet Ministers had been silent. The Primate and Moderator had said nothing. Would I speak at the end of the ten o'clock news?' Eric continues the story of that night:

> I asked what they wanted me to say and for how long. The answer: 'Whatever you like and as long as you like – 5, 10, 15 minutes – whatever time you want to have.' Then they told me they had already in faith during the evening put out a number of news flashes indicating that I would speak at 10.30. They put me into a room by myself and said that I would be called at 10.20.
>
> It was like being in a condemned cell. It was hard to think. I prayed. I jotted down some seeming irrelevancies. Then I was brought to the studio. In the rush I forgot the notes and had to start without them. They were pushed in while I spoke. I cannot remember what I said or how long it took to say it. It did however meet with a quite unexpected response. Ulster Television claimed that it had had a marked and calming effect. In one of their published accounts of the broadcast they alleged that Paddy Scott had finally located me in a gospel hall!

Away from the political arena, Eric was deeply involved in the workings of the Methodist Church in Ireland. He was particularly pleased with some of the decisions taken at the Conference held in Dublin during the second week of June 1969. Firstly, there was approval in principle for the appointment of a full-time Secretary of the Church and Conference. That decision, implemented a year later, Eric felt, indicated that the Church had at long last recognized the folly of expecting a minister with circuit responsibilities to be available to attend all the central committees of the Church year, to carry out all the on-site consultations necessary, to be available day and night for confidential consultation on circuit and personal affairs, to have the ultimate responsibility for the implementation of many Conference decisions, to represent the Methodist Church in the courts and committees of other Churches and Councils, and at the same time to engage in the necessary thinking in depth and give guidance about the future policy and stance of the Church. The nine years he served in this office had given him the authority to make the case for a full-time Secretary: 'I was able to argue for this appointment with vigour and conviction much more easily than had I been in post or the person to be appointed to the position.'

He was also pleased that Conference agreed to the establishment of four central Boards which would recommend policy to the Church through the annual Conference. He had long been convinced that it was desirable to involve more ministers and lay persons in the administration and policy-making of the Church. Previously this had been the preserve of the General Committee, composed of a large number of ex-officio officials and a corpus of seemingly permanent other folk. He was delighted that Conference had decided that the affairs relating to mission in Ireland and overseas, property, stipends and allowances and, finally, general matters should be the responsibility of four separate Boards meeting at least three times annually. That decision was implemented in 1971. However, time often brings changes and eventually two of these 'umbrella' Boards ceased to function. Eric commented, 'Regrettably to my mind the Boards for Mission and General Purposes have been done away with much to the detriment of democratic involvement.'

The third decision he welcomed related to the participation of clergy in ecumenical services. For some years those taking part in such services had often been subjected to criticism and opposition. Conference felt that the time had come to give some measured approval and support to some of those sharing in these ventures and it fell to Eric to draft the legislation providing the guidelines to be followed:

> It is important to understand what an ecumenical service implies and what it does not. It does not imply that each participating Church accepts all that the others believe. It does not imply that they are actively

attempting 'to sink differences' and reach 'a common denominator'. It does imply that each accepts the sincerity of the others, that all believe that God has a purpose and a will for His Church, that each is trying to find out that will and that each has a right to regard itself in some sense, however imperfectly, as a Christian Church.

In the context of a search for God's will for His Church, joint prayer for this end and for a better understanding of each other is not to be repudiated lightly. In principle it is to be encouraged.

Provided always that these facts are recognised, individuals should be free to exercise their discretion with due regard to all the circumstances, not only local but the well-being of the whole Church in this island.[11]

The outbreak of sectarian violence

Following the annual Apprentice Boys' Parade in Derry on 12 August 1969, serious rioting broke out in the Bogside, which lies to the west below the ancient walls of the city. Most sources report that temporary barricades and stores of petrol bombs had already been prepared, but opinions differ on whether they were to be used in defence against possible attack or as weapons to provoke the authorities. Whatever the analysis regarding the circumstances of the rioting that broke out that day, all are agreed that it was the turning-point which ushered in the next 25 years of bitter community violence. Rioting in Derry soon spread to Belfast, prompting the Northern Ireland government to call for the assistance of British troops to deal with the rapidly deteriorating situation. The first troops arrived on 14 August.

That August Eric and Barbara had decided to take their holiday on the north coast in Portstewart and had booked their touring caravan into the caravan park at Juniper Hill. 'We were hardly there before we were called back to Belfast. During the first ten days or so of the month because of urgent calls relayed to us by either the Portrush minister or the police we were up and down the road to Belfast at least three times. After the riots following the march of the Apprentice Boys of Derry we went home once more hoping that within some days we might get back again.'

It was not to be. The situation in Belfast was tragic. However, in the darkest of moments there often appear people of courage, godliness and good common sense. Eric was called upon to demonstrate these qualities when he was asked to come to the aid of the workers in the Harland & Wolff shipyard.

Once the rioting had spread to Belfast, a potential flashpoint was the shipyard, then the largest employer in the city and with a workforce which included men from both the Catholic and Protestant communities. There had been sectarian trouble and mob violence in the shipyard back in the 1920s and also in the 1930s. Some saw it as a cockpit and a barometer for the political temperature in the province. The shop stewards in the shipyard were particularly alert to any signs of sectarian tension and following the violence in the city on the night of Thursday 14 August, they sensed the growing unrest within the workforce. Sandy Scott, Chairman of the Steelworkers' shop stewards at the time, recalls the situation: 'Naturally when the men came into work on the following day, that trouble and that unease reflected itself within the shipyard. One could sense the tenseness in the whole atmosphere. Everyone was very concerned; the men were coming to the shop stewards and asking them what were they going to do about the situation.'[12] Scott was also aware that by virtue of the fact that the shipyard was the major industrial establishment in Northern Ireland other industrial workforces were looking to them for guidance. 'It was against that background that some of my colleagues and myself got together and decided that we couldn't afford to ignore the situation and that it wouldn't go away; and, unless we endeavoured to do something, the situation would escalate and get out of control. So we decided that we should take the bull by the horns and we called a meeting of all the shop stewards and discussed the matter in great depth. We agonised over it because we knew we were in an extremely difficult situation.' They decided to call a mass meeting of all the workers in the shipyard, including management, office workers, catering staff, everybody. Scott and the shop stewards invited three people to address the mass rally: Joseph Foster Cairns, Lord Mayor of Belfast; Roy Bradford, the Minister of Commerce; and Eric Gallagher.

I asked Sandy Scott why he had chosen Eric to speak at the rally: 'Well, I didn't know Eric, but I knew of Eric. I had lived on the Grosvenor Road, a working-class area, and I'd heard of the good work that Eric had done with working-class families. I knew that he was always prepared to associate and identify with a good cause, that he was basically and essentially a man of peace. I'd no reservations whatsoever and no hesitation in deciding that Eric would be the appropriate man if we could persuade him to come along.'

The Lord Mayor was unable to attend the rally but sent Councillor William Hugh Elliot to represent him. Michael McInerney, an *Irish Times* journalist – who had gleaned his information from Sandy Scott – reported the part played by the three speakers:

> After Councillor Elliot had read out an appeal from the Lord Mayor and Mr Bradford had spoken of the relationship between peace and employment, the Revd Mr Gallagher rose. 'His was a most valuable contribution,' Mr Scott told me later. 'His speech was poetic and even romantic, somehow, but it went down very well.' He spoke of 'our beautiful land of Northern Ireland' and how all should work for the welfare of its people, of the need to act in the interests of common humanity and with the highest standards of human behaviour; to act as brothers. There was silence as Mr Gallagher spoke. He was in complete control. He concluded his speech, movingly, by asking the men to join him in a prayer for peace. To the astonishment of everyone in that atmosphere of hard work and toil the men responded and joined him as he said a prayer for peace in Northern Ireland and for all to be inspired to work for brotherhood and happiness. Somehow, Mr Scott

said, the way the men listened to that prayer brought home to him more than anything else their seriousness. 'I was proud of the way the men responded', he said.[13]

Sandy Scott obviously had a high regard for Eric but the feelings were mutual. In a letter to Scott sometime after the shipyard meeting Eric expressed his appreciation and admiration for the key role the shop steward had played: 'I watched the crowd of thousands – they listened as I have never seen any crowd listen. You spoke plainly and directly – you knew what you were talking about – you talked about their jobs and their homes – you showed your pride in your trade – you appealed not only to their own self-interest – you told them about the yard itself and the danger to the whole Province if it went up. You spelled out the consequences of riot and bloodshed line by line and they lapped it up. You spoke in their own language and they understood what it meant.'

While the shipyard escaped an outbreak of sectarian violence it was a different story in other parts of the city, especially in the west. Many were driven from their homes. In the period July, August and September 1969, 1,505 Catholic and 315 Protestant families were made homeless as a result of the violence.[14] This had consequences for Belfast Central Mission as overnight on 14 August it became a refugee centre, offering temporary shelter to 56 persons. Eric recalled those hectic days which he described as a 'dry run' for another emergency in 1970: 'Food and clothing poured in from a generous public, far more than we could use. Joe McCrory [second minister] and my son David set off each morning and shared our surplus with some of the Catholic centres on the Falls and Springfield Roads.' Two other memories remained with him from this critical time. One was of a 'night guest' from the Grosvenor Road whose snoring could be heard all over the buildings and who had to be allocated a room to himself as far away as possible from everybody else; and the other memory:

> Two scruffy-looking individuals who handed in a parcel to Mrs Jones [Secretary] in the lower office. 'Give that to the Revd Gallagher', they said and disappeared

straight away refusing to identify themselves. Mrs Jones was terrified. She thought it was a bomb and alerted me. I rushed down, saw the parcel and thought she could be right. I took it outside the building and phoned the police. They came immediately and had a look at it. It could be a bomb, they said and incredibly lifted it, put it in the boot of their car and took it away for examination. So much for the sophistication of all of us in the summer of 1969.

Next day they brought it back: two lovely pairs of children's shoes, 'probably looted from a shoe shop on the Shankill', they said. We had no means of letting the looters know what we did with them.

On 17 August, the Sunday following the severe nights of rioting and violence, Eric – as Chairman of the Belfast District of the Methodist Church in Ireland – made 'whistle stop visits' to Methodist congregations in areas of tension and danger. It was an attempt to assure them that the Church at large was thinking about them and praying for them and also to encourage everyone to keep calm. Eric notes, 'It was possible by reason of prior arrangement with the ministers concerned to visit several during the times of morning and evening worship.'

Relevance was always a key ingredient for Eric, whether it meant addressing the shipyard workers or his own congregation in the Grosvenor Hall. The tragic events of August 1969 drew from his soul what was possibly one of his best-ever sermons, 'Christ Weeps Over A City', based on Luke 19.41-42, preached in the Hall on Sunday, 24 August. He drew parallels between the situation in Jerusalem just before Christ's crucifixion and the disaster which they had so recently witnessed in Belfast: 'The comparison between Belfast and the smouldering passions and hatreds of Jerusalem is too startling for us to be complacent. Words are almost useless when we try to assess the catastrophe of the past eight days. Foul deeds have been done that will blacken the name of the city for years to come. Fires have been lit that will smoulder long after the last fire engines have gone back to base.' He recalled the vicious consequences which had resulted from false rumours being spread throughout the community: 'Hundreds, indeed thousands, were all too ready to believe what they heard and to take a rough and brutal law into their own hands. And so came action and counter-action, eviction and reprisal, brutality, burning and bloodshed. This was no defence of Protestantism. It was sheer naked defiance of every rule in the New Testament order book that we call our rule of practice. These deeds of lawlessness by whomsoever committed were unworthy of anyone claiming membership of the Holy Catholic Church in any of its sections. Here was Christian betrayal at its worst. It was utter disobedience to everything Jesus tried to teach.'

But all was not doom and gloom. Out of these recent days of violence, causing suffering to so many, especially women and children, Eric was able to pick out things that were positive and good: 'Have you noticed that almost all the victims have paid tribute to the Christian charity and courage of their neighbours of whatsoever faith who were willing to risk threat and danger to protect them and their property?' Police and firemen had also risked their lives in the service of others. And Christians had played a vital role in attempting to bring an element of sanity to the situation: 'There was the moral and often physical courage of Christians – lay and clerical – who faced mob after mob and did their best to make them see a better way.'

Eric emphasized that there were lessons to be learned from the experience: 'All of us are called urgently to wrestle with this foul and wicked monster of sectarianism until we have it wiped out for ever. Common sense suggests this. Our economic future demands it. The Bible leaves us with no alternative.' As in Jerusalem, he suggested, people in Belfast had allowed themselves to be influenced by mob agitators: 'We have listened to the rabble-rousers instead of giving heed to the words of Christ. We have been ready as a people to stone and kill instead of seeking shelter together. Instead of taking the way of love and sacrifice we have chosen hatred in the name of religion.' Eric challenged the congregation to consider the words of Christ, 'If you, even you, had only known on this day what would bring you peace.' And he closed his sermon – as was his custom – with an appeal for genuine commitment on the side of Christ: 'But Jerusalem is made up of people and so too is Belfast. This business has to start with you and me. It only took a few to set Belfast on fire last Sunday. Only a few are needed to put it on fire for God. Where do you stand?'

Eric saw these events in August and September 1969 as the death of a community. Prior to 'The Troubles' there had been a number of working-class areas with 'mixed' housing, Protestant and Catholic. Very quickly a pattern of segregated housing developed. 'A lorry or van load of furniture had only to leave one house and a whole street was on the move.'

Ruth, their elder daughter who is now a senior social worker, was working that summer in the Royal Victoria Hospital. 'I walked up the [Grosvenor] road with her each morning and went back for her in the evening.' It was a hazardous route to take but there was no alternative. Eric faced the same danger in his pastoral visiting. 'Joe McCrory and I learned to take shelter in doorways from flying bullets. Somehow the air-raids seemed more wholesome.'

At the end of June 1970 the Mission was again required as a refugee centre by the Welfare authorities. There had been serious rioting in the east, west and north of the city. Eric recalled: 'Before eight o'clock [on the 27th] dispossessed folk from New Barnsley were arriving by all sorts of transport. They had lost their homes, whether because of being driven out or simply from fear does not matter.' During this crisis the Mission also became a refuge for some of their own members: 'We got word of one elderly handicapped member of the Hall in great danger in East Belfast on the edge of Short Strand. She was confined to a wheel chair. Joe McCrory and I went for her. Terrified, she had lain awake in the small hours of that June morning watching a gunman on the yard wall outside her bedroom window.'

The Mission provided shelter to scores of families throughout the next ten days. Apparently the peak figure at any one time was 138 persons. Eric was thrilled by the volume of voluntary help: 'A band of nearly a couple of hundred people rallied round to help, as did the Welfare Authority, the Housing Executive, the Red Cross and many others.' The extraordinary situation attracted VIPs from Church and State as well as news and television personnel. 'My office was my bedroom by night and HQ by day for the whole period. Barbara master-minded the housekeeping and kitchen side of the operation and we got away for a couple of hours on 30 June to celebrate our silver wedding with the family.'

It was important that the Ad Hoc group had been created before the tragic events of August 1969. At least the principle of some form of consultation had been put in place. However, relationships within the group were not always rosy but this is not surprising given the lack of contact that had existed between Catholic and Protestant clergy for centuries. Eric's Notes indicate that the meetings of the group were often difficult and indeed had almost fallen apart due to hurts and misunderstandings experienced on both sides. He describes their meetings as following a pattern of 'deaf speaking to deaf'. Verbal attacks on Cardinal Conway by various Protestant clergy had been a particular cause for concern and might possibly have resulted in the break-up of the group had not Eric travelled to see the Primate on Thursday, 19 June. The Cardinal had been mystified by the comments made about him. While Eric was not able to erase the damage already done – he volunteered to raise the points with some of the Protestant clergy concerned – he left the meeting with a feeling that the Cardinal had really wanted someone who would listen and empathize with him.

On 14 August the Cardinal had very quickly issued a press release of his own, stating that he 'could not understand why a parade [the annual Apprentice Boys' Parade in Derry on 12 August] – lasting five or six hours and accompanied by dancing women singing party songs and firing off miniature cannons – was allowed to take place in a city which was tinder-dry for an explosion. In the name of God who loves all men, Catholic and Protestant, Jew and Gentile, let no more wood be piled on this destructive fire.'

The Ad Hoc group did not meet on 14 August. It was possibly too difficult in the circumstances to get the group together, decide on a statement, and then recommend it to their respective Church Leaders. Eric relates that he represented both the ICC and the Ad Hoc group at a meeting with those Church Leaders who could be brought together. They decided to issue an urgent appeal. It asked Christians to pray continuously and to speak and act with charity. The appeal concluded: 'We ask all our fellow-citizens to exercise self-restraint in refraining from all inflammatory words and deeds and from acts of retaliation. The full understanding and justice for which we pray can only be attained when the rights and fears of all are recognised and met. In the name of our Lord Jesus Christ we invite the whole community to share this prayer.'

On Monday 18 August he received an urgent message to attend a conference at Stormont Castle that evening called by the Prime Minister. 'Major Chichester-Clark [O'Neill's successor] in a dramatic effort to restore confidence and give the impression of action being taken had called together a very representative gathering.'

Its composition was as follows (the number of representatives in brackets): Belfast Corporation (2), The Churches' Industrial Council (1), The Church of Ireland (2),The Confederation of British Industry (2), The Council of Social Services (1), The Irish Congress of Trade Unions (2), The Londonderry Development Commission (2), The Methodist Church in Ireland (2), The New University of Ulster (1), The Northern Ireland Chamber of Commerce and Industry (2), The Presbyterian Church in Ireland (2), Protestant and Catholic Encounter (1), The Queen's University of Belfast (1), The Roman Catholic Church (2), The Senior Bar (2).

Dr John Carson, the Moderator, and the Revd Jack Weir represented the Presbyterian Church, Archbishop Simms and Canon Eric Elliott the Church of Ireland, Cardinal Conway (absent from the first meeting) and the Revd Padraig Murphy the Roman Catholic Church, with the Revd Harold Sloan and Eric representing the Methodist Church.

Cynics considered the series of conferences – there were 13 in all – a cosmetic or PR exercise. Eric maintains it was more than that: 'The meetings were a means of prodding government and those with responsibility to swift and effective action in certain areas associated with the outbreak of violence. At the initial meeting the PM was supported by five of his Cabinet colleagues, by the head of the Civil Service and the heads of several civil service departments and by high-ranking Army and Royal Ulster Constabulary [RUC] personnel.'

The list of the matters discussed and on which action was promised by Government is impressive. It included medical provision for refugee centres, emergency financial assistance for those in need, compensation for those who had suffered by reason of the outbreak, financial help for those voluntary schools which had been damaged, protection against intimidation, inflammatory news reporting especially by the electronic media, refusal of bail for those charged with firearms offences, late opening of licensed premises in Belfast and emergency housing for the homeless.

Meetings for the most part were held at six or seven o'clock in the evening and a couple were held on Saturday afternoons, thus permitting the members to do their work during the day. Eric recalled some of the significant moments:

> The initial meeting was quite out of the ordinary. We assembled round the large table of the conference room with the Prime Minister at the centre flanked by his cabinet colleagues and the officials seated at the back along the wall. He welcomed all present and thanked them for coming and was proceeding to introduce the business when his chairmanship was challenged. There ensued a long and heated wrangle at the end of which it was proposed and carried that the chair should be taken by Mr Stephen McGonagle of the Londonderry Development Commission, later to be ombudsman. It was a difficult and embarrassing experience. The PM remained for the duration of the meeting. Thereafter a cabinet liaison minister was present in the person of Phelim O'Neill.

And on another evening:

> There was the night when Cardinal Conway attended and spoke of his relationships and those of his Church with Government Departments. He spoke warmly of the way civil servants had dealt with him, making special mention of the Ministry of Education. His big concern had to do with what happened at local government level.

The problem of barricades which had been erected in local areas was one of the most contentious issues they had to consider. 'Father Padraig Murphy insisted that in his area on the Lower Falls the barricades had gone up out of a sense of fear. To remove them without local consultation could do a great deal of harm.' Eric eventually proposed a resolution which first urged voluntary removal but failing this the Army should be asked to discuss the conditions acceptable for a voluntary removal; finally, if all this failed, then the Army should be asked to remove the barricades and in their place put military patrols and checkpoints. There was a majority, though small, against it and it was defeated. However, Eric reports, and, I suspect, with a great deal of satisfaction: 'Padraig Murphy and Tom Conaty, a Catholic businessman and member of the Conference, took the late-night plane to London and in Downing Street next day were able to secure what had been proposed.'

On 28 October Eric was the guest speaker at a meeting of the North-West Council of Churches in Derry and three weeks later he addressed the Dun Laoghaire (12 miles south-east of Dublin) Council of Churches. On both occasions he spoke on 'Lessons for the Churches from the Northern Ireland situation'. He indicated that the Churches had learned a great deal from recent tragic events but they did not learn soon enough. He pinpointed five areas of weakness or failure which had been revealed.

The first and most glaring, he suggested, had been an incomplete understanding of the implications of biblical teaching: 'This in Northern Ireland has been inexplicable and inexcusable. We have prided ourselves on "the open Bible" but we have concentrated on some of it and not on all of it. If we had read and understood Amos and Micah and Hosea, we would long ago have made sure that "justice was running down like rivers". The New Testament in almost every book speaks to our sick society.' Secondly, there had been a failure in teaching, preaching and communication. 'Have our Sunday Schools been the centres of enlightenment they should have been? Has there been the prophetic note in our preaching over the years? It is fatally easy to preach the kind of sermon people like to hear rather than the uncomfortable Word of God.' He lamented the fact that the Churches in Ulster had become increasingly centres of middle-class thought and life, failing to reach out to the working class. Thirdly, the Churches had failed to persuade sufficient numbers 'of the right kind' to enter public life: 'Who can doubt but that if we had had more in public life bringing Biblical judgments to the life of the Province over the last twenty years we would not have been in our present difficulties.' Then he went on to identify what was perhaps one of the most damning criticisms ever made of the Churches in Northern Ireland: 'Perhaps the most tragic weakness of all has been moral blindness or cowardice. Most of us knew that things were not as they ought to be. We allowed ourselves to be silent. We either did not see or kept silent about what we saw.' Finally, he spoke about what he termed 'ecumenical failure'. Despite the fact that a good biblical case could be made in support of inter-Church relationships, clergy and laity had again been silent, allowing misunderstanding and misrepresentation to go unchallenged: 'The result has been an undermining of confidence for which we have had to pay dearly. Charges of compromise and "Romeward trends" can easily be refuted.'

When he had listed the failings of the Church and the lessons to be learned from them he called on his audience to work towards a solution to these problems. Lay Training, he suggested, was vital in this task. And working together as Christians was crucial: 'In the face of riot and murder and bloodshed, denominational differences fade into insignificance. The man in the street is little interested in whether I am a Methodist or a Presbyterian. He wants to know if I am a Christian.'

Protestant Church leaders had generally avoided any personal references to Ian Paisley, considering it preferable to offer criticism in more indirect ways, for example, warning of the danger of 'rabble-rousers' or speaking of the evils of sectarianism. They were never entirely happy with this policy but nevertheless it was one that most followed. It had been thought that Eric was one of the most scrupulous in observing this practice but a hitherto unknown article, 'The Protestant Churches and Ian Paisley' published by the *Abingdon Press* in 1969, suggests that he may have deemed it appropriate to allow an exception to the rule, especially if the circulation of the material was likely to be restricted to the American market. Much of the article concentrates on providing a historical background to the Northern Ireland problem and Eric's portrayal of Paisley is set within this context:

Ian Paisley has of course come to be associated with the political Protestant case, and he now claims to speak for the majority of Ulster Protestants. He is an interesting phenomenon. A forceful evangelistic preacher, he has undoubted gifts of almost hypnotic oratory. He is the only moderator his Free Presbyterian Church has ever had. He never was a Presbyterian. Born of Baptist-Plymouth stock, he was called as a young man to the pulpit of an Evangelical Mission church in Belfast. A born opportunist, he made use of a couple of difficult situations in Presbyterian congregations to found what he called Free Presbyterian churches to which he appointed ministers. He followed this up with a series of tent missions in theologically sympathetic areas. From these efforts he also founded a number of relatively small congregations. Possessed of considerable ambition and seeking prominence and/or power, he has over the years seized on every available opportunity to put himself in front of the public. He has staged public demonstrations on any pretext likely to suit his purposes, and in this context from time to time has been convicted of offences against the law.

A disciple of Carl McIntire, he made the ecumenical movement and the World Council of Churches his Public Enemy Number One. In this he expertly played on the natural fears and susceptibilities of Northern Ireland Protestants with regard to Romeward trends and union with the Church of Rome. One public demonstration against the official Presbyterian Church led to conviction and a prison sentence. This he publicised as the act of a treacherous and corrupt Government against a 'true Protestant' minister.

The current civil turmoil has given him the chance to allege that all the things he had said about the Roman Church were now being proved true. His appeal to the hard-liners of the political Protestant front has been all too successful. Numerically his Free Presbyterian Church is small, but it would be idle to deny the strength of his political following. It is probably true to say that he has heavy support among the militant industrial workers who are for the most part outside the committed membership of the main churches, among the rural population, and among the middle-class Protestants inside the churches.

Eric's portrayal of Paisley is relatively mild and devoid of any sense of overstating his case. It was the typical Gallagher approach of objectivity and fairness. This was in stark contrast to Paisley's attacks on Eric. Since 1967 he had targeted him as the leading clergyman on his 'Black list of Ulster clergymen from all apostate denominations who in word and deed deny their vowed beliefs'.[15] Eric's unease with the policy of not directly criticising Paisley surfaces in the article. One of the reasons for Paisley's popularity and strength, he suggests, might be because:

> The main churches have consistently sent out their calls for a just society. They have not, however, attacked Paisley personally as he has attacked them. This is to their credit, but it has been at a cost of allowing him to get away with it. He is manifestly open to attack on his failure to understand Old Testament teaching on justice and righteousness. His paper, the *Protestant Telegraph*,

reveals in its inflammatory pages a total unawareness of the community implications of Christian love. Again and again this paper has published statements or innuendoes about the leaders of the main churches that fall far below the standards of truth and love.

He goes on to announce what surely amounts to a change of policy in the attitude to be taken to Paisley:

The time has come for the Protestant churches to spell out the biblical reasons why Paisley does not speak for them. His demonstration and speech at Burntollet – the scene of the terrifying brutal January attack on a predominantly student civil rights march – should reveal him once and for all as a political rather than a biblical Protestant.

The hint of a change of policy in dealing with Paisley was never carried through! Others may have advised him against it!

By the end of 1969 the ICC was exploring the possibility of extending its contacts with the Roman Catholic Church. In addition to the Ad Hoc group – whose function was to advise Church leaders in the area of community relations – the Churches Industrial Council had already had a long and useful existence. Hope was being expressed that this pattern of relationship might be extended. Norman Taggart explains: 'The [ICC] Executive sought and received permission to explore the possibility of joint working parties being set up with the RCC "on specific problems such as housing, world poverty, causes of tension in the community, employment, the effects of technological and industrial development on human life and environment, Faith and Order etc." '[16] However, in the process of discussion between the ICC and representatives of the RCC hierarchy this wider perspective on the development of working parties was somewhat reduced. The final remit published on 8 May 1970 read:

The Executive Committee of the Irish Council of Churches, with the approval of the Council, has agreed to a proposal to set up a Joint Group to be appointed by the member Churches of the Council and the Irish Hierarchy to advise on the role of the Churches in Irish Society in such matters as world poverty, employment and housing conditions, drug addiction, alcoholism etc. It is envisaged that separate working parties will be set up on individual topics.[17]

The setting up of the Joint Group was another major step in co-operation between the RCC and the Protestant Churches. It had 30 members, 15 nominated by the RCC, 14 by ICC member Churches, and one – Norman Taggart, the ICC Secretary – appointed directly by the ICC. Canon Robert Murphy and Eric were asked to be Co-Chairmen of the Group. By September the first meeting of the new body had taken place. It was to do much good work in the years that followed, reports being published by working parties on various subjects: drug abuse, (1972); housing in Northern Ireland, [1973]; teenage drinking, (1974); under-development in rural Ireland, [1976]; and violence in Ireland, [1976]. Other working parties followed in later years.

In early September 1970 Eric received a completely unexpected and pressing invitation from an equally unexpected quarter. It was from a group of Swedish members of Parliament who wanted him to address a variety of groups and organisations in Sweden. They particularly wanted him to speak about the Northern Ireland situation from a Church or Christian point of view. He flew out from Belfast on Tuesday, 20 October. Arriving that evening in Stockholm he was entertained to dinner in his hotel by the Chairman of the Liberal Party who passed on the details of the meetings he was to address and instructions about travel and accommodation. 'During the meal he said there was one question he especially wanted to ask and it was as to my opinion about Bernadette Devlin. He told me that I would require to be very careful when referring to her. She had recently visited Sweden and had made a deep impression on students especially and had been entertained by members of the royal family.'

The following day he addressed a meeting of members of Parliament and was entertained at a reception given by a Government minister. During the remainder of the week he spoke to the Council of Churches, to representatives of the Free Churches at Gavle and to a crowded meeting of students in Uppsala where he also met the Archbishop. 'I was mentally prepared to deal with the Bernadette Devlin issue at the Uppsala student meeting but her name was never mentioned. We had an interesting and I think useful meeting during which one student told me that she had spent the previous summer in the Republic of Ireland and that the really big issue was the purchase of Irish farms and property by Germans.' The Saturday and Sunday were spent in Gothenburg. On the Saturday he spoke to the Union of Christian Social Democrats and another student meeting. On the Sunday morning he preached in the Methodist Church and in the evening addressed a public meeting. Next morning he was back in Belfast in time for a meeting at Methodist College at 5.30 p.m.

Links between the Irish Council of Churches and Churches in other parts of Europe developed even as the sectarian violence continued. Dr Glen Garfield Williams, General Secretary of the Conference of European Churches (CEC), visited Northern Ireland in 1970 as did other Church leaders from Germany and Holland. Williams indicated that his organisation would welcome the attendance at its executive meeting of someone from Ireland who would speak on the Northern problem. Eric was nominated by the ICC to go to its meeting in Marseilles on 24 November: 'It was a fascinating but daunting experience: questions from the floor by some well informed members were far from anodyne.'

As time passed other developments followed, most notably an information seminar on the Troubles and the Churches organized by the ICC from 2-4 December 1971 in the Edenmore Hotel, Whiteabbey, near Belfast.[18] It was attended by 40 church-related representatives from ten European countries, most of them with media responsibilities. Taggart tells us that visits were arranged to troubled areas in and around Belfast. It met under the chairmanship of Archbishop George Simms who had succeeded Eric as ICC Chairman. Other speakers in addition to Eric included: Padraig Murphy of Corpus Christi Church, Ballymurphy, Belfast; Alf McCreary, journalist; Robin Baillie, the Newtownabbey MP and Stormont Minister of Commerce; and David Bleakley, soon to become the full-time ICC Secretary. A comprehensive range of topics covered the historical background to the Troubles, political attitudes, the Orange Order, the minority's attitude towards Northern Ireland, community relations, and the position of the Churches. Eric was pleased with the outcome of these various meetings: 'Out of this came the Churches' Emergency Fund for Ireland which to date has been the means of grant-aiding peace and reconciliation projects in this country to the tune of over £700,000.'[19]

At its Summer Graduation ceremony on 8 July 1971 the Queen's University of Belfast – the university in which Eric had served as Methodist Chaplain during his ministry in University Road Church – conferred an honorary Doctor of Divinity on him. The scores of congratulatory letters he received from different parts of Britain and Ireland all emphasized that the honour was well earned and deserved. Professor J.A. Faris, Dean of the Faculty of Theology, in his citation declared: 'In his ministry there have been interwoven several distinguishable strands of activity and interest.' Faris outlined Eric's pastoral and administrative work in the Methodist Church and across the denominations, highlighting his bridge-building work between Roman Catholics and Protestants. He also referred to his immensely impressive record of social service, his distinctive contribution in public affairs and his continuing interest in education.

Brian Faulkner had succeeded Chichester-Clark as Prime Minister in March 1971. Five months later on 9 August, his government introduced internment without trial which proved without doubt to be the main factor in his own downfall and the prorogation of the Stormont Parliament in March 1972. Possibly the Prime Minister and his advisers had been encouraged by memories of the success of internment in the late 1950s, but on that occasion it had been introduced on both sides of the border by both northern and southern governments, a similarity noticeably missing in August 1971. Apart from the wisdom or otherwise of introducing the measure in the first instance, other factors such as poor military intelligence and an imbalance in the ratio of Republicans detained to Loyalist detainees further contributed to a worsening situation. Within a few days 7,000 people, mostly Catholics, were reported homeless, and the number of killings in the remaining months of 1971 far outnumbered that in the months prior to 9 August. One of the most damning indictments of the measure was the propaganda weapon it presented to the IRA, which now claimed to be the victim of an unjust and corrupt regime.

Eric first heard the news that internment had been introduced when he received a telephone message on the morning of 9 August from William Slinger, the Permanent Secretary of the Ministry of Community Relations: 'He told me that the Government had not only introduced detention without trial, it had also put a ban on marches and processions of whatever kind. It was feared that some loyalists might defy the ban. The Government would welcome a statement by a Church leader or leaders encouraging compliance with the ban. He enquired if I could do anything to ensure such a statement.'

As Convenor of the Ad Hoc group Eric interpreted the situation as one in which he must call the other members together. He immediately ran into difficulties. Only two others, Eric Elliot and Harold Allen, were able to come to the Grosvenor Hall. Patrick Walsh was at his mother's home in Andersonstown (West Belfast) but he said the place was like an armed camp, preventing movement in or out of the area. Eric promised to keep in contact with him. Repeated attempts to contact Denis Faul were unsuccessful. There is no reference to any attempt to reach John Radcliffe.

Eric discovered that all the Protestant Church leaders were on holiday but he was able to invite their appointed representatives: Bishop Arthur Butler of Connor representing the COI Primate Archbishop Simms, the Revd Jack Weir standing in for the Moderator, Dr John Carson, and the Revd

Harold Sloan for the President, the Revd Charles Bain. The meeting started at two o'clock with only Protestant clergy present: three members of the Ad Hoc Group and three designated representatives of Protestant Church leaders. The noise of gunfire and explosions from the nearby Lower Falls could be heard all afternoon during the course of their discussions. Eric recalls some of their thoughts: 'None of us welcomed the introduction of internment. We were convinced, quite mistakenly as it turned out, that it would be applied right across the board.' During the course of the discussion news must have come through that the Apprentice Boys had agreed to observe the ban on marches so this was not as crucial an issue as it first appeared from William Slinger's phone call.

Further contact was made by phone with Paddy Walsh but he was still unable to leave Andersonstown. By teatime those present had agreed a statement for release to the media. It read:

> We recognise that because of the continuing violence and bloodshed for which there can be no Christian justification, the Government in its duty to all citizens has no option but to introduce strong measures which must be distasteful to many.

> We regret the necessity for the introduction of internment. We note, however, that there is already provision for an Appeals Committee. This is designed to safeguard the rights of law-abiding citizens.

> The right to peaceful demonstration should be the mark of a mature society but in present circumstances there is great danger in asserting all our rights. Christians should be sensitive to the true wellbeing of the whole community. We welcome the acceptance of the Government's decision by those planning the proposed march for Thursday next.

> We welcome the Prime Minister's urgent call to all the people in Northern Ireland to play their part in developing our country. Violence and fear are the enemy

of us all. This is a time for persistent prayer by everybody.

Patrick Walsh heard the statement over the phone and relayed it to the Cardinal, also reached by phone. The Cardinal was not convinced that he could sign it so it was released carrying only the signatures of the Protestant Church leaders. Conway issued his own statement, appealing to the Catholic population 'not to allow their feelings at the present time to lead them into situations where they could suffer serious injury or death'. A day or two later he spoke of the 'abhorrence of internment'.

The statement by the Protestant Church leaders – or, to be more correct, those who had signed on their behalf – had a mixed reception throughout the country. In the Republic Roman Catholics and Protestants were critical. Northern Catholics and some Protestants saw little merit in what had been done. Some of the media criticisms were quite scathing. Eric was particularly annoyed by the editorials in the *Irish Times* entitled 'The Right to Speak' which appeared in the days following internment, especially the editorial on 11 August: 'The statement of Monday night on internment from the leaders of the three main Protestant Churches – the Church of Ireland, Presbyterian and Methodist – is not good enough. If Protestant clergymen over the years of the Stormont regime had protested against the inequalities and injustices in the Northern State, they would be on firmer ground, and they would be listened to with more respect today. If they had marched with the Civil Rights Movement, instead of with the Orange Order, their words would carry more weight.' Eric prefaced his lengthy reply by voicing his appreciation for the careful reporting and analysis which had characterized the *Irish Times* over the years, 'I am a Methodist who, following the example of my mother, reads the leaders in the *Irish Times* each day as carefully as the Bible. This discipline has taught me much about Irish and international affairs and I greatly acknowledge my debt to you and your predecessors over the last forty years.' However, the rest of his reply made it clear that he deplored what he regarded as irresponsible editorial comment on the right of the Protestant Church leaders to speak on the Northern Ireland situation. Regretting the limitations of space available for him to reply, he succinctly endeavoured to outline the track record of the mainstream Protestant Churches since 1966 regarding their condemnation of injustices and support for reform which would implement human and civil rights. He concluded: 'You may think all this confers no right to speak – others may think differently.'

Archbishop George Simms possibly received the severest criticism, coming from various sources, including those within the Church of Ireland. It pained Eric to read and listen to the criticisms made, especially when he knew that Simms had not even been present, a fact which the Archbishop never disclosed!

There is no doubt that Eric later regretted the statement on internment: 'In the after light I am convinced that the statement would have been differently worded had we known more about what was going on. It was days before many of the facts came to light and months before others were known, the bungling of the whole operation, the one-sided arrests, the interrogation methods, the treatment of those arrested and the delays and difficulties associated with appeal.'

The internment issue could well have wrecked the already fragile existence of the Ad Hoc Group. Indeed, it is amazing that Eric for the second time in two years – the first being on 14 August 1969 – had persevered with an exclusively Protestant Church leaders' statement when he himself had been the chief architect of the machinery set in place for presenting joint statements from both Catholic and Protestant Church leaders. Even before 9 August Denis Faul had expressed doubts about his continuing as a member of the Ad Hoc group. On Friday evening 20 August 1969 he again expressed his feelings to Eric, coupling these with his concern regarding the ill-treatment of detainees under interrogation. He shared with Eric, and later that evening with Harold Allen, some of the stories of ill-treatment that had come his way. Harold Allen was able to pass these concerns on to Brian Faulkner, insisting that the truth of the situation be uncovered. By the following Monday an enquiry had been ordered. The same day Eric wrote to Denis, telling him of Harold Allen's approach to the Prime Minister and concluding, 'Denis, we need you. You can help us far more by telling us what you think than by staying away.' Eric notes, 'He stayed.'

In contact with the IRA

During the early autumn of 1971 Barbara and Eric had discussed on several occasions whether or not he should try to make a personal approach to the IRA. Such a meeting could provide an opportunity to give his own Christian reflection on the situation, share with them the view that their military approach was really counter-productive in that there would always be a loyalist backlash, and make an appeal to try a political route to achieve their objectives. Within the context of these husband-and-wife discussions there then followed what Eric describes as 'an almost unbelievable set of coincidences'.

That autumn he was one of three Irish clerics – the others being George Simms and Jack Weir – who were invited to speak about the Irish situation at the meeting of the British Council of Churches in Dunblane, Scotland. Following the session dealing with Ireland he was informally approached that evening by two BCC members – Dr Ernest Payne, then General Secretary of the Baptist Union in Britain, and the Revd Edward Rogers, General Secretary of the Methodist Division of Social Responsibility in British Methodism – who quite independently of each other suggested that violence in Ireland would not stop until someone was prepared to reach out to the IRA and talk with them. They both thought that Eric was the one who should do this and asked him to think about it.

Sitting at breakfast in the hotel next morning, he was called to the telephone. 'The caller was Father Desmond Wilson from Ballymurphy. He told me that some "hard men" would like to talk to me and he said I would know what he meant by "hard men". He wanted to see me as soon as I got home.'

Eric met Desmond Wilson soon after he returned to Belfast. The two had known each other since the late 1950s when they had both shared in the inter-community clergy group called together by Robert Murphy. Wilson indicated that the Provisional IRA leadership wanted to talk to Eric and another Unionist 'about the possibility of bringing the struggle to an end'. This information must have come as something of a surprise to Eric because less than two years had elapsed since the PIRA had split from the IRA in a disagreement over policy: the question of whether to follow physical-force Republicanism or the political method. In December 1969 the IRA Army Council had voted to recognize three Parliaments – Westminster, Dublin and Stormont – and in January 1970 the Sinn Fein Ard Feis in Dublin had voted in favour of the army council decision. Those against walked out to form the 'Provisional' IRA, determined to continue the physical force tradition and steer the movement away from what it considered was an extreme form of socialism whose ultimate objective was 'a totalitarian dictatorship of the left'.[20] The leaders of this breakaway group – by now undoubtedly the major force of the two – were evidently wanting to explore ways of bringing their armed struggle to an end.

After some further discussion with Barbara, Eric agreed to meet with the PIRA but indicated he was prepared to act as a messenger, not a negotiator. He was alarmed when he learned they wanted him to bring Ian Paisley with him. Eric recalls: 'I declined on two grounds. If they wanted to speak to Dr Paisley they could make the approach themselves. In the second place I was quite sure he would not go and I was not prepared for him to know that I was going.' Eric suggested an alternative name which was accepted but the person agreed was unable to go.

In the Curate's House of St John's parish Wilson introduced Eric to 'Jim', described as a messenger on behalf of others. Jim said that there were those in the Belfast leadership who felt that the struggle was getting nowhere. Young people on both sides were being sucked into it. Some of the Belfast leaders were looking for an acceptable way out of the morass. Jim indicated that some moves along those lines were likely to be made at the Army Council the following day and produced a document which he said was the introduction to a resolution likely to be moved. Eric notes, 'He asked me to read it and told me that I could keep it, adding that the leadership wished to talk to me.' The statement provides an insight into a section of PIRA thinking at the time:

> The situation in the North continues to escalate. The death toll rises while Irish men and women on both sides of the divide and holding extremely conflicting views suffer death, injury and imprisonment, British soldiers also die or are injured doing a job they don't understand or want.
>
> Each of us are victims of a situation that we seem unable to arrest or affect.
>
> Whatever the claims being made now by spokesmen for the establishment or for the IRA as to the success or otherwise of their different campaigns, the fact remains that there are no victors in the present struggle, but that the great mass of the people continue to suffer and that we will all lose if we are each content to retire behind our own wall of prejudice and regard any move toward peace as being futile or unworthy of the sacrifice already made by our people. Peace can and will come but not until we are all prepared to admit that possibly we have had something to contribute to the creation or sustaining of the present situation. True peace is not merely the absence of violence but also the creation of a society where legal force is minimal.
>
> It is not our intention to pontificate as to who is responsible for the lack of peace, nor can we condemn, condone or apportion blame. All that we ask is that we approach the situation as it is and not as we would wish to have it.
>
> The proposals for peace in the community are made after giving consideration to the following facts and are only practical if the same credence is given to these facts by those who will have to implement the recommendations:

1. No military solution is possible for either side. This means that no military machine is capable of inflicting enough damage on the IRA or on any guerrilla army in a situation similar to this one, which will render the guerrillas incapable of inflicting damage on the economy or killing or injuring establishment personnel in one degree or another for an unspecified period of time. In reality even if the forces at present acting in support of the Stormont administration were to completely destroy the IRA (which means killing or imprisoning all their personnel and destroying all their supplies – a feat which is regarded as being impossible by all military tacticians) a new generation would resurrect the ideal and the struggle would continue for our children. No one on either side wants that.

   Similarly the IRA are not capable of inflicting enough damage to the British economy to force changes in British policy in relation to the six-county area, nor of killing enough British army personnel to force a change in the immediate future but they have the potential to continue the campaign on indefinitely causing irreparable harm to the Northern Irish economy and extolling [sic] an ever increasing toll on the forces ranged against them, on the civilian population who will die as a result of the situation, and inevitably on their forces.

2. Just as 1,000,000 Unionists cannot be bombed into a united Ireland, no more can 500,000 Nationalists be coerced indefinitely into a state which is diametrically opposed to their aspirations, but that there is enough innate goodness in the people of both sides to make a solution possible.

3. The eventual reunification of the country is an accepted fact on both sides of the divide either through the natural process of an increasing birth rate on the Nationalist side combined with a decrease on the Unionist side (due to socio-economic factors

operating on the more prominent middle class in any advanced capitalist economy) and again due to the rapid transfer of power to larger and more international groupings on both the political and economic front which will eventually make the partition of the island both irrelevant and impractical.

4. That while both Britain and Eire can contribute in varying degrees either to exacerbate or conciliate, the solution in the final analysis can only lie in the hands of the people who are both the creators and the sufferers of the status quo.

Eric read the document and they talked together till midnight. 'I shared with him something of my own Christian beliefs and convictions about violence and my own concern for the good name and wellbeing of my country as well as his. Jim revealed himself as a sensitive person, well informed and deep thinking.' But there was another side to Jim: 'He spoke almost casually about the training of recruits and the need to "get them blooded"'.

Some days later Desmond Wilson contacted Eric and told him that the Army Council had not reached the anticipated decision. However, the IRA leadership still wanted to meet him. They had suggested Tuesday, 9 November. Eric's reaction is revealing: 'The date was out of the question as far as I was concerned. We had had no real holiday since 1968 and I had promised Barbara that we would take some days in the Lake District on my way to Edinburgh via Newcastle-upon-Tyne for a meeting of the Scottish Assembly of the Royal Institute for International Affairs at which I was to speak. I was to leave Barbara in Newcastle with Ruth who was doing a post-graduate course in the university.' He told Wilson that they were due to leave Larne on the Tuesday morning and that he was not willing to break the arrangement. The date was rearranged for Monday, 8 November!

Wilson drove Eric and Jim to the meeting which took place in the Imperial Hotel in Dundalk. At the Border crossing point south of Newry they were stopped by an army patrol but immediately waved through when it was seen that there were two clerics in the front seats.

Eric found it somewhat ironic that they were meeting in the *Imperial* Hotel! It wasn't long before the first member of the IRA leadership appeared: 'Suddenly a tall man clad in green army-type drill trousers, strong brown boots and Aran sweater, was beside us. Jim spoke to him and then he asked us to go with him. He brought us upstairs and on the way he told Jim that he was not required and that he should come back in a couple of hours time.' The 'tall man' introduced himself as Sean MacStiofan, Chief of Staff of the Provisionals.[21] Soon they were joined by Ruairí Ó'Brádaigh, President of Provisional Sinn Fein, and Joe Cahill, Belfast Commander of the PIRA.[22]

They wasted no time in pleasantries but got down immediately to business. Eric was asked to speak first:

> I told them who I was and where I came from. I mentioned that my father had not signed the Ulster Covenant but had counted himself a good Protestant and had been a loyal citizen of the state until his dying day. I was in the same mould. Along with my Protestant co-religionists I had been born in this country. I loved it: I belonged to it. I had nowhere else to go and I counted myself both Irish and British. The campaign of violence troubled me. I could see no justification for it: it was against my understanding of the New Testament. I wanted to see it ended so that all of us could live and work together in what could be the best country in the world.

MacStiofan was the next to speak, followed by Ó'Brádaigh, who – in Eric's judgement – was the most voluble of the three Provisionals. He records that Cahill had almost nothing to say. 'His sole contributions were made every half-hour or so: he would produce an ear piece from his pocket, put it in his ear and after listening for a minute or two would say that everything so far was quiet. What everything was we were not told. And what he was listening to I do not know, whether Radio Eireann, BBC, Downtown or some link of their own.'

The Chief of Staff indicated that the leadership was anxious for a ceasefire leading to a complete cessation of hostilities. If the British could find some way of reducing army activity in response to lowered activity by the Provisionals, and then take the army off the streets altogether, the IRA would respond. Indeed, if the ceasefire lasted long enough it might be possible to end the campaign. This could happen, Eric was told, 'If at some time convenient to themselves the British were to say that by a given date they would leave the country altogether. That date did not necessarily need to be soon. It could be into the next century.'

It was obvious to Eric that this last point was the crucial one. He had earlier indicated that he did not see his role as a negotiator but on hearing the suggestion of a British withdrawal he felt compelled to speak: 'I pointed out the problem from a British point of view but more particularly from that of the Northern Protestants who were conscious and proud of their British citizenship.'

When Eric asked them what they wanted him to do they requested that he convey the message to Harold Wilson. He was somewhat puzzled that they did not want the message to go to Edward Heath, the Prime Minister. 'Their reply amazed me. They knew enough, they said, about the way the British work to realise that if Wilson got it, he would pass it on.'

Eric and Barbara enjoyed their few days away, but that Sunday evening while in Newcastle at the home of the Revd and Mrs Kenneth Waights he received a phone call from their son, David. The message was that Major Robert Stephens, secretary to the Governor, Lord Grey, had been on the phone. 'He told me that Lord Grey had invited me to lunch on the following Tuesday to meet Mr Harold Wilson who would be visiting Northern Ireland. David had told Major Stephens that he did not think I would be able to accept the invitation as I would not be back until Monday evening and that I would have a big backlog of work to see to.' Eric reflects on David's message: 'It was moving to have a son who considered his father's backlog of work more pressing than the Governor's invitation to meet the Leader of the Opposition and next Prime

Minister. I asked David to phone Hillsborough next morning and say that I hoped to be back in Belfast by six o'clock on Monday and would be happy to speak with Major Stephens, if he so wished.'

The not unexpected phone call came soon after they had returned home on Monday evening. Major Stephens said that the Governor wished to speak to Eric personally. 'I understand you are very busy,' said the Governor, recalling the message David had given to his secretary! Lord Grey expressed the hope that Eric might be able to accept the invitation to lunch next day at Hillsborough. Eric indicated that he would be very pleased to accept. The Governor went on to say that there might be another guest, Tom Caldwell, the Unionist MP who represented Willowfield at Stormont.[23] On hearing this Eric felt it necessary to indicate that he had an important and confidential message to pass on to his chief guest, Harold Wilson: 'Lord Grey said he would do his best to facilitate me. If the other guest did not come, he would certainly manage it. If he did come I would have to take my chance. Next day I found out what taking my chance really meant.'

There is a certain element of mystery attached to Harold Wilson's visit and to Eric's invitation to lunch at Hillsborough. Why did Lord Grey invite both Tom Caldwell and Eric Gallagher to Hillsborough? W.D. Flackes and Sydney Elliott in *Northern Ireland. A Political Directory 1968-1993* suggest that in 1971 Tom Caldwell met PIRA leaders in the Republic in a bid 'to stop the killings'.[24] Was this before or after the Hillsborough meeting? Certainly, according to Eric, Caldwell told Harold Wilson at Hillsborough that the IRA wanted a ceasefire but denied having had contact with them. Despite the smallness of the luncheon group Eric found it very difficult to speak to Harold Wilson on his own, even though Lord Grey did his best to take Caldwell out of the frame and give Eric the chance to pass on his confidential message! Eventually, just before the group broke up, Eric was given his chance:

> Harold Wilson and I were left together. In the time that was left I said that the information he had received [from Caldwell] was correct for I had met 'these men'.

His response was instantaneous. 'Name them,' he said. I did so and the next question was when and where the meeting had taken place. I told him and he said emphatically that this was the most important piece of news he had had since he had come to Ireland. I asked about the Prime Minister. 'Don't worry about Ted,' he replied. He went on to indicate that before he left London he had asked that he should be accompanied by the assistant secretary of the Cabinet and that the latter had been instructed to report back all that would take place. 'I'll tell Cairncross about this and Ted will know it by teatime.'

Eric was content that he had completed his task. The Manchester *Guardian* reported next day that he had been seen going into Hillsborough Castle for lunch but it did not attach any significance to the visit.

The meeting of the Scottish Assembly of the Royal Institute for International Affairs on Saturday, 13 November 1971 in Edinburgh had a historical significance all of its own. There were three speakers: Professor Paul Rose, who referred to his publication *Government Without Consensus*, which basically held out no hope of any future government by consensus in Northern Ireland; and two others, Father Desmond Wilson and Eric Gallagher.

Eric entitled his address 'The Future of Northern Ireland'. He immediately made clear his disagreement with Professor Rose's conclusion that no answer to the Northern Ireland problem seemed to be possible: 'A solution that makes a reasonable life possible for all must be found.' Eric proposed both a short-term solution in the first instance and a long-term one after that. In the short term he suggested there should be a plebiscite to decide the question of the border, followed by one every ten years: 'Let the people say whether or not they want the border to continue. If the opinion of the majority is for the continuation of the Northern Ireland State, let security for the ensuing period be in the hands of the United Kingdom completely.' In the long term he asked: 'What is there to prevent the Northern Ireland Government getting on with the business of day-to-day politics?' He saw no reason why, if the total Northern Ireland budget in a given year was fixed, the Northern Ireland people could not get down to 'the politics of priorities in expenditure'. He went on: 'If there was a real discussion, dialogue and controversy over the expenditure on Education, Agriculture, New Industry, Housing, Social Services, possibly Postage and a Civilian Police Force, this could make all the difference in the world of day-to-day politics.' Then came the insight which would later be implemented – with strong degrees of similarity – in the creation of the 1974 Power-Sharing Executive and a similar form of shared government following the signing of the Belfast Agreement in 1998: 'With the introduction of a proportional representation system, an enlarged House of Commons and an enlarged Senate and with the reflection of political strength in the Cabinet, there is no reason whatever why people with long-term differing ideals would not serve in the same Government.' Eric saw this as a means of encouraging people to hold and cherish their own political ideals while still providing a method of government by consensus: 'In the long term each party should be free to have its political ideals and aims. The only thing that should be required of it is to undertake to pursue those aims constitutionally and legally.'

He was conscious that his proposal might be ridiculed but he asked that it be considered: 'The pundits may well say that my suggestion is completely impossible. I can only say that to continue the present situation is not only impossible but intolerable. Government policy at the moment is to gain a military victory before discussions begin.'

To my knowledge Eric's suggestion of a Cabinet which reflected the political strength of parties elected by proportional representation is the first time that this principle had been seriously made by anyone looking to the future of government in Northern Ireland.[25] He was, among other things, a political analyst of the highest calibre. Historical records should recognize the prophetic, political contribution he made at Edinburgh.

Eric Gallagher age c.11.

Graduation at Trinity College, Dublin, 1936.

Edgehill Theological College Ministerial Community.
Eric is second on the left in the second row.
Dr Alec McCrea, Principal, is in the centre of the front row.
Dr William ('Barney') Northridge is second on the left in the front row.

Eric with the children and teachers of
Woodvale Sunday School, c.1939.

Eric and Barbara's wedding, 30 June 1945.

*Eric (left) and the Revd Brian Cobbe examine the model of the
new church buildings at Glenburn, c.1953.*

*Family photo.
Left to right:
David, Ruth
and Helen.*

Family on holiday:
David, Helen and Ruth.

Eric and his father 'RH'.

Past Presidents at Eric's Induction Service as President of the Methodist Church in Ireland, 12 June 1967.

Eric and the Revd Robert Brown, PCI delegate, at the Fourth Assembly of the World Council of Churches, Upsala, 11 July 1968.

Sandy Scott, the shop steward who invited Eric to address the shipyard workers on 14 August 1969.

With Barbara at Buckingham Palace to receive his OBE in 1972.

Attending the 1983 Methodist Conference in Enniskillen. Left to right: Revd Kenneth Best, Dr Stanley Worrall, Eric, Revd Dudley Cooney and Revd David Houston.

At a meeting of the Wesley Historical Society, Edgehill Theological College in 1992. Left to right: Cardinal Cahal Daly, Mrs Marion Kelly, Eric and the Revd Derek Ritchie.

Attending a meeting of the Wesley Historical Society [Irish Branch].
Left to right: John Frost, Fred Jeffrey, Eric and Jack Weir.

Three past Secretaries of the
Irish Methodist Conference.
Left to right:
Eric, Dr Edmund Mawhinney
and the Revd Charles Eyre .

In retirement at
9 Cloverhill Park, Lisburn.

12

Political analyst
1972-73

Words like provocation and crisis are far too mild for what is happening at the present time. Every news bulletin screams out a new tragedy. Life has been cheapened and humanity is being dragged deeper into the gutter every day. The death toll is increasing all the time and there are more innocent victims than guilty ones. You would almost think that some creature out of hell was stalking the streets of Ulster deliberately bombing, wounding, goading its long-suffering people into a blind mad fury. You could be forgiven if you came to the conclusion that his only purpose was to put us at each other's throats. He has been handing out a devil's brew, absolutely determined to poison the hearts and minds of decent people whose only wish is to live at peace. Some fiendish minds seem hell-bent on making the Protestant and Catholic people of the Province to burn each other out of house and home and to torture and slaughter each other by the thousands.

So many people have said to me in recent weeks 'Isn't it terrible? What can we do?' There is something practical every one of us, Protestant and Catholic, can do. The advice of the good Book is so simple as almost to be disarming. Here it is: 'Encourage one another so that no one is made stubborn.' I know that the cynic will want to laugh this to scorn. And yet he would be wrong. The people of Northern Ireland – Protestant and Catholic alike – need courage and encouragement more than anything else. You know how quickly rumour spreads and does its dirty work. Why not spread a bit of encouragement to many people who desperately need it? There are too many about these days who seem determined that nothing will succeed. We need people who will try and encourage others to try. And we need them on both sides of the great divide. I want my Protestant friends and my Catholic friends to encourage me to keep struggling for what I know to be right. I want every Catholic and every Protestant who holds out against pressure and intimidation to know that he is not alone.

That is God's call to every Northern Ireland Christian today. Stand up: stand erect and unafraid, for what you know to be right, and when you do stand up, you will encourage others to do the same. That is the Holy Spirit's call to Ulster on Whit Sunday 1972.

Extracts from Eric Gallagher's
Whit Sunday sermon, BCM,1972

The events of Bloody Sunday, 30 January 1972, when 14 Catholics – 13 died on the spot, one later – were shot dead by soldiers of the Parachute Regiment in Derry at the end of a Civil Rights rally, are etched indelibly into Irish history. Controversy still exists as to who may have fired the first shots but, whatever the verdict on this question, unarmed civilians lost their lives as a result. A few days later the Church leaders – Cardinal Conway, Archbishop George Simms, the Revd Dr James Haire (PCI Moderator) and the Revd Charles Bain (MCI President) – issued a joint statement in which they shared the grief and pain, and recognized the depth of feeling. They said: 'In face of everything we once more ask our people to make a greater effort to understand each other's point of view and to accept one another in our differences.'

Eric could see little evidence that people were in a mood to listen to what the Church leaders were saying. The following month Ulster Vanguard was launched by William Craig, the former Northern Ireland Minister for Home Affairs, and on 18 March he addressed a 60,000 strong rally in Ormeau Park, Belfast, warning that 'if and when the politicians fail us, it may be our job to liquidate the enemy'.[1] On 4 March a bomb placed in the Abercorn Restaurant in Belfast resulted in the death of two people and injury to more than 130, including two sisters who were shopping for a wedding dress, both of whom lost both legs. The tragedy deeply affected Barbara who made it the subject of one of her poems in *Embers from the Fires of Ulster*.[2] In it she tried to articulate the last thoughts and words of the dying. There is a poignancy and finality in what she wrote:

> If I could move, O God, I'd leave this horror
> If I could speak I'd shout out loud my fear.
> But as it is I must lie still and listen
> To anguished screams of torture that I hear.
>
> Time is a dream extended like a nightmare;
> What happened? When? Or where? Or even why?
> If this is death, why should it be so cruel? –
> No one I know or love to say goodbye.
>
> Have I lost limbs? – I don't have any feeling,
> What of my sight? – O God, why was I born?
> I can't shed tears, I'm drifting into limbo ...
> Wait! – the lights went out inside the Abercorn.

Eric writes of that year, the bloodiest of the Troubles: 'Tragically before 1972 had run its course, hundreds were to breathe their last with no one they knew or loved to say goodbye.'

He had received no information from any government source since his conversation with Harold Wilson on 16 November 1971. Eric was naturally keen to know if there had been any follow-up to the message he had passed on at that time so he phoned Mr Howard Smith, the UK representative, on Saturday morning 11 March, and was invited down that afternoon to his home at Laneside, Craigavad. He gave Smith a full account of his meeting with the IRA leaders in Dundalk and left a copy of the detailed IRA statement which Jim had passed on to him. Smith returned the copy to him a couple of days later, expressing his thanks but providing no further information as to what he had done with it. Eric commented: 'It was the kind of reply I have come to associate with Government when it does not wish to disclose its hand.'

On 22 March a massive car bomb exploded at the Great Victoria Street bus station, causing much damage to the premises and also to nearby buildings, including the Grosvenor Hall itself. Miraculously members attending a women's meeting in the Hall had seconds earlier dispersed, so the absence of fatalities was a great relief and a cause for much thanksgiving. However, Eric was now faced with the frustrating problem of dealing with bomb damage claims – he writes that at one point they had 22 claims outstanding with the Northern Ireland Office.

Two days later, Edward Heath, the Conservative Prime Minister, announced the suspension of the Stormont Parliament for one year, following the refusal of the Faulkner government to accept the handing over of all security powers to Westminster, despite the implicit provision for such a hand-over in the 1920 Government of Ireland Act. It marked the end of 50 years in which successive Unionist governments had ruled Northern Ireland and it was greeted with jubilation in Republican and Nationalist areas. Unionists, however, were stunned and shocked.

William Whitelaw was appointed the first Secretary of State for Northern Ireland and he made it clear from the beginning that he wanted to initiate a period of political dialogue. It was a process Eric had already started and he was aware of the significance of the new situation: 'Nationalists as well as Unionists had to engage in a new round of hard thinking. And so had the Churches.' Writing in the *Methodist Recorder* of 20 April he reflected that as yet there had been no prophetic word from the Churches but concluded: 'Ulster 1972 can be an exciting, pregnant experience, if you have faith and courage. If you have neither, it is grim and soul-destroying.'

In June Eric was once again addressing the Royal Institute for International Affairs, this time at its meeting in London. His talk was entitled 'Religious Factors in the Northern Ireland Situation'. He attempted to outline the positive developments that had taken place, especially the growing co-operation between Protestant Church leaders and representatives of the Roman Catholic hierarchy. He explained the benefits that the setting up of the Ad Hoc Group had brought: 'For three years now officially-appointed representatives of the Cardinal and of the main Protestant Churches have been meeting at least monthly with the sole purpose of advising their leaders about what action they can take to improve the situation in the field of community relations. Those meetings have produced some interesting results – a number of joint statements and appeals and a very definite and emerging relationship between the leaders themselves.' He also referred to the existence of the Joint Group set up by the RCC Hierarchy and the Protestant Churches and the various working parties which were being formed on subjects important to the Churches: housing, unemployment, drug abuse, alcoholism and other related matters.

However, he did not attempt to gloss over the problems which had existed in the past and still remained. Despite the positive attitude of Church leaders he lamented the fact that at the grass roots, especially in Protestantism, little had changed: 'Few have the courage to take their stand against a narrow and totalitarian attitude to the Bible. Equally few have had the courage to deny the frequent allegation that the Catholic Church is completely corrupt, devious, treacherous and dangerous. It has often been said that most Northern Ireland Protestants fear the Church of Rome more than they fear the devil. And in this simple statement lies the secret to the hostility of the great majority of Northern Ireland Protestants to any idea of a United Ireland.' Eric indicated that this was the kind of context in which Ian Paisley had thrived. He acknowledged that the mainstream Churches had possibly misjudged Paisley's ability to manipulate the situation: 'Part of the problem lies in the slowness of the traditional Churches and the political leaders to recognise his ability and amazing staying power. For far too long he was regarded as a buffoon and ephemeral 'rogue elephant'.

On 22 June the IRA announced a ceasefire. There was a condition attached, namely, 'provided that a public reciprocal response is forthcoming from the armed forces of the British crown'.[3] The statement expressed the hope that the ceasefire would lead to 'meaningful talks between the major parties in the conflict'. Eric made a public appeal that everyone should give the ceasefire a chance and use it constructively as an opportunity to find a better way forward. Politicians, journalists and broadcasters should avoid saying things that would cause offence. And he saw it especially as an opportunity for the Churches to 'redeem their name' and be seen to practise reconciliation: 'There is no point in beating about the bush: we in the Christian Churches will sign our own death warrant if we don't take seriously what the New Testament says about the gospel of reconciliation.'[4]

As a result of the ceasefire a top-level meeting took place in London on 7 July between, on the one hand, William Whitelaw and other British ministers, and, on the other, six IRA leaders: Seamus Twomey, Sean MacStiofan, Dáithí Ó Conaill, Gerry Adams, Ivor Bell and Martin McGuinness. Though Eric had politely warned the IRA leaders against it, their main demand was for a British withdrawal from Northern Ireland by 1975. Bew and Gillespie, in *Northern Ireland. A Chronology of the Troubles 1968-1993*, have recorded Whitelaw's comment on the discussion : 'The meeting was a non-event. The IRA leaders simply made impossible demands which I told them the British government would never concede. They were in fact still in a mood of defiance and determination to carry on until their absurd ultimatums were met.'[5]

An end to the IRA ceasefire – which had lasted just two weeks – followed the breakdown of the London talks.

On Friday 21 July Eric and Barbara attended a civic luncheon in the City Hall. As they walked back to the Grosvenor Hall they heard one bomb after another exploding. That day the IRA had set off 26 bombs, killing 11 people and injuring 130. The scenes of carnage in various parts of Belfast were horrific. Two days later the editorial comment in the *Sunday Independent* was scathing: 'We fostered the men who planned the murders of innocent men, women, boys and girls in Belfast on Friday. We fed these people with propaganda. And because we are not a morally courageous people, we never seriously tried to stop their terrible excesses.' It described the consequences of what became known as 'Bloody Friday' as 'a black sin on the face of Irish Republicanism that will never be erased'.

The escalating violence and intransigence distressed Eric as it did many others. He comments: 'It was hard to see any light at the end of the tunnel.' He put pen to paper and attempted to articulate his thoughts. He decided to share his reflections with a wider public and placed them in the form of a letter – two typewritten A4 pages – which he sent to all the Belfast and Dublin daily papers. All the dailies printed it in full and gave it a great deal of publicity. It was a moving and sensible letter which included a word for most within the community.

He began by saying that he wrote as an Ulsterman: 'I belong here. I have no other home and I want no other. Northern Ireland – Ulster – I don't care what you call it – is one of the world's most beautiful places.' He referred to the violence that all had seen: 'We have more murders in a day than we used to have in a year. Our Province is tearing itself limb from limb. Death, destruction, intimidation, fear and hatred are stalking through every town and village.' And he asked what was the purpose of it all. The IRA and the Ulster Defence Association (UDA), he said, had claimed that force would produce results but all he could see was more houses being bombed and burned, more factories destroyed, unemployment continuing, and men, women and children being killed.

Moving on to real politics he said he had heard talk that Britain should leave Northern Ireland to settle its own affairs – no doubt referring to IRA demands for a 'British withdrawal' and some Loyalist sentiments that they should be left to themselves to sort out the problems – but he commented: 'This talk terrifies me.' He voiced a theme which British Government Ministers would later, much later, express: 'I am convinced that *Britain has no strategic or any other interest in staying in Northern Ireland* [my italics] a day longer than she is wanted.' He went on to suggest that as Britain had had its share in creating 'our problems' then it followed that Britain had also an obligation to contribute to the solution of the problems.

Eric then underlined the need for people being prepared to sit down and talk through their political problems because it was increasingly obvious that 'no side in Ulster can have things its own way'. He declared: 'No party, no group, no organisation can settle the Ulster problem on its own terms. Two possibilities are starkly clear. Shoot it out or talk it out. The first is so terrifying that we dare not contemplate it. The other is what we should have gone for at the very beginning – discussion, negotiation and eventually some kind of meaningful reconciliation of interests between our respective communities.' He gave no hint that this would be a process that the Government would soon be initiating but his appeal for dialogue would certainly have helped to prepare the ground for some form of inter-party talks. He stressed the urgency of talking together: 'At the end of the long day people will have to get round the table and talk and talk until they arrive at some workable understanding. Why can't they do it before the holocaust destroys us all?'

He appealed to both the IRA and the UDA to end their violence. To the IRA he said: 'Even if you succeed in your campaign, what kind of country would you have? The bitterness and the division we have today would be nothing to what we would have tomorrow.' And to the UDA: 'Stop to think of the inevitable result of a collision course.' But having underlined the importance of dialogue he had a special word for the politicians. They had been voted into positions of leadership and responsibility so now was the time for them to demonstrate these qualities: 'Show your leadership. Exercise your responsibility and do it now. Give posterity the chance to say that you were big enough for the challenge of Ulster's most dangerous hour. I plead with the leaders of every Ulster political party to say now – privately or publicly doesn't matter – "We are ready to talk. We are ready to seek some way out. We are willing to work whatever arrangements we reach. All we ask is fair play for everybody."'

Finally, he made a plea as a Christian to 'all my fellow Christians of whatever communion' that whatever the future might hold each of them should resolve to avoid saying or thinking anything which would be 'at variance with what we have learned of God in Jesus Christ'.

It is not surprising that having asked the politicians to talk together Eric himself continued to think of ways in which this could be implemented. During his holidays in August he worked on draft proposals for what he termed 'a Consultative Assembly' elected on a proportional representation basis with all the parties participating. He envisaged the Assembly having two functions:

1. To hammer out some constitutional proposals to put to the sovereign government.

2. To accept responsibility for whatever functions might be allocated to it e.g. supervision of the work of the Area Boards.

He circulated copies of his suggestions to a fairly wide and representative group of people: the Secretary of State, William Whitelaw; James Callaghan, Merlyn Rees and several British MPs; BCC (British Council of Churches) and ICC personnel; and several local people. He was encouraged by the number of favourable responses he received.

Two developments soon followed and one is tempted to think that Eric's address at Edinburgh in November 1971 to the Scottish Assembly of the Royal Institute for International Affairs, his letter to the papers in July 1972 and his draft constitutional proposals of August 1972, might have played some small part in the process. Firstly, William Whitelaw convened a Constitutional Conference near Darlington from 25-27 September but it was doomed to failure as it was boycotted by the Social, Democratic and Labour Party (SDLP), the Nationalist and Republican Labour parties – all of whom were protesting against the continuation of internment – and the Democratic Unionist Party (DUP). Secondly, despite the failure of the Darlington Conference or possibly because of it, at the end of October the Northern Ireland Office circulated a Green Paper, *The Future of Northern Ireland,* for discussion. For the first time the suggestion of an 'Irish Dimension' was floated, undoubtedly influenced by the SDLP's recent publication, *Towards a United Ireland*, which had called for joint British and Irish sovereignty over Northern Ireland. But there was another notable suggestion: 'There are strong arguments that the objective of real participation should be achieved by giving minority interests a share in the exercise of executive power.'[6] This is remarkably similar to Eric's proposal 11 months earlier at Edinburgh: 'With the introduction of a proportional representation system ... and with the reflection of political strength in the Cabinet, there is no reason whatever why people with long-term differing ideals would not serve in the same Government.'

It is not surprising that a deputation from the Methodist Church in Ireland which met with the Secretary of State on 4 December welcomed the Green Paper and made its own appeal to the political parties to 'submit constructive proposals and to show some flexibility in their approach'. The suggestion of an Irish dimension was noted but, while not rejecting it, the MCI considered it would be 'inadvisable to overstate it'.

Eric had been unable to attend the meeting of the Conference of European Churches in Puchberg, Austria, from 24-27 October, so he sent a tape recording of his speech. He reported on the situation in Northern Ireland over the past 12 months since he had attended the Symposium in Whiteabbey and earlier their Council meeting in Marseilles. He spoke about the violence, the destruction of lives and property, and about Government attempts to initiate dialogue despite the growing polarisation in the community. Referring to the continuing role of the Churches he acknowledged that they now had a diminishing influence in the community. He cited a joint call from the Church Leaders for public meetings of prayer for reconciliation and peace on the first Sunday in October which had largely gone unheeded in the North. His explanation as to why this had happened is itself rather strange and sad: 'When the call to prayer was issued a great deal of fear and consternation arose in some quarters. Not unnaturally some of the ministers and clergy and priests felt that public meetings for prayer between Catholics and Protestants would do more harm than good. In quite a number of places there was no response beyond an indication that people were praying in their own churches.'

Another part of his speech reveals some of the innermost thoughts in Eric's mind. Referring to the future of Christianity in the Province he hinted: 'There may well be the emergence of some kind of confessing Church.' Many clergy, he said, were being faced with a series of questions: 'Am I a representative of my people? Am I to identify with my people? Am I to lead them? Am I to be a priest or a prophet or a pastor? Or if I am one, can I be that thing without doing it at the expense of the other two?' It is a fact of history that a confessing Church in Ireland did not emerge as it had in Germany in the 1930s. However, it is worth noting that Eric had raised the question of its coming into existence. In sharing his thoughts with the CEC he was undoubtedly speaking to a more sympathetic audience than he would have had in Ireland. This was not a brief casual reference for he went on to speculate on possible developments if a confessing Church were formed:

> If this confessing Church emerges, as it very well may emerge, we may find all sorts of unexpected groupings inside the Christian Churches of Ireland. Increasingly the churches will have to concentrate far more than they have ever done on their teaching function, on their prophetic function, on their obligation to lead the people for whom they have responsibility into a more Christian concept of politics and of community relations. It may well be that we are reaping the harvest of the years, years of insensitivity to the basic knowledge of what the Church and the ministry are all about.

In early November Eric received yet another invitation to Hillsborough House, this time to meet the Prime Minister, Edward Heath. Included among the 36 at the function were Lord and Lady Grey, and Mr and Mrs Whitelaw. There were six tables and six courses; at the end of each course the Prime Minister moved table so that everyone present had an opportunity to talk with him. Eric recalls a funny side to the evening: 'He [Heath] arrived at our table a little prematurely.

Someone at the preceding table had so annoyed him that he moved on as soon as possible. We treated him warily but found out quickly that he was well informed.'

At the end of the meal Lord Grey announced that everyone was welcome to stay on for a time and speak with the chief guest. Eric had teamed up with Jack Withers. As they moved around they discovered that the person who had so annoyed the Prime Minister during the meal was once again tackling him 'with considerable verbal animation'. The two churchmen decided this was a time for action! 'So heated and prolonged was it that the two of us decided we should endeavour to break it up. We did and then went home.' With typical diplomacy Eric's Autobiographical Notes do not disclose the identity of the troublemaker!

Before Christmas Eric's thinking once again turned to the wisdom or otherwise of a Consultative Assembly. He shared his thoughts with some ICC Executive members and also some within the BCC. The result was a letter to *The Times* in London. So often an optimist, on this occasion he expressed his doubts that Whitelaw's constitutional talks with representatives of the Northern Ireland political parties would produce a consensus. In these circumstances he suggested the Secretary of State would have two options: he could produce a White Paper outlining his proposed solution, which Eric saw as an 'imposed' solution; or alternatively by a 'significant political initiative' he could 'play for time and perhaps succeed in identifying the "middle ground"'. Eric warned against the first option: 'If the imposed solution is unacceptable to large numbers on either side of the Northern Ireland spectrum it would be folly to discount the possibility of determined armed resistance to it.'

He hoped that the Secretary of State would adopt the second option:

> Mr Heath and Mr Wilson have repeatedly called for the 'middle ground' to assert itself. Unfortunately it has never been given the chance. Mr Whitelaw can offer it the opportunity. If his talks produce no consensus he can test the strength of the various points of view at the ballot

box. He can call for an election to a 'consultative assembly'. The responsibility of this assembly would be to give the Secretary of State the needed conditions and structure for a renewed attempt at consensus. He and everybody else would know who speaks for whom.

In January Eric wrote another letter on the same theme, this time sending it to the Irish papers, with copies to Mr Whitelaw, several MPs at Westminster and Stormont, and others whom he regarded as 'well informed'. This time he backed up his plea for a Consultative Assembly by reminding his readers that it was almost four years since the 1969 General Election and that it was important 'to let Mr Whitelaw know what weight to attach to the different political parties'. He suggested that direct rule, without local parties and spokesmen interpreting and supporting it, would result in a political vacuum which was far from satisfactory. He pleaded, prophetically as later events were to prove: 'Some form of political activity and expression of opinion is urgently required. To go to the polls on the basis of a White Paper, for which the community is not yet ready, could well produce tragedy no matter how well intentioned and argued the Paper is.'

Accompanying copies of his letter Eric enclosed another detailed document, 'A Consultative Assembly for Northern Ireland. Why? How would it work?' In this he claimed that the election of a Consultative Assembly would make possible what he termed a 'Darlington Mark Two' but this time there would be a difference: 'This time the elected representatives of the parties will have a mandate and the British Government and everybody else will know what weight to attach to their stances.' He envisaged the Consultative Assembly sending delegates from its parties to a 'Constitutional Conference' whose task would be 'to hammer out a solution which can be guaranteed to find adequate popular and party support'.

William Whitelaw personally thanked Eric for forwarding his proposals. However, as the coming months unfolded it was evident that there were differences in the pathway proposed by the Secretary of State and that outlined by the Superintendent of Belfast Central Mission!

On Monday, 22 January Eric was one of the main speakers at the Greenhills Study Conference, Drogheda, attended each year by Protestant and Catholic laity and clergy. His topic was 'The Christian in Politics'. A significant part of his presentation dealt with the role of priests and clerics in politics. These reflections were to be repeated, sometimes at other conferences or in conversation. And it is possibly true to say that in Irish Methodism they became unwritten guidelines for its ministers. Eric explained his views on the subject by relating how he personally had understood his ministry. He accepted without question that a minister of religion should be concerned about the world and its affairs, including at times the necessity for political action. However, although he saw his role as one who should encourage others to be involved politically, he believed that as a minister he should not be active in the field of party politics: 'I should place on myself the self-denying ordinance of abstention from the field of party politics. I must be accessible to everybody who wants me or needs me. For me to join a political party would place constraints on my ministry which should not be there.' He went on to explain how he had enjoyed ministering to people of all political persuasions – a privilege which might not have come his way had he been involved in party politics: 'I am a Methodist Minister – non-aligned. From time to time, Unionists of all 57 or less types have felt free to come and talk to me and share more than their merely political concerns. So too have Socialists and Nationalists, Liberals and Republicans. I have valued that ministry.'

Another section of his paper examined the record of the Churches and their degree of culpability for the present chaos and violence. He acquitted the Irish Churches of any charge of deliberately propagating sectarianism but stated that the Churches were guilty in another respect: 'I accuse them, however, of not being sufficiently perceptive theologically and sensitive politically to recognise the evils in society which have bred the sectarian bitterness and horror that have made us suffer as we have done.' He related how he had carried out a little research into the official statements made by the Methodist Church in Ireland over the past 60 years and he was shocked by his findings. Yes, there were a few utterances regarding issues like housing and unemployment. The O'Neill-Lemass conversations had also been welcomed. But much had been left undone: 'There is no sign in the documents and I have no recollection of the enunciation of those prophetic principles in season and out of season in such a way that Irish Methodists could not avoid the challenge to social and political action. We did not educate. We did not analyse. We did not challenge. We did not criticise – all this relatively of course and in the field of social and political action.' Above all, the Methodist Church had failed to encourage people to get involved in politics: 'We failed to lay our hands on this man and that and tell him as we would have been ready to tell someone to go into the ministry – "For God's sake and for men's sake get into politics."'

Not necessarily connected with his comments at Greenhills – for acceptance of blame for the Church's failure to address the menace of sectarianism was occasionally one of Eric's themes – the (Belfast) *Newsletter* reported in January that Methodist members of Vanguard were threatening to sever their church membership if certain ministers did not cease from placing partial guilt for the present problems in Northern Ireland on the Protestant people. They named both Eric Gallagher and George Morrison, at that time the Chairman of the Londonderry District, as ministers voicing these sentiments. The Vanguard members suggested that comments from these ministers had been one-sided: 'The Methodist people in common with all other Protestant denominations demand an explanation from their Church leaders as to why they have been silent on the many occasions on which the Roman Catholic Church had extended the privileges and ritual of the Church to known IRA murderers.'

On 7 February the Vanguard Party supported the Loyalist Strike called after the detention of two loyalists under the Detention of Terrorists Order. They had been arrested in connection with the murder of a Catholic man, making them the first Protestant internees. Eric's description of the consequences of the strike give some indication of the disastrous effect it had on the Province. He declared: 'Few things in Northern Ireland's history have done more damage than the events of last Wednesday.' He referred to the intimidation of workers, shooting at the security forces and the fire service, killings, the destruction and desecration of churches, the terrorizing of school children, the placing of hospitals in jeopardy, and old people's and children's homes without heat or light. 'Is it any wonder', he asked, 'that the great majority of people in the Province today are bitter and ashamed?' He went on to indicate the effect that a strike of this nature could have on public opinion in Britain: 'I can understand also the growing reluctance in Great Britain to pour money into the Province and to keep its soldiers here any longer.'

Further invitations and appointments in 1973 extended the diversity of Eric's responsibilities. Towards the end of 1972 he had been invited to become a member of the Religious Advisers Panel of the Independent Broadcasting Authority. He had been approached about such a possibility some five or six years previously but, although he had indicated an interest, nothing had come of it! The assignment entailed approximately nine one-day committees each year in London. He found them interesting and 'occasionally stimulating' but he often wondered what real influence the Advisers were able to exert. By the time any specific proposal for a programme or series of programmes reached the attention of the Advisers, preparation and filming were often well in hand and it was more than difficult to obtain any change or indeed deletion. He recalls: 'Probably our best contribution was in the fight – at that time successful – to maintain the "God slot" in prime time on Sunday evenings and to have some influence on the kind of future programming.'

Eric had already been serving on the Belfast Education Committee but in 1973 with the reorganization of Local Government it went out of existence. Like all other Education Committees it was replaced by an Education and Library Board. He welcomed the new arrangement in that it now included members appointed because of a known interest in education or libraries. The Methodist Board of Education asked him to continue representing the Methodist Church in the new arrangement and nominated him for appointment to the Belfast Board by the Minister responsible for education.

Involvement as a member of the Board of Governors in the Training Schools at Rathgael (Bangor) and Whiteabbey was another service which Eric gave to the wider community. Indeed, he felt his attendance at these Training Schools gave him a new appreciation and understanding both of the work of the staff and the nature of the young people in them: 'It was encouraging to witness the efforts being made by dedicated staff members to help young people who had suffered at the hands of society and who in their turn had made society suffer in some way.' He particularly admired the Very Revd Dr Gibson's chairmanship of the Board and also staff members like Frances Moffitt and her colleagues in the girls' school at Whiteabbey.

In the early seventies the Training Schools were faced with a growing problem associated with young people for whom a more specialized education was required. Rejection by society, alienation from it, behavioural and domestic problems – all had had their effect on the teenagers within the Schools, and, as they were to discover, these problems were also found in the two corresponding Catholic Schools: St Patrick's on the Glen Road, Belfast, and St Joseph's at Middletown, Co. Armagh.

Staff in each of these establishments were increasingly aware that their open and relatively liberal regime was not necessarily the best for a small minority who required more individual care and guidance and who could benefit from treatment that was more secure, both physically and emotionally. Hence the proposal for a fifth school which would care for some young people from all four schools. A Working Party was formed from Board members and staff from the four schools to consider the possibilities and, along with government officials, to recommend future policy. Eric was appointed as a representative of the Rathgael and Whiteabbey Board. He speaks positively of the contacts established between representatives of the four schools: 'The consultations and negotiations with the Catholic members could not have been more harmonious and successful. We learned a great deal from each other. The relationships we built up at that time were maintained when we became members of the Board of Management of the new school at Lisnevin, Newtownards.'

In March 1973 Eric addressed the Conference of European Churches (CEC) in Austria. Although the title of his address was 'The Churches' Witness and Service for Peace in Europe' his focus once again was Ireland. On most occasions when he spoke to other nationalities about the Northern Irish problem he gave an historical introduction and this was no exception. However, one of the significant differences in this presentation from other historical reviews he had given was his insightful analysis of the parties involved in the creation of the Northern State and the attitudes that had persisted after its creation. He pointed to the creation of partition in Ireland in 1921 as one of the factors which 'sowed the seeds of future trouble'. Partition, he declared, had left the Roman Catholics in Northern Ireland with a sense that they had been betrayed: 'They felt themselves captive in a Protestant state and their goal of a self-governing Ireland had not been realised. From the beginning they were reluctant citizens.' But the settlement of 1921 did have the potential of being an interim solution rather than becoming – as it now was – 'a political time-bomb'. Not all the blame could be ascribed to the Unionist majority and ascendancy: 'All the parties contributed to the series of crimes and tensions which finally erupted on the streets of Northern Ireland in 1969 – and by all the parties, I mean not only the political parties – North and South – but also in their own way the Churches.'

Eric maintained that the two main parties to the 1921 settlement had had their obligations but to a greater or lesser degree had not fulfilled them. The British Government claimed in the Government of Ireland Act (1920) to retain full, complete and total responsibility for the affairs of Northern Ireland. The powers of the Northern Ireland Parliament were declared to be subject to the sovereignty and ultimate responsibility of the British Parliament. However, this did not happen: 'In practice Britain allowed Northern Ireland to act more or less as if it were a sovereign state – at least as far as its domestic affairs were concerned.' Likewise the Republic of Ireland Government had been at fault as it had failed to meet its responsibilities: 'It did singularly nothing to allay the fears of Protestants as to what might happen to them if they were included in a United Ireland. It left the British Commonwealth. It remained studiously neutral when Northern Ireland was suffering during World War II. It promulgated a Constitution which recognised the Catholic Church as having a special place in the State. It did little to convince Protestants that they would be living in anything but a Catholic State organised in Catholic ways for a Catholic people.'

These are only short extracts from a lengthy paper but they provide at least a glimpse into Eric's superb grasp of Irish history and his very perceptive understanding of some of the origins of the Northern Ireland problem.

Eric was now addressing conferences and public meetings about once a month. In addition to all his other work it was a punishing and demanding schedule and it was a pressure which would continue for some time. The tragedies of 'The Troubles' meant that people both inside and outside Ireland wanted to understand and analyse the problems that were resulting in the loss of so many lives. Following the Greenhills Conference in January he had been in Longford on a speaking engagement for Bishop Cahal Daly, the Roman Catholic Bishop of Ardagh and Clonmacnois.

March was another month when he had a second major engagement to fulfil: on 23 March speaking in Dublin to the Irish Association for Cultural, Economic and Social Relations. His subject on this occasion was 'Inter-Denominational Trust'. Once again he highlighted the menace of sectarianism: 'The curse and blight of Ireland has been the recurring sectarian strife of recent centuries. It has dirtied the name of our race across the world. We are known as a bitter, cantankerous people.' It was a problem which the Churches needed to address because their mutual distrust and suspicion had helped to create an atmosphere and environment in which sectarianism could grow. He declared: 'Unless the Churches do something urgently about increasing inter-denominational trust, all hell will break loose again inside another generation.'

The Churches, their leaders and members must engage the minds of people and alert them to the need for change: 'We must hammer home with all the intensity of which we may be capable that greater tragedy will certainly follow the present holocaust, if we do not act now.'

One of the misconceptions that should be corrected was the false caricatures Catholics and Protestants had of each other. For example, many Protestants believed that the Roman Catholic Church wanted a Catholic-dominated Ireland based completely on a Gaelic-Catholic culture. On the other hand Catholics thought of the Protestant Churches as being synonymous 'with the Unionist Party at prayer' – even though there was now a problem of discerning which brand of unionism! 'Catholics', he said, 'are convinced that the old idea of a Protestant province ruled by a Protestant parliament for a Protestant people is not yet dead.' In the face of these misunderstandings Eric had a suggestion to make:

> Has the time not come for the Churches to declare unambiguously, simultaneously and possibly jointly where they stand: that they recognise the ecclesial rights and integrity of each other; that they have no political stances as such except those that are calculated to encourage full human rights and dignity; that they are not seeking any form of government that will give them a built-in advantage over others; that they want fair play and justice for everybody and not just for their own members; and that they are not seeking any and every opportunity to subvert or proselytize the others or to gain an advantage.

He was convinced that such a declaration willingly made right across the board would do a great deal 'to sweeten Irish life'. And he acknowledged the significance of what he was asking: 'It would be a milestone in inter-denominational relationships.'

Picking up the spirit of much that had already been said in Vatican II's *Decree on Ecumenism* he went on to encourage Churches and their members to co-operate in whatever joint activities might be possible. It should be possible to share in some common acts of worship without any compromise of essential principle. He suggested common Bible study and common lay training. He was convinced: 'People who work and worship and study together begin to know and respect each other. There is no greater enemy to interdenominational trust than ignorance and isolation.'

He also recommended that the Churches should face up to the really divisive issues. 'To do this will be dangerous. It could be explosive and devastating in its effects.' He listed the issues that troubled Protestants: Catholic attitudes to the pluralist society; aspects of education; mixed marriages; the *Ne Temere* decree; basic human rights; Catholic influences on the State; and the Church's attitude to the IRA. And he attempted to itemise the topics which might be of major concern to Catholics: Protestant attitudes to and involvement in the Orange Order; the attitude to sectarian politics; the choice of State schools; laxity about divorce; and a seemingly Protestant obsession with contraception.

Finally, he closed by reminding the Association that the topic of interdenominational trust was by definition one that called them to focus on the divine. All that they were considering was directly related to the practice and proclamation of the gospel of Jesus Christ. He therefore ended by declaring: 'I know of no better recipe for inter-denominational trust than a fuller practice of the love of Christ by those who profess to regard him as Lord and who claim to be his disciples.'

The Dun Laoghaire Council of Churches never seemed to weary of having Eric Gallagher as their speaker! On 11 April he was back with them again, this time speaking on 'Northern Ireland – What violence has done and what should be done about violence'. Possibly for the first time in his addresses on the Northern Ireland situation he focused on the street demonstrations of the mid-1960s as a contributory factor in the upsurge of violence which started in 1969. He did not suggest that the demonstrations were the only cause of the violence which followed but he was prepared to identify them as playing a part: 'They helped in no small measure to create the environment of unrest, fear and suspicion in which the violence of 1968 and 1969 finally erupted and from which the much more brutal and costly violence that was to follow was bound to develop.' In a very interesting comment he claimed that it was violence which had driven Terence O'Neill from office. The consequences of his removal were grave: 'That act had removed whatever little chance remained of a peaceful solution to the developing crisis.'

He prefaced his remarks on the consequences of violence by first affirming clearly what violence had failed to achieve. PIRA violence had, he claimed, failed to achieve its objective: 'If the purpose of the Provos was to achieve a United Ireland based on good-will and consent, they have lamentably failed. That goal is farther away tonight than at any time in my memory.' Similarly, loyalist violence was counter-productive: 'If the purpose of loyalist activists was to cement the union with Great Britain and make secure some kind of perpetual Protestant ascendancy they also have failed.'

In the main body of his presentation Eric listed 16 consequences of violence and then went on to elaborate and comment on some of them. In a rare glimpse of how he often worked he explained how he had arrived at the list of 16: 'In preparing the notes of an outline of this address, I jotted down a list of items just as they occurred to me. They are not in order of significance. I stopped because the phone-bell rang – not because I had run short of ideas.'

The 16 consequences of violence provide as comprehensive a list as you might find in any record of 'The Troubles':

- Appalling cost – hundreds of lives lost, bloodshed, suffering, millions of pounds worth of property destroyed, jobs lost, livelihoods.
- Increasing desensitivity – 'the only one or two people killed last night' mentality.
- Corruption of a whole community – what has been done to women, young girls, youths, children. What

has happened to truth and honesty? The corruption of human attitudes.

- Counter-productive and spiralling amount of violence.
- Emigration of the best young families – the type a community can ill afford to lose.
- Increased bitterness, growing hatred and sectarian strife.
- The disruption of ordinary social life.
- The production of young fanatics in the cult of violence and the perpetuation of violent attitudes and actions into another generation.
- The general breakdown of law and respect for authority.
- The disastrous effect on the witness and effectiveness of the Churches and the credibility of the gospel.
- The growth of sectarian ghettos and the disappearance of mixed area experiments.
- The increasing involvement of girls in acts of violence and murder, as, for instance, in the brutal and revolting murder of the three British Sergeants.
- The brutalising of the security forces, torture and other reprehensible methods.
- The growth of the prison population: increasing number of young prisoners and young terrorists.
- Nervous disorders and drug dependence.
- The growth of illicit drinking dens and clubs with all that goes with them.

The Christian Church was called to live and witness within this new situation. A number of things was needed: a proper teaching ministry; encouraging of women and men to take up the life of politics; living out the two great commandments of Jesus; practical co-operation and witness between all the Churches. He closed with these words: 'Either we work and live and pray together or we fail. If violence teaches us that, then God will have brought good out of evil and for that we shall be thankful.'

Eric had been a member of the Tripartite Conversations – comprising representatives of the Church of Ireland, the Methodist Church in Ireland, and the Presbyterian Church in Ireland – since its inception in January 1968, and of the Bipartite Conversations which had preceded it. The three Negotiating Committees published a *Declaration of Intent* on 28 March 1968 – later approved by their governing bodies – which unanimously decided 'to seek together that unity which is both God's will and His gift to His Church'. The declaration had clearly stated: 'Without this unity the fulfilment of Christ's mission to the world is being hindered.'

Working under the remit of the *Declaration* the members of the Tripartite Conversations had drawn up various agreed statements and throughout their conversations had endeavoured both to inform and consult the membership of their respective Churches. It was therefore with some degree of hope that they submitted the report *Towards a United Church* in 1973 to be considered by their governing bodies in May (COI General Synod) and June (MCI Conference and PCI General Assembly).

Each of the governing bodies – and the local congregational church courts who were also asked to consider the report – appeared to receive quite favourably the first four sections of the report dealing with 'The Divine Revelation and the Scriptures', 'The Church', 'The Sacraments', and 'The Creeds and later Historical Statements of Belief'. Among Presbyterians and Methodists problems arose with the fifth section entitled 'The Ministry'. Basically, it recommended a threefold order of ordained ministry: bishops, presbyters and deacons, although the last of these – termed 'Associated Ministries' – was written in such a way as to encompass Deacons and Lay Readers in the Church of Ireland, Ruling Elders in Presbyterianism, and Class Leaders and Local Preachers in Methodism. There was a clear distinction between the ministry of bishops and the ministry of presbyters. The Episcopate, it said, shall be both conciliar and historic:

a)   By conciliar is meant that Bishops shall be appointed and shall perform their functions in partnership with the Ministers and People, and in relationship to and responsibility towards the representative councils of the Church.

b) By historic is meant an episcopate which contains continuity with the life and faith of the early Church.

It went on: 'As chief shepherds, under Christ, of the Church bishops have oversight of the proclamation of the Word both within and beyond the Church, and of the administration of the Sacraments, and have pastoral oversight of other pastors and the whole People of God in a given area.'

Of the ministry of Presbyters, it said:

Presbyters, in the spheres assigned to them, shall give leadership to the Church in the fulfilment of its vocation and apostolic mission in the world. They are called to proclaim the Gospel of Christ, to preserve sound doctrine, to administer the Sacraments, to serve the Church's ministry of reconciliation, to strengthen and enlarge the People of God and to lead members of the Church in their Christian witness and service to mankind.

Comments in Gallagher and Worrall, *Christians in Ulster 1968-1980*, possibly reveal Eric's reflections on the rejection of the report: 'The outcome was disappointing. The local debates revealed either a profound apathy or a deep-seated suspicion about the whole matter.'[7] However, apathy and lack of enthusiasm for the report did not put an end to the Conversations but it did indicate the immensity of the task which the three Churches had undertaken. In 1974 the PCI General Assembly suggested that the participating Churches should examine the feasibility of a declaration that they 'fully and freely recognise the efficacy and spiritual reality of both ordination and sacraments as administered in the other Churches, and that this recognition includes permission for intercommunion'.[8]

If the lack of enthusiasm for the Tripartite report was a disappointment for Eric, the publication by the June Methodist Conference of *A Better Way for Irish Protestants and Roman Catholics. Advice from John Wesley* was certainly an encouragement! In 1749, following a riot in Cork in which Methodist property and persons had been attacked, John Wesley wrote *Letter to a Roman Catholic* in which he made a strong appeal that Catholics and Protestants should show Christian love and concern for each other. Towards the end of the *Letter* Wesley had appealed: 'Let us resolve, first, not to hurt one another ... secondly, God being our helper, to speak nothing harsh or unkind of each other ... thirdly, resolve to harbour no unkind thought ... fourthly, endeavour to help each other on in whatever we are agreed leads to the Kingdom.'

The idea of publishing the *Letter* along with Wesley's sermon *Catholic Spirit* had come from members of the Mission Board of which Eric was Chairman. The Board asked him to write the introductory chapter underlining the relevance of the two documents to the present problems in Ireland. Eric's keen knowledge of Wesley enabled him to draw on an incident which illustrates Wesley's willingness to practise the forgiveness and love which he preached. Around 1780 Wesley had engaged in a pamphlet war with a Capuchin Father O'Leary. The controversy related to the question whether or not Catholics could be regarded as good reliable citizens – honouring their word – and whether Wesley was guilty of persecuting Catholics. However, when he was back in Cork in 1787 he had a chance to meet O'Leary and now formed a completely different impression of him. Eric quoted Wesley's comments on the encounter: 'A gentleman invited me to breakfast with my old antagonist Father O'Leary. I was not at all displeased at being disappointed. He is not the stiff, queer man that I expected, but of an easy, genteel carriage, and seems not to be wanting either in sense or learning.' The conclusion Eric drew from the incident was straightforward: 'Wesley the controversialist and polemicist had given way to the Wesley of the Catholic Spirit – and the ecumenist before his time. He discovered, as many another has discovered since, that when you come to know a man and respect him, somehow, although you do not change your convictions, you begin to take another attitude to the man as a person. Attitudes and relationships take on a new dimension.'

Eric was also pleased with other work accomplished by the Mission Board. There was the recommendation, accepted by the Conference, regarding a fit and suitable order of service to mark the arrival of a minister on circuit. The Conference also accepted a proposal for a full-time chaplain to the Dublin universities. And another draft document on the role of the minister was approved by Conference and commended for study and implementation. He attributed much of the success of the Board to the work of its Secretary, the Revd Robin Roddie: 'I was able without any hesitation to leave him to get on with the implementation of the various decisions we took at a number of residential Friday night Saturday morning meetings.'

World awareness of the problems in Ireland manifested itself in a new venture, 'An Ecumenical Initiative to Promote Understanding and to Pray for Peace in Ireland', launched at Pentecost 1973. The call for prayer was co-ordinated by the Secretariat of SODEPAX, the Roman Catholic/World Council of Churches Committee on Society, Development and Peace. The appeal, signed jointly by John Cardinal Willebrands, President of the Secretariat for Promoting Christian Unity, and Dr Philip Potter, General Secretary of the World Council of Churches, stated:

> This initiative is an invitation to Christians throughout the world to join in prayer. It is intended to be an act of religious solidarity that would express the deep feeling of brotherhood and sympathy which Christians in all parts of the world have with the people of Ireland. A concerted effort of prayer would contribute to the atmosphere in which peace can grow and it would be an encouragement both to the Church leaders in Ireland whose task is such an onerous one and to the groups and individuals who are working for peace and reconciliation.

Eric welcomed the initiative. Undoubtedly the knowledge that Christians throughout the world were praying for peace in Ireland was one of the major factors which sustained him and others through the decades of violence and community strife.

The first meeting of the Irish Inter-Church Meeting at Ballymascanlon, near Dundalk, on 26 September 1973 was certainly historic. This was yet a further development between the Protestant Churches and the Roman Catholic Church, following on from the setting up of the Ad Hoc Group in 1969 and the Joint Group in 1970. The initiative appears to have come initially from the ICC and contacts established between its organising Secretary, Norman Taggart, and Cardinal Conway. Some ICC members had been talking of the value of a conference attended by representatives of the Irish Episcopal Conference and the ICC. It was envisaged that such a gathering might be used to consider contentious issues, the problem of mixed marriages possibly being uppermost in the minds of ICC members. The outcome of Taggart's meetings with the Cardinal eventually led to an invitation being issued from the Secretary of the Irish Hierarchy, the Bishop of Meath, Dr McCormack. In July 1972 the Bishop wrote: 'What is contemplated is a general review of relations between the Christian Churches in Ireland and the possibilities of further dialogue on both practical and doctrinal issues ... It is envisaged that working parties might subsequently be set up to further such dialogue.'[9]

Eighty-three delegates, lay and clerical, met under the co-chairmanship of Cardinal Conway and Archbishop Simms, who had succeeded Eric as ICC Chairman. There were five main papers: Archbishop Dermot Ryan on 'Church – Scripture – Authority'; Eric on 'Social and Community Problems'; Bishop Cahal B. Daly on 'Christianity and Secularism' and a second paper on 'Inter-Church Marriage: the Position of the Irish Episcopal Conference'; and the Revd Professor John Barkley speaking on 'Baptism – Eucharist – Marriage'.

The meeting had just started when the delegates were informed that the Revd Ian Paisley and his supporters wished to hand in a protest. It was received by the Revd Joseph Dunne, one of the press officers to the conference, and a reply was given to Mr Paisley by Mr Dunne on behalf of the joint chairmen. Paisley told reporters that there could be no middle ground between Roman Catholicism and Protestantism. The Roman Catholic Church was based on a system of idolatry which was contrary to the teaching of the Scriptures. The meeting, he declared, was only 'a bit of clerical acrobatics' to get unity through a smokescreen.[10]

The Irish papers gave good coverage in reporting the event, none more so than the *Irish Times*. Its editorial, like the others, noted the significance of the event: 'Officially, it was an inter-Church meeting; in the popular mind, it was a Church leaders' summit conference; historically it marked a crucial, although far from dramatic, stage in Irish Church life; to the Revd Ian Paisley and his followers it was a sell-out to Rome; to the organisers it was an amicable and positive beginning; to the observer it was a modest success.'

Eric's remit on 'Social and Community Problems' gave him the opportunity to comment on a number of issues. On violence he said: 'Ireland has suffered far too much from an emotional and extravagant adulation of its gunmen.' He acknowledged that the Churches had not encouraged violence but he was convinced that they had not done enough to discourage it: 'There has been an ambivalence in the attitudes of all of us to the situations and conditions which have produced violence and indeed to violence or the threat of it when it has been used successfully.'

He also referred to the sensitive issue of mixed marriages, expressing the hope that the Conference would undertake a careful consideration of the whole question. He said the differences between the Churches on mixed marriages had often resulted in the partners of the marriage having no Church connection whatever. In the Republic there was 'the steady erosion of Protestant presence and witness, a significant proportion of which is considered to be attributable to Roman Catholic requirements in the matter of mixed marriages'. In Northern Ireland there were also serious consequences: 'There is in the North the grave threat, if not of death itself for one or other partner to a mixed marriage, at least of the virtual ostracizing of one or other or both by their respective communities of origin.'

He went on to consider the nature of education in the country, particularly the question of whether segregated education was a contributory factor in the present troubles. In a useful examination of the topic, avoiding the temptation to come down categorically on one side or the other, he appeared to hint that the present form of segregated education might have a part to play in the uninformed attitudes which Catholics and Protestants had towards each other. He suggested: 'I am not convinced that segregated education is at the root of our divisions. But I must ask: If it is not at the root of our problems, is it not in some way mixed up in them?'

During 1973 the British government had pressed ahead in its attempts to find some kind of political consensus in Northern Ireland. On 20 March it had published its White Paper, *Northern Ireland Constitutional Proposals*. The main difference between these proposals and Eric's plan for a Consultative Assembly was essentially the method by which government by consensus would be reached. Eric's proposals in the latter half of 1972 and the beginning of 1973 called for the election of a Consultative Assembly which would 'hammer out some constitutional proposals to bring to the sovereign government'. The method suggested within the White Paper also contained proposals for an Assembly elected by proportional representation – multi-member constituencies were suggested – but the guidelines within which a future form of provincial government would function were clearly defined and set out, a feature only hinted at in Eric's plan. The White Paper clearly stated: 'It is the view of the government that the executive itself can no longer be solely based upon any single party, if that party draws its support and its elected representation virtually entirely from only one section of a divided community.'[11] Eric had hoped that the outcome of discussions by representatives of political parties would be that people 'with long-term differing ideals' would agree to serve in the same government. The hoped-for outcome was the same but the pathway to that solution was different.

The White Paper – like the Green Paper of October 1972 – also referred to an 'Irish Dimension' but this time the suggestions were more fully developed. It referred to a Council of Ireland in which areas of mutual interest such as tourism, regional development, electricity and transport could be considered. The White Paper went further: following the Assembly elections the British Government planned to hold discussions with the Government of the Republic in which representatives from the elected parties in the Assembly would participate. It was hoped that these discussions would reach agreement on the present status of Northern Ireland, consensus on the most effective means of dealing with terrorism, and a clear understanding of how effective consultation and co-operation could be set in place for the future. Should these talks be successful then an executive could be formed and the Secretary of State would devolve responsibility for areas such as social security, education, industry, agriculture and planning to the new executive. Bew and Gillespie explained the British Government's strategy: 'The British pursue a carrot and stick approach. The unionists regain responsibility for many of the areas they had controlled under the Stormont parliament [security being the major exception], but to do so they must share power with a nationalist party, and come to an understanding with the Republic.'[12]

From the outset Ian Paisley opposed the proposals set out in the White Paper, suggesting that the real intention of the Westminster Government was to lead the province into a United Ireland: 'It makes Ulster men and women second-class citizens in the United Kingdom, and is a half-way house to a United Ireland.'[13] He described the power-sharing proposals as 'an attempt to destroy democracy'. Soon a coalition of Loyalist/Unionist groups opposed to the White Paper was formed. And opinion within the Unionist Party, led by Brian Faulkner, the former Stormont Prime Minister, was divided.

The results of the Northern Ireland Assembly elections on 28 June resulted in a clear majority of elected members being in support of the White Paper but also revealed the deep division of opinion within the varying shades on unionism. Parties favouring the White Paper polled 63 per cent while 32 per cent voted for parties which were against the proposals. On 22 November the formation of an executive was announced: it would consist of 11 members, six being 'Faulknerite' Unionists, four Social Democratic and Labour Party (SDLP), and a member of the Alliance Party. There would also be four non-voting members of the administration, two SDLP, one Unionist and one Alliance.

To facilitate conditions laid down in the White Paper, namely, that the creation of devolved government depended on agreement being reached on matters providing for an 'Irish Dimension' between representatives of the British and Irish Governments and the parties prepared to serve in an Assembly Executive, a tripartite conference comprising representatives of these three constituencies was held at Sunningdale in Berkshire from 6-9 December. The most significant area of agreement related to the formation of a Council of Ireland. It would have representatives from the Republic and Northern Ireland and consist of a Council of Ministers and a Consultative Assembly. As a concession to the Faulknerite Unionists it was conceded that decisions of the Council of Ministers would depend on a unanimous vote. However, Brian Faulkner's pre-Sunningdale suggestions that the Republic's Government should rescind Articles 2 and 3 of their Constitution – which laid claim to jurisdiction over the whole of the island of Ireland – were not accepted. Instead Liam Cosgrave, the Taoiseach, offered a declaration 'that there could be no change in the status of Northern Ireland until a majority of the people of Northern Ireland desired a change in that status'.[14]

As the year ended the decisions of the Sunningdale Conference and the formation of an Executive provided some hope for a better future in the Province. But there was also much foreboding lest opposition to these decisions should eventually succeed and overturn the progress made to consensus government.

13

Taking Risks
1974

123 Springhill Avenue
Belfast BT12 7QF

My dear Eric,

Thank you for going to Feakle. I hope you will have great peace in spite of whatever controversy there may be. I know how much this visit may have cost you and how heartbreaking it can be to be misunderstood or not understood. Thank you for the many things you have done for the people. And I hope you will have a very peaceful Christmas. Every good wish to all the family and very especially to Mrs Gallagher who has been so kind to me so often.

Sincerely,

Desmond Wilson

Letter from Father Desmond Wilson,
late December 1974

The hope which Eric felt at the beginning of 1974 was tinged with an element of uncertainty. The Power-Sharing Executive led by Brian Faulkner had just taken office. Eric comments: 'Many in the Churches – myself included – wished it well on Sunday 6 January.' But he was very apprehensive because two days earlier the Ulster Unionist Council had rejected the concept of an all-Ireland Council at a crowded meeting in the Ulster Hall by 427 votes to 374. Brian Faulkner realized that he had lost control of the UUP and resigned as leader of the party on 7 January. Harry West, elected as Faulkner's successor, now swung the entire Unionist Party machine against the Sunningdale Agreement. A month later the unexpected Westminster general election revealed a massive groundswell of Unionist opposition to the Agreement when the United Ulster Unionist Council (UUUC), comprising Harry West's

UUP, Bill Craig's Vanguard and Ian Paisley's DUP, won 11 of the 12 seats.

A situation had now developed in which a majority of elected members of the Stormont Assembly still supported the Sunningdale Agreement but an overwhelming number of MPs from the Province were opposed to it. Tensions and differences within the pro-Sunningdale group – which had existed in varying degrees from the start of the process – were now exacerbated. On 4 March the Unionist pro-Assembly group decided that they could no longer support all the steps necessary for the ratification of the Agreement, particularly the setting up of the Council of Ireland. They insisted that there could be no moves in this direction unless Articles 2 and 3 of the Irish Constitution were repealed. The SDLP who all along had had their own problems in working the Agreement – notably with the continuing existence of internment – were naturally unhappy about this and demanded the implementation of the whole package.

The Ulster Workers Council (UWC) strike which began on 15 May, following the Assembly's rejection the previous day of a motion condemning power-sharing and the Council of Ireland by 44 votes to 28, has generally been seen as the main factor in the collapse of the Executive. The actual announcement of the planned strike had been made by the UWC at the meeting of a 'study group' of the UUUC attended by representatives of the Ulster Defence Association (UDA) and the Ulster Volunteer Force (UVF) and presided over by Ian Paisley.[1] The co-ordinating committee which directed the strike included the UUUC leaders: Paisley, West and Craig. Most now accept that intimidation practised by the paramilitaries was a significant feature of the strike. Gallagher and Worrall confirm this aspect of paramilitary involvement: 'That there was intimidation is unquestioned, and behind the UWC, giving the orders, stood the "Ulster Army Council" enforcing them, in some cases with proven acts of violence.'[2] Ken Bloomfield, the civil servant who served as Secretary to the Executive, similarly states: 'This committee (UWC) argued that it relied on the moral force of a popular mandate derived from the Westminster election. In reality it also relied very heavily on muscle: the paramilitary muscle of men in dark glasses armed with pickaxe handles and other inducements to co-operation, and the industrial muscle of loyalist cadres in essential services such as the generation and distribution of electricity and the distribution of petrol and fuel oils.'[3]

Church leaders did not stand idly by during the strike. Among the various initiatives tried was a delegation to see the Minister of State, Mr Stan Orme, led by Bishop George Quin, a contemporary of Eric's at Trinity College, Dublin. Eric was a member of the group: 'What exactly we wanted him to do we hardly knew. It was a kind of desperation exercise asking him to do what no one else had been able to accomplish, namely persuade the strikers to stop.' And, unusually for Eric, he found himself getting into an argument: 'I got into an argument with him [Mr Orme] after he said something about the immutability of stated positions. I made no headway in countering with the comment that politics should be in the nature of things flexible, if it had anything at all to do with the art of the possible.'

On 28 May Brian Faulkner and his Unionist colleagues requested the Secretary of State, Merlyn Rees, to enter into dialogue with those responsible for the strike. When this recommendation was turned down Faulkner resigned as Chief Executive, effectively ending the Power-Sharing venture. On 30 May the Assembly was prorogued though it was not officially dissolved until 29 March 1975.

Eric was obviously deeply disappointed by the failure of this attempt to make government in Northern Ireland more inclusive of both Nationalist and Unionist aspirations. However, his Autobiographical Notes bear no trace whatever of what might be termed an 'If only' or 'I told you so' mentality. He had proposed a different pathway to that which the Westminster Government had set out in its White Paper. He had recommended a more gradual progression towards finding a solution: a Consultative Assembly elected by proportional representation which would send delegates from its parties to a 'Constitutional Conference' whose task would be 'to hammer out a solution which can be guaranteed to find adequate popular and party support'. His proposals relied on the encouragement of leadership within the local political parties. It was more in the nature of a 'Northern Ireland solution' in contrast to the policy of the White Paper which laid down basic principles and parameters within which a solution might develop and which involved representatives of the British and Irish Governments at an early stage, namely the Darlington Conference.

One cannot resist the temptation to speculate what the possible outcome might have been if Eric's ideas had been followed. Is it unrealistic or naïve to think that leaders of political parties in Northern Ireland – and he had hoped that proportional representation would produce some MPs who were more representative of moderate opinion – might have been able to draw up proposals for government more inclusive of minority opinion and acceptable to the Westminster Government? Undoubtedly the British Government was convinced that the Northern Ireland political parties would be unable to reach this kind of agreement on more inclusive government without a prior laying down of basic principles on which agreement might be founded.

By July the British Government had issued another White Paper, *The Northern Ireland Constitution,* which followed part of Eric's proposals: the election of a Constitutional Convention to draft an agreed plan for the future of government of Northern Ireland. But the basic principles which the elected members were to follow were once again stipulated in advance: some form of power-sharing and arrangements which would take account of Northern Ireland's common land frontier and special relationship with the Republic of Ireland.

Significantly, the 22nd Annual Summer School of the Social Study Conference held at St Augustine's College, Dungarvan, County Waterford, from 3-10 August, chose 'Sectarianism – Roads to Reconciliation' as its overall study topic. Of the ten major papers presented during the week, Eric's 'Roads to Reconciliation – A Protestant Contribution' was the ninth, given on Friday, 9 August. His definition of sectarianism is as good as any that have been produced over the years: 'By sectarianism I mean a factionalism based on religion, or more properly a misunderstanding of religion, which produces in the members of the faction an attitude of superiority to others and which results, at best, in self-imposed isolation from others and at worst in acts of hostility and violence against those others from whom the sectarians are isolated most of all.'

He indicated that he had been invited to include in his address a confession of Protestant guilt for sectarianism. He explained why he was not going to do this: 'I must decline the invitation, not because I consider the Protestant Churches guiltless. That would not be true. They share in the guilt for sectarianism in Ireland. But they only share that guilt.'

He lamented the fact that the Protestant Churches had very little hold or influence over the young or the working class. Regarding the former he declared, 'The Sunday of the Protestant Church galleries teeming with teenagers has gone. They just are not in the churches in overwhelming numbers any more.' And of contact with the working class, he said: 'Equally the day has passed, if it ever existed, for the Protestant Churches to claim that they are Churches of and for the workers. If you examine the street leadership in the traditional Protestant strongholds and the new estates of the North, you will find some interesting facts. If it has an active religious background of any kind, it is more likely to be associated with the anti-ecumenical and/or anti-ecclesiastical wings of the Churches in question.' In light of the fact that sectarianism was finding a breeding ground among young people and workers, he suggested that it was imperative for the Protestant Churches – quite apart from the biblical commandment to evangelize – to re-establish contact and influence over those two sections of the population.

Throughout his life, in the various circuits on which he had served, Eric had continually advocated the importance of lay training and education. At Dungarvan he returned to the theme: 'The mission of the Church is not completed by persuading men and women and boys and girls to attend a place of worship. A properly mounted and sustained programme of Christian education, spelling out in political, economic and sociological terms the implications of the simple statement "God is Love" would do more to remove sectarianism than any other single thing I know.'

When Eric was addressing the subject of lay education and training he made the rather interesting proposal that there should be an Irish Churches' Residential Conference Centre. He reported that there was a growing demand for residential weekend and mid-week conferences and seminars. He asked: 'Can all the Churches possibly do something about this? The need is evident: there is firm indication that there is a demand. If a centre were available, I have no doubt about its economic viability.'

This was not idle speculation! The ICC had been considering the possibility of such a Centre since the previous April. They had learned that the seminary of the African Fathers at Drumantine near Newry might soon be available. The Executive decided to send a group of its members, Eric included, to investigate the possibility of acquiring it, in whole or in part, on rental terms. The group went down to see the site on at least two or three occasions so it was evidently a serious proposition for some time. They felt it was a good site with great potential: 'We were deeply impressed with what we saw. Few more attractive or better-appointed centres can exist.' There was a suggestion that if the project came off Barbara and Eric might think of becoming resident wardens. They may have been interested in pursuing this possibility but the scheme was dropped: 'It did not come off and we were spared what could have been a difficult vocational choice.'

The danger of triumphalism was another of Eric's themes at Dungarvan. He suggested that there was a tendency in the Protestant Churches to 'do their own thing', and to 'go it alone'. Such attitudes and actions were fostering the spirit of sectarianism: 'Every decision to act in isolation prompts the other Churches to do the same. It drives them in upon themselves, spending their time, talents and energies on separating – and sectarian-producing activity. It creates isolation, unawareness, foundationless concepts of superiority, rivalry – in a word sectarianism. For this reason, if for no other, denominational triumphalism is an unacceptable face of Protestantism.'

He made a plea that the Protestant Churches should take more seriously the concept of working together. And he extended this to the whole area of relationships between Roman Catholics and Protestants. There should be a basic attitude of mind that insisted on doing things together, particularly where conviction did not require that they be done separately. He suggested that people should not be hesitant in putting the case for co-operation. For far too long those who believed in co-operation had been silent and timid: 'They have left the running and the shouting to the wreckers and all of us have paid the price. By our silence and inactivity we have acquiesced in the propagation of sectarian prejudice. We have allowed wild statements and charges to go by default. And this seeming conspiracy of silence has persuaded many puzzled people that the accusations and objections are well founded. Silence breeds sectarianism. We must learn the art of public relations and courageous commendation of others.'

Finally, Eric turned his attention to the urgent need for someone or some people to establish contact with those on both sides of the sectarian divide who were involved in violence. Ireland was a beautiful country and the men of violence must surely have some sort of love for it. The Churches must make some effort to contact these men: 'Has the time not come for the Churches instead of making statements and speaking, no matter how sincerely, to make some kind of attempt to find these men? Can someone with the authority of the Churches behind him not find a way to meet them in the name of God – someone who can speak to the activists on either side in plain words they can understand and who equally can appeal to whatever love, however misplaced, they have for their countrymen. The Man of Nazareth would have found a way. Increasingly I am convinced that we too must try.'

On Tuesday 24 September Eric attended a meeting of the Management Committee of Gort-na-Mona Secondary School at the top of the Springfield Road. He had been appointed to the Committee by the Belfast Education and Library Board. It was his very first experience of sharing on the Management Committee of a Catholic School and he discovered that it was their first experience of a Protestant cleric in their midst. He was somewhat apprehensive: 'The Committee seemed to be made up almost completely of priests and Christian Brothers. I can well imagine Catholic lay folk finding as I did the experience daunting or as the French would put it "formidable". That evening I think we measured each other up.' He need not have worried! 'Before long I felt and was made to feel at home.' On one occasion he was asked to chair an appointments committee. He remarks: 'I considered I had arrived. I came to have the highest respect for what Brother O'Connell and his staff were doing for the boys in that difficult area of the city.'

During the summer of 1974 slender links between the various paramilitary organisations – with the exception of the UVF who refused to participate – had been initiated by the Community Relations Commission. Dr Stanley Worrall, former Headmaster of the Methodist College, was appointed chairman of a committee which organized a weekend conference at a seaside hotel in County Donegal for some 150 members connected to these organisations. Worrall later recorded his first-hand account of this meeting: 'Men who openly boasted they would shoot each other in the streets of Belfast shared tables in the hotel dining-room and danced with their respective wives and sweethearts for half the night.' But it was not all partying – important as this was to help create a friendly atmosphere: 'In a three-hour plenary session on the Sunday morning it emerged that everyone was appealing to the Provisional IRA to call off the violence, "to get off the backs of the working class", so that talks on the basic problems could take place.'[4]

In September there was another significant meeting, this time in Holland. It was a smaller, more secretive gathering compared to the event in Donegal, only about 20 attending. Paramilitaries, or those with links to paramilitary organisations, were present. Some weeks later the *Belfast Telegraph* reported on developments at that meeting: 'On the first day some refused to speak to each other, or sit at the same table.' But this icy atmosphere had changed by the fourth day when a wide range of Protestant/Catholic community schemes were mapped out. The *Telegraph* declared: ' Paramilitary men from the IRA Provisional movement and militant loyalist leaders were said to have reached a new determination to work together in their communities.'5

One of those present in Holland was the Revd William (Bill) Arlow, Associate Secretary of the Irish Council of Churches. On the plane coming home he had sat beside Jimmy Drumm, a leading member of Sinn Fein, whose wife Maire was the Sinn Fein Vice-President. Bill and Jimmy talked together about what had been said at the meeting and Bill got the impression that his companion was anxious to see a stop to the killing and bombing. They promised to keep in touch and a short time later Bill received word that the Provisional IRA leadership would welcome the opportunity of meeting and talking with a group of Protestant churchmen with a view to considering the possibility of a ceasefire.

Bill Arlow shared his news with the Revd Ralph Baxter, ICC Secretary, and they decided to ask Eric for his opinion on the matter. 'I could not but say that it should be followed up.' They then asked him if he would be prepared to be a member of such a group. Eric wanted to know why there was no suggestion of the IRA meeting a group of Catholic clerics or of having some Catholics in the group. Baxter and Arlow indicated that it was a question of Protestant clerics or no one. Eric comments: 'In the light of my previous meeting [with the Provisionals], my answer had to be in the affirmative. For me there was no alternative.'

There then followed weeks of preparation which centred on 'assembling a Church-related team' and finding a suitable location for the meeting. Eric had been in favour of a meeting outside the country, possibly Holland. Initially the Provisionals agreed to this but later changed their minds because they were aware of tighter security at the ports and airports. They feared that some of them could be recognized or arrested. Agreement was eventually reached that they should meet at some remote location in the Republic.

As Ralph Baxter had ministered for some time at Shannon he was asked to reconnoitre and report back. Baxter already knew the Smyth Village Hotel in Feakle, County Clare, an ornately and traditionally furnished cottage-style hotel situated on the brow of the hill overlooking the village, so he went in person and enquired as to their ability and willingness to house a conference of clergymen and others over a three-day period in December. The Provisionals agreed that this would be a suitable venue.

It is interesting that Stanley Worrall records in Worrall and Gallagher, *Christians in Ulster 1968-1980,* that he contacted the British Government through the British Ambassador in Dublin to tell them that an invitation had been received to meet the Provisional leadership and that it was intended to accept it. He reports: 'The authorities neither encouraged nor discouraged the move. It was not done behind their backs, but no suggestion emanating from the authorities was carried to the rendezvous.'[6] Obviously he thought it right to inform the British Government but one wonders what effect this had on the supposed secrecy surrounding the meeting. We have no information whether he told the Provisionals that he had been in contact with the British Embassy. Certainly Eric's record of the meeting suggests that all the arrangements were shrouded in secrecy: 'So secret were the arrangements that only the car drivers involved were told of the venue beforehand and that at the last possible time.' And later he comments: 'Naturally all of us hoped that we could keep the meeting secret. We realised of course that there was always the possibility of a news leak.'

The only one Eric told what was afoot was his wife! 'As always she reacted with her completely full but somewhat fearful approval. Her support and love over the years never wavered.' However, they agreed not to tell the family until all was over.

The team chosen represented both British and Irish Church leaders. There was one layman, Stanley Worrall. In addition to

Eric and Stanley, and the two ICC Secretaries, Ralph Baxter and Bill Arlow, there were four others: Dr Arthur Butler, Church of Ireland Bishop of Connor; Dr Jack Weir, Clerk of the Presbyterian Assembly; Dr Harry Morton, Secretary of the British Council of Churches; and the Right Revd Arthur McArthur, Moderator of the United Reformed Church in England. The Provisionals were represented by three PIRA activists – Dáithí Ó Connaill, Chief of Staff; Seamus Twomey and Kevin Mallon – and three from Provisional Sinn Fein: Ruairí Ó Brádaigh, SF President; Maire Drumm, SF Vice-President; and Seamus Loughran, Belfast organizer.[7]

The meeting at Feakle started on Monday evening 9 December. Eric reports that it began with a 'getting-to-know-you' session but in these circumstances there were obvious limitations: the Provisionals could know who the church leaders were but for security reasons their own identity was hidden. During a conversation with Eric, two of the Provisionals drew attention to Stanley Worrall sitting in another group: 'They wanted to know who he was. I replied that he was the former Headmaster of Methodist College, Belfast. They commented that he looked like a British Army officer to which I replied that they might be re-assured if I told them that he had been a pacifist during the Second World War and had worked as such in the coal mines. "That's enough for us", they said. Indeed it was so good that they were ready to accept him next morning as chairman.'

The informal session broke up about 11 p.m. and both groups then reflected separately on the next day's business. Eric had missed the final preparation meeting for the 'Feakle team' so he was surprised to learn that it had been planned that he should open the proceedings in the first formal session. 'No one had been asked to tell me and no one had.' He relates how he coped with this news: 'I went to my bedroom which was shared with Ralph Baxter but it was a considerable time before I went to bed. We talked about what should be said: they had asked that I should "kick for goal". Eventually I got notes written on paper.' Those notes – though written late at night – reveal Eric's capacity for clear and constructive thinking:

1. We are a group of persons – interested and concerned. Not here at behest of any party. I speak personally as a Christian and as a minister of a Christian Church – also as an Irishman.

   No claim to be better than anyone else – but my Christian faith makes me convinced there must be a better way.

   As Irish – proud of Irish birth and land I love. No other homeland. As passionately devoted to it – though in some ways I have been denied half my heritage – so too with others.

   In discussion none of us wishes to make judgments on integrity or motives of anyone else. But right that our stances and attitudes should be known.

2. Present campaign as we see it:
   1. War no one can win – all losers.
   2. Has produced and is producing more polarisation – put back possibility of reconciliation.
   3. Has put well-being and safety of NI minority in jeopardy – always possibility of Protestant backlash – this seen in UWC strike [refined form] but more violent form always potentially present.
   4. Full-scale civil war – Irish form of scorched earth – possible.
   5. Not union –but re-partition – much smaller Protestant enclave.
   6. Harm being done to Ireland – at home and abroad – deaths, destruction, personal injuries.
   7. Corruption of whole communities – break down in standards and morals.

3. All this adds up to the need for a political solution – cessation of violence. Everybody on hook – Big Question – How can all sides get off hook? Has Provisional IRA the key?

4. Have heard demand for withdrawal of army. We have no illusions about army being blunt instrument – not designed as police force. When community rejects police it gets army.

   But what is alternative? If army is withdrawn – immediate bloodshed. What do you mean by withdrawal? What then do you propose regarding maintenance of order? What is replacement?

5. We are convinced of need for political solution – how do you see it? We take it that it is recognised that a settlement which is imposed by duress has seeds of trouble in it – recipe for greater disaster.

   We must all seek modus vivendi – where justice is done and seen to be done.

6. Role of Churches – [a] in seeking to promote [Christian] attitudes among members [b] in seeking to promote quest for peace. Dr Weir to speak later.

7. Grateful for present opportunity – recognise you have honoured us by coming – we make no claims – except that of being ready not only to convey if we can any instruction that commends itself to all of us to either British or Irish governments but also in whatever way we can work for solution that may be acceptable.

Eric must have had little or no sleep that Monday night! 'Such were the notes – I thought them over and over again during the night and went over them again early in the morning and again after breakfast.'

At breakfast the churchmen were seated before the others arrived so they had an opportunity to observe the full Provisional team as they entered the room. Seamus Loughran was the only one whom Eric knew. However, he thought one of the others appeared familiar to him: 'He had a wig and was fitted with contact lenses. I looked at him at length and as I left the room I went over to him and said I thought we had met in

Dundalk a couple of years previously and that I surmised he was Ruairí Ó Brádaigh. With no great reluctance he said I was correct and then I told him I had kept the promise I had made to him and his two companions.'

Eric describes the room in which their discussion took place: 'There was a small table at the head of the room with Dr Worrall sitting behind it. The Provisionals were seated along one side and beyond the end of it and the Churchmen on the other.' Stanley Worrall introduced the churchmen and then Ruairí Ó Brádaigh, known as 'Peter', said that it would be convenient to identify his side, nearly all of whom were disguised, by false names. Worrall then asked Eric to speak: 'I developed the notes I had made stressing my conviction that violence was the antithesis of the gospel.'

O'Brádaigh was the next to speak. Eric's Autobiographical Notes summarize it as follows:

> Their campaign was justified, he said: it was a legitimate military operation on behalf of their oppressed minority. The only solution was for Britain to get out – they were not asking for an immediate withdrawal – the date could be negotiated – the republican movement would put forward its political solution – and a cessation of hostilities would follow. They wanted to see a democratic socialist republic under public control with worker participation.

Then Dr Weir followed:

> He spoke passionately about mirror images. He said that Protestants had an attachment to these islands as well as to this island. The Provisionals distrusted London and England – Protestants had a distrust of Dublin and the South. A declaration of intent to withdraw by Britain would mean a cutting off of Protestant roots. There were deep emotional depths in Protestantism. He agreed that there was a military stalemate and stressed his concern about a civil war. He referred to the increase in sectarian killings – it was a case of blind hitting back. He said we

did not want to talk in those terms. It was a question of where do we go from here.

The dialogue continued courteously and quietly, with a break for coffee, until lunch time. Before they adjourned it was agreed that they should start the afternoon by meeting separately so that each side could take stock of what had been said so far.

During lunch a couple of men appeared at the dining-room door and beckoned to Ruairí Ó Brádaigh and Dáithí Ó Conaill. They got up and went outside. After some time they returned to say that 'their man in Dublin Castle' had alerted them to the fact that Dublin knew about the meeting and that a detachment of the Special Branch was on its way to the hotel.

The three 'activists' left but the Sinn Fein officers remained. Everyone was now concerned what would happen to the discussions. They decided to have two sessions: a plenary session of the churchmen and the Sinn Fein officers together, followed by a separate session for each to assess their positions. Eric found the joint session valuable: 'The joint discussion enabled us to discover at least in part what kind of situation might persuade the IRA to call off the campaign. When we were on our own we talked over the whole situation as far as possible objectively taking into account what was about to happen.' Despite the coldness of the upstairs room in which they were meeting it was a creative session. As had been the custom in so many discussions in the past when important business was being considered – and this would continue to be the pattern for some time to come – Eric was the one who put pen to paper and jotted down the suggestions being made: 'As we talked and waited I jotted down what seemed to be a possible basis for something to put to the three downstairs. We worked at it and over it, changed this and that, added and took away while we listened to every sound and followed the beams of car lights on the road.'

Just as they finished a possible draft, Bill Arlow who had left the room came back with the news that the Special Branch were coming up the drive. According to Eric the next couple of hours were memorable: 'Doors were pushed open, there was noise and shouting. We could hear the men downstairs being questioned. All the bedrooms were searched: drawers turned out and furniture pushed about.'

While this rumpus continued the churchmen were left alone: 'The stairway leading to our room had not been noticed.' Apparently the raiding party had been convinced that they would find the top men of the IRA and could not understand that the only ones to be seen were O'Bradaigh and his 'political' companions. Eventually O'Bradaigh, who had thrown his wig under the counter and had put on his spectacles, told the Special Branch that they would find the men they were looking for upstairs! Eric continues the story: 'Our moment had come. There was a rush up the stairs: the first thing we saw was the muzzle of a sub-machine gun and then the man who held it followed by three or four others. What followed would have been farcical had it not been deadly serious. Instead of the top brass of the IRA whom they expected to be fully armed, they discovered a seemingly harmless group of clerics most of whom were well past middle age!'

Special Branch were puzzled that churchmen should be talking to the IRA. They had to produce their driving licences to prove their identity and for some moments it seemed that even this was not enough: they were asked for their home phone numbers and told that calls would be made to their homes to find out if they were the people they said they were. 'Bishop Butler asked that the phone call to his wife should be discreet and not in any way frightening. He did not wish his wife to be alarmed. I made the same request.' Fortunately, after reflection, Special Branch decided that the phone calls were not necessary.

However, there was another surprise: 'They produced montages of photographs of suspected IRA men and wanted to know if any of them applied to the men who had left. Whether they did or not we will probably never know. The disguises had done their work: we certainly did not recognise anyone.'

Finally, Special Branch wished the churchmen well. They were told that a guard would be placed on the hotel overnight and were instructed not to leave until the next day, Wednesday.

Following the departure of the Special Branch the two parties reassembled in another plenary session. The churchmen presented the draft statement which had been completed just before the arrival of the police. A few alterations were made to it and the three Sinn Fein officers indicated that it could be put to the Army Council with a hope of some kind of positive response, though they made it clear that nothing could be guaranteed. 'We on our part promised to follow the thing through and make the government aware of what had happened.'

In the statement the British Government would confirm:

1. HM Government solemnly re-affirms that it has no political or territorial interests in Northern Ireland beyond its obligations to the citizens of Northern Ireland.

2. The prime concern of HM Government is the achievement of peace and the promotion of such understanding between the various sections in Northern Ireland as will guarantee to all its people a full participation in the life of the community, whatever be the relationship of the Province to the EEC, the United Kingdom or the Republic of Ireland.

3. Contingent upon the maintenance of a declared ceasefire and upon effective policing, HM Government will relieve the Army as quickly as possible of its internal security duties.

4. Until agreements about the future government of Northern Ireland have been freely negotiated, accepted and guaranteed, HM Government intends to retain the present armed forces in Northern Ireland.

5. HM Government recognises the obligation and right of all those who have political aims to pursue them through the democratic process.

On the Wednesday morning the churchmen left the hotel and went their separate ways. Eric and Stanley Worrall travelled to Dublin for a scheduled meeting of the Tripartite Conversations. Later that day they returned to Belfast.

Eric had not considered the possibility that news of the Feakle meeting would be leaked to the media: 'It never occurred to us to discuss contingency plans in the event of the news leaking – proof the critics will say that we were completely unsuited to the task.' The BBC had the news on the early news bulletins on Thursday, 12 December and that evening the *Belfast Telegraph* had the whole front page devoted to news of the Feakle meeting, describing it as an 'Amazing Summit'. The writer of 'Viewpoint' in the same newspaper supported the initiative: 'By at least talking to the IRA the churchmen were implying that clerical statements from pulpits, fine as far as they go, do not go far enough. Preaching must be backed by action, even if that means confronting the men of violence with the implications of their continued action.'[8]

All in all there was a fairly mixed reception to the meeting. Vanguard and DUP spokesmen condemned the Church leaders for what they considered 'peace at any price'.[9] In contrast to this, Mr James Molyneaux, the UUUC leader at Westminster, said he saw no harm in the talks.

However, what disappointed Eric considerably was the official response of the Methodist Church to the initiative. On Thursday, 12 December, the Revd Henry Holloway, press officer for the Church, declared: 'Both the Revd R Desmond Morris [President] and the Secretary, the Revd Harold Sloan, have dissociated themselves from this approach to the Provisional IRA because it is an approach to men outside the law and who are wanted by the law.'[10]

The annoyance felt by the Methodist Church officials was undoubtedly linked to the fact that news of the Feakle meeting broke on the same day as the launch of the Joint Peace Campaign planned some time earlier by the mainstream Churches. Full-page advertisements announcing the Peace campaign had appeared in most Irish papers that day. The Church leaders said:

> We sincerely ask you, as members of our own or other Churches and as men and women of goodwill, to join us at Church Services on Sunday, 15th December in earnest prayers for peace in our land; and personally thereafter daily at noon or any other convenient time.

> Speak up for this cause every day to your family, your friends and neighbours and to the strangers you may meet.

> As we approach the Christmas season, when we celebrate again the coming of the Prince of Peace, we appeal to you, to make a special effort in seeking a cessation of the violence in our land. Help us now to begin something which may yet last when Christmas is gone.[11]

Some saw the Feakle meeting as the practical outcome of praying for peace but others felt that the media interest in Feakle reduced the publicity for the Church leaders' appeal.

Each of the Feakle participants had a particularly unpleasant personal price to pay: abusive phone calls. On the Thursday evening before Eric left the house to go to an appointment Barbara answered a phone call which informed her that her husband would be dead by midnight. Eric writes: 'For better or for worse our phone went out of order for a couple of days: Barbara at least was spared the abusive phone-calls that came to all of us – I got at least a share of mine at the office.'

Eric was the only churchman at Feakle who had a direct responsibility for the pastoral care of a congregation. He was not sure how the Grosvenor Hall congregation had reacted to the news of churchmen talking to the IRA. He knew his ministerial colleagues on the Mission staff stood by him but he was apprehensive about the feelings of the congregation. He need not have worried! In *At Points of Need. The story of the Belfast Central Mission 1889-1989* Eric recalled the thoughts he shared with the congregation on the morning of 15 December, the first Sunday after he had returned from Feakle: 'I reminded them of what I had said the previous Sunday evening ['Blessed are the peacemakers'] and told them of how we had reasoned with the Provisionals and had pleaded with them to call off their campaign. Then I said: "I don't expect that all of you will agree with what I have done. I have valued and enjoyed your friendship for the last sixteen and a half years and you have had mine. I sincerely hope that you are still my friends." ' At the end of the service the congregation made a point of leaving by one door only. 'Without exception, each shook me by the hand and almost every one of them had a word of approval for what had been done.' The experience of that Sunday morning reminded him of the privilege he had in being the pastor of this congregation: 'To serve such a people was the greatest honour the Church could bestow on any of its ministers.'[12]

The Mission Christmas Appeal that year was a record. The Christmas Eve Street Collection formed a major part of that appeal. Eric positioned himself as usual in Donegall Place, standing there with his collecting box from eight in the morning until after five in the evening, with a short break for lunch. Again, he had been apprehensive of how people would treat him: 'Not one hostile word was spoken to me during the day and my total collection was also a record.'

The Feakle participants received countless letters as well as phone calls, some supporting the venture and some opposed to it. Eric was no exception. He replied sensitively to all the letters he received. One particular letter came from a member of a former congregation. Her son had been kidnapped and murdered by the IRA and she was deeply distressed that Eric had been talking with representatives of his murderers. Eric relates the contents of his letter to her: 'I told her what she did not know. The night I heard that her son was missing I had tried to get a message through to the IRA pleading for his life. I said that I had gone to Feakle to prevent, in any way I could, other young men suffering the same fate.' The lady replied to Eric very quickly: 'As I stood on the street on Christmas Eve an urgent letter was delivered to me by hand. Now she saw and understood.'

The days following the Feakle talks appear to have been filled with intense negotiations involving various groups: the British Government, the Dublin Government, the PIRA/Sinn Fein and some of the Feakle churchmen. One of these meetings involved representatives of the Feakle group going to Westminster to see Mr Merlyn Rees, the Secretary of State, on 18 December. They wanted to give Rees a first-hand account of what had transpired at Feakle. Eric was surprised at the outdated conditions in which he worked: 'We were amazed at his cramped and uninspiring accommodation and the primitive telephone system that was incapable of resisting incoming calls. He had to take the receiver off the hook and smother the mouthpiece with his handkerchief.'

Phone calls and secret meetings continued for some time both before and after the PIRA had declared a temporary ceasefire on 20 December. Sadly all the talking did not produce a permanent ceasefire and the 25-day break in the IRA campaign came to an end on 17 January 1975. Merlyn Rees denounced the return to military action by the IRA: 'I will not be influenced by any views which are backed by the bomb and the bullet.'[13]

In his Autobiographical Notes Eric reflects on the value or otherwise of the Feakle talks:

> What good came of it all? It is hard to say. The initiative was attempted in all good faith. Undoubtedly lives were saved and further destruction avoided at least for a time. We have been criticised as being naive: the charge does not stick. All of us held responsible positions: as one letter-writer to the press put it, we put our reputations on the line; we knew the risks. We believed and had reason to believe that there was at least a fifty-fifty chance and perhaps more than that of an end to the violence. It was a chance we had to take. Government, I feel, could have acted more positively. Most certainly the sudden break-up of our meeting was

unfortunate. Had we been able to reach an agreed statement with the military side of the delegation things might well have turned out differently. Who knows?

The meeting at Feakle between 'unofficial' Protestant leaders and the Provisionals will surely go down in history as a significant attempt by Christian leaders to both listen to republican paramilitaries and, at the same time, share with them their conviction regarding the futility of their military campaign. The fact that it did not result in a permanent ceasefire does not diminish the significance of their action. Eric had already shown himself ready to listen to them in 1971. Other initiatives involving individuals or small groups were to follow in the 1980s and early 1990s but Eric was not involved in them. All are examples of the Christian Church being prepared to listen as well as to proclaim its message of love.

14

Perseverance
1975-79

What are God's commandments all about? Basically, they are about rights: human rights and divine rights, or perhaps better the other way round – God's rights and other people's rights. They are about priorities – about what you think is really important.

Jesus summed them all up for us in two sentences. Love God. Love your neighbour. And so the question to ask ourselves is this: is it just possible that a large part of our troubles comes from a basic failure to put God first and to work that out in practical terms as far as our neighbour is concerned. Obviously, you don't put God or your neighbour first when you plant a bomb in your neighbour's shop or factory. You don't put God or your neighbour first if you shoot him or get someone else to shoot him. But it's not only bombers and gunmen who don't get their priorities right. You don't put God and your neighbour first if you make up your mind to get all you can no matter who suffers as a result. You don't obey when you concede absolutely nothing either to God or man and do as you like. It's a poor kind of loving God and loving God's children when you build walls or barriers around yourself and so cut yourself off completely or even partially from meaningful contact with either God in all his fullness or your neighbour in all his need. A society that does that kind of thing is bound to destroy itself. People talk about being 'For God and Ulster' or 'For God and Ireland' – if they mean anything worthwhile, they can only mean 'For God and my neighbour'. Until we practise that in all its fullness we can never really have the peace we want.

BBC Broadcast Service, Chapel of Unity,
Methodist College, Belfast, Sunday, 14 October 1979

Early in 1974 Eric had accepted the invitation of the Carrickfergus Circuit to be minister in Whitehead following the Conference of 1975. The Mission's Executive Committee consequently began to think about possible successors. They had two or three ministers in mind but enquiries and direct approaches revealed that for one or another good reason none of them would be available either in 1975 or at all. By the time the list had been exhausted it had become increasingly clear that because of ministerial shortages Whitehead was to be left without a minister for the year 1975-76. In these circumstances the Mission committee unanimously invited Eric to continue as Superintendent until his retirement which he thought would be in 1979 or 1980.

He had become Superintendent of the Belfast Central Mission in 1957 – 18 years earlier – but he clearly welcomed the Mission's invitation to continue with them until his retirement: 'I had looked forward to the thought of Whitehead but was more than pleased to be asked to continue in the Mission. In any case I had little relish to be left without an indication as to where I might be sent, particularly as I had no wish to undertake new, heavy work. The Mission's work was arduous but I knew it and that was enough.'

Once the uncertainty had been settled he started to reflect how he would spend the remaining years of his ministry at the Mission. Things had changed considerably since 1957, and especially after 1969. The years of strife and urban renewal had already dealt a heavy blow as far as congregational work was concerned. Week-night work in a down-town situation had become almost impossible. Parents were unwilling to allow their children to be exposed to the hazards of a city at war. Eric knew this at first hand as it had affected his own children: 'Our own children never knew normal night life in their adolescent years. Like most of their peers they were virtual prisoners after dark.'

This affected the numbers attending evening services in the Mission. Smaller evening congregations in turn influenced the degree of media interest: 'The opportunities for major utterances and appeals to the community consequently declined and media interest and demand for Church statements went into reverse.'

Congregational numbers had also been reduced by the effects of urban redevelopment. Progressively housing in the lower Shankill, the Grosvenor Road, Sandy Row, parts of East Belfast and other areas from which the Mission had drawn large numbers, was cleared with little likelihood of its residents ever coming back. Eric explains: 'The Government had introduced its resettlement grants – some people called them bribes – as part of their policy to reduce the size of Belfast.' Demographic changes also had their effect. Several mixed areas –notably the Grosvenor Road – had become predominantly Roman Catholic.

On top of all this Grosvenor Hall had suffered from the effects of several bomb incidents. Its location in Glengall Street meant that it was right in the centre of a major target area. By 1975 Eric had a number of bomb damage claims outstanding with the Northern Ireland Office.

Eric's assessment of the situation was that he should aim to hold the congregation together and at the same time endeavour to provide some measure of pastoral ministry for those who had moved away and had not yet settled into other churches. Increasingly the pastoral list included addresses in Bangor, Carrickfergus, Lisburn and the estates on Belfast's periphery. He commented: 'For the last four years of my active ministry, along with my colleagues, I was a roving pastor.'

In other areas of the Mission's work there were problems to be faced and new initiatives to be taken. The UWC strike of 1974 had demonstrated just how vulnerable were the residential homes as far as electricity was concerned. He applauded the staff in Castle Rocklands and Childhaven who had displayed exemplary commitment to the old folk and children in their care. Day by day they had defied road blocks and intimidation to get to work and had been able to have enough food in store to get through the difficult period. But oil without electricity to fire the boilers was of no use whatever, and it was the same with the electric cookers. Permanent auxiliary generators were clearly needed. And so Eric had to negotiate grants with the appropriate authorities for their installation, making the homes secure against similar eventualities.

Building plans were also undertaken at the two homes during this period. The bungalow colony at Castle Rocklands was completed and an attractive terrace of staff accommodation and provision for young people to commence independent living was erected at Childhaven – again with the help of generous grant assistance, all of which had to be negotiated.

One of the most time-consuming exercises Eric faced at this time arose out of a request from the central MCI authorities that both the BCM and the Donegall Square Circuit should explore and discuss a possible amalgamation. Eric recalled: 'It was to take its toll in mental, spiritual and physical demand. The discussions, while always pleasant and harmonious, were lengthy and time-consuming.' Difficulties emerged right from the start: 'It was early evident that the Donegall Square building, which was listed, had not adequate accommodation for the Mission's administrative and other needs. It was also felt that the Grosvenor Road/Glengall Street site was more appropriate for the Mission's non-congregational work, placed as it is at one of Belfast's community inter-faces.' Despite these problems both the Mission Committee and 'the Square's' Quarterly Board Meeting – the latter by a majority vote – agreed to the amalgamation. The two congregations were to remain separate but share in a united evening service. Both expressed the hope that they would eventually unite.

The Methodist Conference of 1976 approved the merger and also suggested that discussions might take place with the Sandy Row Circuit. Time was to prove, however, that the will for the merger was not strong enough to overcome the difficulties: 'Sadly, for whatever reason, the two congregations never really "gelled" in spite of bona fide attempts on each side to chart out an acceptable common future.' During the ministry of Eric's successor, Dr Norman Taggart, Donegall Square reverted to its original status and the Sandy Row Circuit became part of a larger Belfast Central Mission Circuit.[1]

The 1970s was also a time of staffing changes at the Mission. For a long time the Church had always appointed three ministers whose work was specifically related to the Grosvenor Hall congregation and various Mission activities. In addition to this a fourth minister was appointed to serve the Springfield Road congregation in the west of the city, this congregation being part of the Mission Circuit. After 1972, Conference withdrew the third Hall-based minister and the Deaconess Order in England, which for many years had seconded one of its members to the Mission, no longer appointed anyone to serve there. To counteract this reduction in staffing personnel Eric managed to persuade a retired minister, the Revd Jim Pedlow, to give some part-time service: 'It was an inspired appointment. He brought with him years of wisdom and experience and a pastoral concern that meant a very great deal to the many old people on his visiting list.'

After 1969 the Springfield Road Church often found itself literally in the firing line between two warring factions. It was a dangerous place in which to serve, especially as the Manse was located fairly close to the church. Eric notes: 'Again and again members of the congregation faced gunfire on their way to church.' He had a particular admiration for the ministers who served this congregation in the 1970s. Of Malcolm Redman he says: 'Throughout it all Malcolm Redman and his wife Nessie never flinched. They stayed by their post when many another would have sought a change.' In 1975 he was succeeded by the Revd Robin Roddie: 'He too never flinched and brought his own distinctive gifts to a congregation that responded to his leadership.' Roddie's contacts with Eric affected his perception of his new Superintendent: 'Before I was stationed in Springfield Road my impression of Eric was that he was an austere person but I discovered on becoming his colleague that both he and Barbara were an enormously warm and caring couple who made their home available to me.'[2]

The Revd Joe McCrory's period as second minister in the Hall between 1963 and 1975 was undoubtedly one which cheered the hearts of the Mission congregation and that of the Superintendent Minister. Joe had a distinctive humour which brought a sparkle to his ministry. There was obviously a close bonding between Eric and Joe: 'They were years [1962-75] of great enjoyment and fellowship for me and, I believe, also for Joe. The friendship we formed lasted until his all-too-early death in 1980.' It was no surprise that Vera, Joe's widow, asked Eric to give the address at the funeral. He found it a difficult and emotional experience. He had an enormous appreciation for Joe's ministry: 'No words are adequate to describe the quality of the work Joe McCrory did in and for the Mission. Always a delightful companion he was ever completely loyal. I owe him much.'

Joe was followed by the Revd John Nelson who stayed until 1978 when he was appointed chaplain at Campbell College, a prestigious grammar school in the Belmont area of east Belfast. His place was taken by the Revd Arthur Parker who had earlier served as the third minister in the Hall. Eric appreciated both men: 'John was a boy at school when I was at University Road. He brought his enthusiasm and splendid tenor voice with him. Arthur Parker, always anticipatorily wise, used his expertise in property to good effect.'

Three months before Joe McCrory left the Mission there had been the retirement of 'Sister' Mary Gihon. Mary had never belonged to the Wesley Deaconess Order but has been described as one of the old-style 'Mission Sisters'. Eric explains her background and the circumstances of her original appointment: 'Self-taught and self-trained, she had been appointed away back in 1948 by the late John N Spence, a shrewd assessor of character and ability.' For most of her years in the Mission she had supervised the bulk of its social work, had organized and managed the yearly holiday programme in Childhaven, was the founder of a successful Girls' Brigade Company before handing it over to Marjorie Gill, had run the Women's Club and weekly meeting and had been, as Eric describes her, 'the recognised authority on all matters affecting the congregation and the traditions of the Mission'. She had been a committed member of the Woodvale congregation during Eric's ministry there. Her immense contribution and value were readily recognized by her Superintendent: 'There is no telling what she could have achieved had she had the benefit of the post-war educational system. It was a rare privilege to have such a person as a colleague.' After her retirement it was decided to employ a person to have specific responsibility for the holiday programme and caring for the elderly.

One appointment remained unchanged during Eric's ministry in BCM. Esther Fyffe became Secretary to the Superintendent in 1962 and remained in this position long after Eric had left in 1979. He could not have wished for a better Secretary and a more efficient or loyal colleague.

Eric was conscious of other changes that he believed now affected the nature of his ministry. He no longer held high office in the Methodist Church or at inter-church level and he concluded that this made him less newsworthy: 'By 1975 I had become one of the lower forms of ecclesiastical animal life. No longer a Secretary or President of the Church and now a former Chairman of the Belfast District, public utterances were not expected from me and indeed were, I thought, resented in some quarters on the occasions when something I said was publicised.'

Changing values in what was becoming a more secularized society added to his sense of having a more diminished leadership role. He declares: 'What is more by that date the media were rarely looking for statements by churchmen.'

It is interesting to observe Eric's self-analysis at this stage in his life. It will certainly come as something of a surprise to many of his younger colleagues whose respect and appreciation for him were increasing rather than decreasing. He was increasingly being regarded as a Church statesman of the highest calibre whose ministry, more than most, was appreciated by those both within the Christian Church and outside it.

Invitations to address major conferences or important civic services continued to arrive on Eric's desk but not with the same frequency as before. In March 1975 he preached at a

Special Church Unity Service in St Anne's Church (COI), Dublin, attended by ministers of the Republic's Government. In his sermon, widely reported in the press, he drew attention to the menace of sectarianism: 'Sectarianism in its subtle, sophisticated form, or in its naked viciousness, has been responsible for murders, discrimination and the religious apartheid that are destroying our country. And yet inexplicably the Churches have so far shown little sign that they recognise the monster in their midst.' Eric had been alerting the Church to the dangers of sectarianism since before the outbreak of the Troubles. He and others had been trying unsuccessfully to persuade the Joint Group set up by the Irish Council of Churches and the Hierarchy to mount a study of sectarianism. In St Anne's he decided to go public in calling for greater action by the Churches: 'What Ireland needs urgently is a programme to combat sectarianism and we need every Irish Church involved in that programme up to the hilt.'

His appeal appeared to fall on deaf ears! The Irish Churches did not heed his call for some considerable time. Since his participation at the Social Study Conference at Dungarvan he knew that the secular world was beginning to wake up to the problem. Not so the Churches! It caused him great pain: 'Tragically it took another seventeen years before such a study appeared under the aegis of the Department of Community Affairs of the Irish Inter-Church Meeting. That study revealed all the insidious poisonous characteristics of sectarianism: sadly the programme to combat it has still to be mounted.'

Why were the Churches so slow to move on this issue? Eric does not address this question but his concluding comments on this topic at this point in his Notes may indirectly give us the answer: 'There is a streak of sectarianism in all of us not very far beneath the surface. None of us, individual or Church, can afford to be complacent.'

On Saturday, 18 October 1975 Eric gave the address at a Service for World Peace in Westminster Cathedral in which Christians, Muslims, Hindus and Buddhists all participated. He began carefully by stating what he believed they all held in common: 'We are declaring our belief in God. We are not saying that we all believe the same things. We are not saying that we are united. Quite the contrary. We are declaring our manifold and important differences of belief and practice.'

Despite their differences they were all united in their desire for peace and real peace meant a new regard for the value of human life: 'Human life has been cheapened. Human beings are today the pawns and stock-in-trade of hi-jackers, terrorists and kidnappers.' Eric acknowledged that Northern Ireland was a glaring example of this cheapening of human life: 'In my own country the value of life has been debased and we must re-establish the basic right of every man to life. You can let a man rot in prison or in a ghetto or an internment camp and he would still be alive. So life itself is not enough.' He offered a succinct definition of the human rights to which everyone was entitled and suggested that this was an objective which would unite them in prayer: 'Every man has the right to the full life, a right to participate in the significant decisions which affect his life, his family and his future. And that must be what we pray for – or our prayers mean nothing.'

Paramilitary activity in early January 1976 ensured a chilling reception to the new year. On 4 January two Catholics were murdered at their farmhouse near Whitecross, South Armagh and another three Catholic men were killed by loyalist gunmen at Ballydugan, County Down. In a possible act of retaliation on 5 January ten Protestant workers were murdered by the IRA at Kingsmills, South Armagh, as they returned home from work in a minibus.[3]

Eric was alarmed about the escalating level of violence. Writing in the *Methodist Recorder* on 10 January he warned that the country was on the brink of civil war:

> Make no mistake about it! Ulster is on the brink. By the time these words are in print, there may be no brink left.

> Everything adds up to a crisis greater than anything yet known. Civil war is more possible now than at any time since the 1920s. One Loyalist paramilitary organisation has openly declared its preparedness, if

driven to it, to engage in all-out war, where the final victory will be hollow for the few survivors.

> The long years of blasted hopes have now brought the bloody murders of the New Year, and now there is an aftermath of despair on the part of ordinary people.[4]

Not surprisingly Eric was also concerned about the deadlocked political situation. Elections to the Constitutional Convention the previous May had given the UUUC 47 of the 78 seats, a result which appeared to guarantee implacable opposition to the British Government proposals for power-sharing. This was borne out when the UUUC used its majority to persuade the Convention in November 1975 to accept its call for a return to the majority rule system. On the Irish dimension issue the UUUC report recommended 'good neighbourly relations' but rejected anything resembling 'institutionalized associations' with the Republic of Ireland.[5]

He saw the continuing violence as militating against any movement towards community co-operation or the development of shared government. In this situation, he told his *Methodist Recorder* readers, politicians were unwilling to take risks:

> Politically, the more things change, the less the politicians seem to change. Of course, all of them are on thin and tricky ice. If only they realised the need to give – just the slightest bit. If only they saw themselves as leaders, rather than as representatives.

The emergence of the Peace People in August 1976 inspired a level of hope among many. The movement had been prompted by massive public reaction to a tragic incident in West Belfast on 10 August which resulted in the death of three young children. Mrs Anne Maguire had been out with her three children – the youngest a six-month-old boy in his pram – when a gunman's getaway car crashed into them in Andersonstown. The driver had been shot dead by troops, causing the car to run out of control, mount the pavement and crush two of the children to death against a fence. The third child died the following day.[6] It was the children's aunt, Mairead Corrigan, and two others, Betty Williams and Ciaran McKeown, who founded the peace movement, declaring their methods and objectives as 'a non-violent movement towards a just and peaceful society'.[7] With cross-community support encouraging their initiative, they organized marches and rallies in Belfast, Dublin, London and throughout Northern Ireland.

The 13th World Methodist Council was held in Dublin at the same time as the Peace People were emerging in Belfast. Eric and Barbara managed to support both organisations! On Friday, 20 August Eric addressed a plenary session of the Council which met in the large hall of the Royal Dublin Society at Ballsbridge but next day both of them travelled back to Belfast and joined the peace marchers on their way to a rally – with an estimated attendance of 20,000 – in Ormeau Park.

Eric's address at the World Methodist Council followed a similar pattern to those he gave when speaking to people from overseas: an historical analysis of the origins of the Northern Ireland problem followed by an assessment of the role of the Churches in the situation. But he also included an appeal to the gunmen: 'If they love this country as some say they do, I ask, for God's sake let us live in peace, let us put our energies and our abilities into healing and binding the sores and wounds that have destroyed and ravaged this country for centuries.'

He concluded his address with the suggestion that a World Methodist Peace Prize should be initiated. Next day the Conference implemented his suggestion, deciding that the first recipient should be from Ireland. Sadie Patterson, a Trades Union activist and tireless peace worker, was the one chosen.

Violence in Ireland, the report of the fifth Working Party set up by the Irish Council of Churches/Roman Catholic Church Joint Group on Social Questions, was undoubtedly one of the most significant inter-church publications of the 1970s.[8] The report was launched on 7 October 1976 and received fairly wide press coverage in both Britain and Ireland.

Dr Cahal Daly, at that time Bishop of Ardagh and Clonmacnois, and Eric were Joint Chairmen of the Working

Party, which included some of the best thinkers in all of the Churches: Mr Denis P. Barritt, the Rt. Hon. David W. Bleakley, the Revd Robert N. Brown, Mr Jerome Connelly, the Revd Dr Michael Crowe, Professor Norman J. Gibson, the Very Revd Dr James L.M. Haire, Miss Kathleen Kelly, the Revd Michael McGrail, the Revd Dr Kevin McNamara, the Revd Columb O'Donnell and Dr A. Stanley Worrall.

The Working Party had started its work in early 1974 and had met in 14 plenary sessions. However, the interaction of so many brilliant minds on the subject of 'Violence' does not appear to have made it any easier to reach agreement! Eric comments: 'At times it looked as if no report of any kind would be possible or that the most we could hope for would be majority and minority reports.'

Possibly the friendship and good understanding which existed between the co-chairmen may have been a major factor in the group's ability finally to reach agreement. Eric and Dr Daly had known each other since the late 1950s when they were both part of the informal monthly inter-church clergy group in Belfast brought together by Robert Murphy. Their friendship had continued and, indeed, grown as time passed. Dr Daly had invited Eric to attend his consecration as Bishop of Ardagh and Clonmacnois in 1967 and had understood when Eric explained that his attendance could cause difficulty in some sections of the Methodist Church. In January 1973 – during the Week of Prayer for Christian Unity – Dr Daly had invited Eric to an Ecumenical Service in the cathedral and then later to deliver an address in the parish hall. Eric had apologized for not being able to attend the service but said that he would be there for the talk. Later Eric told Dr Daly that he had actually been standing at the back of the cathedral during the service. Dr Daly recalls: 'Eric explained to me with great sadness that he had in fact been present incognito in the back of the Cathedral and he felt very deeply the pain of being unable to take public part in the service in his robes. The reason was that he felt this would cause so much pain to some of his cousins and extended family and that he did not feel he should inflict this pain on them because they simply wouldn't understand and would be very upset by Eric's taking part at that time in Roman Catholic worship.'[9]

These experiences and others had created a special bonding between the two men. Dr Daly affirms this very clearly: 'You know how it is that that kind of chemistry exists between people who naturally feel an affinity and Eric for me was always one of these.'

The report – 128 pages in total – was very comprehensive in its analysis of the causes of violence and how the Churches should respond to it. It certainly never attempted to exculpate the Churches from its share of the responsibility for the violence. This was clear when it asked direct questions regarding the underlying reasons for the community's inability to establish consensus government:

> But if the efficacy of 'majority rule' depends, in Western democracies on a voluntary consensus of the whole people or society, then how far is the lack of consensus, indeed the deep division of allegiance, to be equated with a religious division – a division between Catholics and Protestants? How far are the terrorists of both sides 'extensions of us', in the sense that we have made do with an uneasy co-existence where we should have sought long since a positive reconciliation? Is terrorism a rejection of the ethos of our society? Or is it, as some of us would regretfully think, a manifestation of that ethos?[10]

Both Eric and Dr Daly – and, indeed, most members of the Working Party – had been wanting the Churches to initiate a programme to combat sectarianism. Underlining the need for such a programme it went some way in laying the foundations for it when it made seven specific proposals to the Churches:

1. The Churches and their members must *act justly themselves.*

2. The Churches and their members must *uncover injustice fearlessly* whether perpetrated by political

institutions or by other interests or groups in the community.

3. The Churches must be prepared to *come to the aid of victims of injustice.*

4. The Churches should *encourage and prepare their members to take legitimate action to overcome injustice.*

5. The Churches cannot escape the obligation *to give guidance to their members about methods of direct action alternative to violence,* and not open to the same condemnation.

6. The most distinctive task confronting the Churches is to *promote and support reconciliation.* Reconciliation will mean acknowledging our own sins, being ready to forgive wrongs done against us and recognising that we have all, as individuals and institutions, things to repent of – acts of omission, words ill-spoken and acquiescence in evil acts.

7. [The Churches must encourage] *Community Development and Reconciliation.*

Eric was both pleased and disappointed with the reception the Churches gave to the report. Some things the Churches tried to implement. An early direct result was the setting up of the Peace Education Programme by the Irish Council of Churches in conjunction with the Catholic Commission on Justice and Peace, with its subsequent study guides and projects for schools and youth groups. An indirect result was the development of the Northern Ireland Department of Education programme of Education for Mutual Understanding. And Cahal Daly introduced an ecumenical emphasis into the Down and Connor schools when he became bishop of that diocese in 1982. However, there is no mistaking his overall sense of disappointment at the lack of action by the Churches: 'The Irish Churches have yet to tackle individually and jointly the threat to the credibility of the faith posed by their insistence on going their separate ways. There continues to be failure to tackle the different facets of the implications of the gospel. I am aware now as I have always been of the distinctions that divide us and I know that they must not be blurred or ignored but I long for the day when all of us will be willing to do together those things that conscience does not demand that we do separately.'

In the spring of 1977 Eric found himself involved in an embarrassing personal situation at the Irish Inter-Church Meeting held in the Ballymascanlon Hotel, near Dundalk. In the morning session he had made a plea for much greater concentration by the Churches on the more difficult and divisive issues. He suggested a well-planned 'Christian Peace Summit' which would need to be more than 'a well-publicized ecclesiastical cosmetic exercise'. His speech was followed by a strong protest from Bishop Eamonn Casey of Galway who asserted that Eric was endeavouring to pressurize the Conference. Eric recalls: 'I was completely taken aback by his broadside, especially as we had formed a good relationship, having shared not only a session with him at the first Ballymascanlon Conference but also by having shared a youth vigil in Downpatrick Cathedral at 3 o'clock in the morning of a previous St Patrick's Day. Suspecting that he was speaking for more than himself, I was completely at a loss.'

Later he discovered what lay behind Casey's intervention. Prior to the session, one of the Church press officers had asked Eric if he intended to speak. When Eric replied in the affirmative, the press officer enquired if he could have a copy of what he was going to say. 'I facilitated him, in all good faith, thinking that it would be used for press purposes only.' What Eric did not know was that it had been copied and circulated to a number of those present before he spoke. 'There was no good reason for it not being made available but had I known I would certainly have made my wish clear not in any way to pressurise.'

Over the lunch interval Eric thought hard and long about what he should do and at the beginning of the afternoon session he requested permission to make a personal statement. Casey's response was favourable: 'As soon as I had finished Eamonn Casey went straight to the podium and in a most warm-hearted speech accepted my statement unreservedly, saying that he would not in any way wish anything to come between him and his friend.'

The *Irish Press,* reporting the incident, said: 'The whole episode had about it an air of unreality, and even gave rise immediately after the end of the conference to questions about the usefulness of these meetings.' The correspondent went on to suggest that Ballymascanlon might justifiably be seen as an ecclesiastical 'talking shop'. Eric felt he had been involved in an awkward and embarrassing incident. He reflected: 'Whether as much was learned from it as should have been, I am not too certain.'

Barbara felt keenly the suffering of people affected directly by the years of community violence. In the early summer of 1976 she started to jot down in an old diary what she imagined were the thoughts and feelings of the dying, the bereaved, the injured, and other ordinary Ulster people. She didn't tell any other member of the family what she was doing. For a long time it was a secret she kept to herself. It was her son David who made the discovery! He was at university at the time: 'I would come into the house and say, "I'm home", and get an automatic reply. Mum would come out of the room, wherever she was, and greet me.' Then, on a number of occasions, he noted there was a delay and thought it was a bit strange. Some days he noticed the housework hadn't been done as well as it normally was. Then slowly he discovered his mother's secret: 'Once or twice as I was approaching the kitchen I could hear a shuffling of papers and a drawer being closed. One day she wasn't quick enough! I said, "What is this? What is this?" and asked her to take out the papers from the drawer. She said they were only some scribbling, some jottings.'

David asked his mother to read what she had been writing. As she read one or two of her poems they both started to cry: 'She was crying, and I was crying. I said, "Mum, this is very good; you've got to do something about this."'[11] Other members of the family were supportive and encouraged her to get the poems published. *Christian Journals* brought out the first edition of *Embers From the Fires of Ulster* in 1977. The poem

'Little Belfast Girl' illustrates the sense of fear which many a child experienced during the 1970s:

> I'm a little Belfast girl –
> I'm frightened.
> When the doorbell rings at night –
> I'm so frightened.
> When Mum and Dad are late,
> Or a stranger's at our gate –
> I'm frightened.
>
> When I'm going off to school –
> I'm frightened.
> Though I never break that rule –
> I'm too frightened.
> When they're kissing me goodbye,
> though I hold my head up high –
> I'm frightened.
>
> We leave Mummy all alone –
> I'm frightened.
> I can't use the telephone –
> I'm too frightened.
> I don't stay at school to play
> And as I run home all the way –
> I'm frightened.
>
> If we do go out at night –
> I'm frightened.
> In our street there's not a light –
> I'm frightened.
> Army jeeps go racing by,
> helicopters in the sky,
> and I know the reason why –
> I'm frightened.[12]

Towards the end of June Eric addressed what was known as the Methodist 'Big Meeting' in Durham Cathedral. He appreciated the privilege of speaking in this historic cathedral:

'It was a daunting but memorable experience to speak from that famous pulpit.'[13]

In September he once again teamed up with Bishop Cahal Daly when they spoke at a Methodist District Conference held in Radcliff Hall, Sandymount, Dublin. Eric's address was entitled 'The Opportunities and Difficulties of Co-operation'. Throughout his speech he centred on the need for conviction when attempting co-operation. Six things, he suggested, were needed:

1. An awareness of the nature of modern society and the place of the church and religion in it. We must take nothing for granted in a world which increasingly thinks it can do without God.

2. A realisation that the attack is on us all – the good of one is the good of all. The loss of one is the loss of all. If Roman Catholicism were to disappear from Ireland – it is doubtful if the Protestant churches would benefit. It is more likely that they would disappear as well. If Protestants forsake their churches – it is not very likely that they would flock into Catholic churches.

3. Acceptance, not only of the desirability, but the necessity of common witness for the sake of survival.

4. A realisation that Ireland, North and South, for the sake of any meaningful future, needs that mutual relationship.

5. A new honesty about each other's ecclesiology and Christian bona fides. Meaningful and honest co-operation must be motivated by more than the need to survive.

6. A new awareness of what 'membership in Christ' means for all of us.[14]

In the course of his address Eric referred very openly to his own pilgrimage in coming to a better understanding of other Christians:

I, like all of us, am a creature of my environment. For too long I lived in our divided society and my eyes were blinkered. Sometimes I saw and did not realise. Other times I did not see, and because I did not see, I did not realise. Today it is different. I have seen, and now I know as I did not know then, 20 years ago, what our divisions have done to us. And because I have seen and realised, I dare not stand idly by. The call is clear and I must try to make an answer, however imperfect or hesitating that answer may be.[15]

The address was published in full in the October and November editions of *The Methodist Newsletter* so its message reached a wider public than the 70 or so members attending the District Conference.

Eric and Barbara were given VIP status when they visited the USA in November at the invitation of the Board of Global Ministries of the United Methodist Church and the National Council of Churches. Thanks to the good offices of the Revd David Bowman of the NCC Irish Desk and by courtesy of the British Consulate General, they were met immediately they got off their plane by New York-based diplomatic staff, thereby avoiding the hassle of immigration and customs procedures. The visit had been under consideration for some time and when the time finally arrived both Eric and Barbara found that a hectic schedule of meetings, services, lectures, and radio and television interviews had been planned.

Eric preached in Memphis (Tennessee), Manchester (Connecticut) and Evanston (Illinois). He spoke in Memphis at a National Pax Christi Conference and in a number of universities; he addressed the staff and student body at Garrett Theological Seminary in Evanston, and spoke at the Law Faculty of the North Western University and the Chicago Council of Churches.

Three speaking engagements he particularly appreciated: addressing the National Council of Churches Annual Meeting in New York; addressing a political 'think tank', also in New York; and finally, meeting and speaking with a number of groups when they were in Washington DC.

On many of these occasions Barbara read some of her poems. Everywhere they went they found an intense interest in what was happening in Northern Ireland. Eric comments: 'I tried as best I could to give a balanced and objective account of the causes and reasons for the turmoil and unrest. They were most keen to learn what the Churches were doing in this situation.'

Eric's 22 years as Superintendent of the Belfast Central Mission came to an end in June 1979. On 22 June members and friends of the Grosvenor Hall congregation met to celebrate his ministry among them and to express their thanks for all he had done for them over that time. But it was not only thanks to Eric but to Barbara and the whole Gallagher family.

It is not surprising that the main feature of the entertainment that evening was music by the Grosvenor Hall Military Band. The Mission Secretary, Mr William H. Patterson, chaired the proceedings and following the musical entertainment invited various people to pay tribute to Eric's wide-ranging ministry. Mr Jack Weir recalled the circumstances of Eric's call to the ordained ministry and also his appointment to the Mission congregation in 1957. Mention was made of the various honours that had been heaped on their minister: the Presidency of the Methodist Church; an OBE from the Queen; and an Honorary Doctorate from the Queen's University of Belfast. However, it was not a purely Methodist gathering: Professor James R. Boyd from the Union Theological College, Belfast, and Dr Arthur H. Butler, Bishop of Connor, also paid their tributes to Eric.

Eric concluded his ministry on Sunday, 24 June. There were large congregations at both morning and evening services that day. The Mission records include these comments: 'For all of us it was a sad day, but a day of grateful thanksgiving for the ministry of such a man who had been with us for 22 years, and for most of us was not only minister but friend and counsellor. In all the work he has been fully sustained and supported by Mrs Gallagher and their family.'[16]

15

Family

Family matters to me. Family has always mattered. I have been fortunate in a supremely happy marriage and we were both grateful, and I still am, for our three children whose love and support to both of us have been outstanding.

Eric Gallagher: his unpublished
Autobiographical Notes

The ties of love and loyalty within the Gallagher family were very strong. This was the unit which gave him the love and security he needed in order to engage in his wide-ranging ministry. His unpublished Prayer Notes, which record his daily prayers and meditations during part of the 1970s, include frequent appreciative references to his family. They affirm the depth of love which he had for Barbara and each of their three children: Ruth, Helen and David. On Saturday, 18 December 1976 he wrote: 'I'm happy tonight at the prospect of Helen coming home. The family will be together again – complete. The noise and conversation will make it hard to concentrate on any one of them. But you know, God, how it is. You know what fatherhood – parenthood – means.'[1]

Occasionally Eric referred to little incidents at home to illustrate a point he was making in a sermon or short address. Speaking on Ulster Television's 'End The Day' slot on Sunday, 2 October 1960 he told his viewers about a book which one of his daughters was reading: 'One night about three weeks ago, long after she had gone to bed, I went upstairs to get something. On my way up I saw a light under her bedroom door and wondering if something was wrong I opened the door quietly. But I needn't have worried. "I'm just reading," she said, and she showed me this book of children's poetry by Robert Louis Stevenson. "Would you like me to show you the ones I like?" she asked. I said "Yes".' Eric went on to name the poems his daughter liked and read from one of them to make the point he wanted to share with his television audience.

The love which Eric felt for his family was clearly reciprocated. Helen expresses the feeling vividly: 'Our whole family was bathed in love. We were so aware of how much Mum and Dad loved each other despite Dad being out of the house so much. We knew how much we all mattered to him.'[2]

Eric's long hours of working might well have affected the relationship of love within the family. But this was not the case. His work routine appeared to mirror that of his father: he worked in the mornings – after 1957 this meant a daily trip to the Grosvenor Hall; returned home for lunch; out again in the afternoon, returning for evening meal; and out in the evening to attend some church organisation or meeting.

He may even have worked longer hours than his father! 'RH' played golf on Monday mornings but the only golf Eric played was the pre-Conference golf tournament – even this was denied him while he was Secretary of the Conference – and the early-morning rounds of golf he played with David while on holiday in Portstewart.

Eric was conscious to some degree of the problem created by his long hours of working. He admits: 'Too often during the years of my active ministry I was conscious of the lack of time I could give to my family. This was particularly true of the period when I was Secretary of the Conference and of the Church at large coupled with the superintendency of the Mission.' He had hoped that after his Presidential year, 1967-68, he would have more time to spend with the family but he declares that circumstances prevented it: 'In the autumn of 1968 the Civil Rights movement was gaining momentum. The dream of more family and leisure time was illusory.'

He must have been aware of Barbara's concern about the effect that his long hours of working would have on his health. We will recall that during the period when he carried the dual responsibility of being Secretary of the Church and Superintendent of BCM, he had arrived home one evening to find that she had enlisted the support of the family doctor in an effort to persuade him to reduce his workload.[3] At that time he had acknowledged he worked an 84-hour week.

One wonders if Barbara was also experiencing a degree of loneliness. Most clergy worked long hours and were frequently engaged in church meetings in the evenings in addition to daytime work commitments. But few, if any, worked an 84-hour week! Was the Methodist Church at fault in expecting Eric to cope with both the secretaryship of the Church and the superintendency of the Mission? Or was Eric personally responsible for accepting this heavy burden for nine years? In the 1960s he made it clear to the Church that the dual responsibility was too much for any one minister to carry and his successor as MCI Secretary, Harold Sloan, was appointed full-time to the post.

Eric's sense of call as a servant of his Lord and the Church may have been the reason for his shouldering this heavy workload for so long. And it may also explain why things did not noticeably change after his Presidential year. With the outbreak of the Troubles in 1969 he continued his long hours of working! He felt that the problem of violence in the Northern Ireland community and the suffering which it brought demanded a major part of his time and energy. He believed he had a specific mission to fulfil. Barbara knew that the work he was doing was important and she supported him in every possible way, but there must have been occasions when she longed to have him spend more time at home.

Ruth, the eldest – not really the eldest, as Barbara had had a stillbirth prior to the birth of Ruth and this little one was always remembered in the family – had her own method of ensuring she enjoyed her father's company. During the school holidays she accompanied him in the car when he went visiting: 'This was a big treat. He was very strict about confidentiality so I never knew what he was going to do, but it was a chance to talk with him about the issues that were around. He was very concerned about justice. When visiting Crumlin Road prison I used to sit and wait in the car. He would come out and we would talk about capital punishment and all sorts of issues. I think I learned an awful lot from him.'[4]

Ruth suggests that these and other chats she had with her father possibly had an influence on her decision to follow a career in the Social Services. She is now a Senior Social Worker married to David Twyble, a teacher, and is stepmother to Miriam. Her comments about her love for her father reflect the feelings which her sister and brother also had for him: 'I had a very close relationship with my father, a very great respect and love for him, and I thought he had that for me.'

The long hours Eric worked did not particularly trouble David. During the holidays he saw much more of his father and felt he came closer to him at these times. He was never conscious of feeling deprived of his company during the rest of the year: 'I wasn't annoyed about it. I wasn't concerned about it. That was just the way it was, that was family life.'

Helen was not so accepting in her attitude to her father's intense work routine: 'Of course we resented a lot of the church mid-week meetings and things that he had to go to. I think I probably resented the fact that he didn't make it to school functions unless he was actually going as a Governor or perhaps an invited guest.' She was particularly upset that he never made an effort to go to parents' evenings: 'I remember asking why he wouldn't go to parents' evenings. He would just say, "Well, if I want to know something I can just ask so-and-so." Yes, there were tensions, there's no doubt!'

Perhaps the explanation as to why this family was 'bathed in love' really lies with their mother! Barbara was the central figure in the family, always available to her children. Ruth comments: 'My mother was just a remarkable person – a very selfless person. Somebody whom I never really can ever remember looking for anything for herself. Her family, I think, was her Number One priority. Mother was the central part of the home.' Helen echoes similar feelings: 'We just adored Mum and we knew she utterly adored us. She lived for us.'

Barbara, like many women of her generation, had never taken part-time or full-time employment and was able to devote her time to the care of her family. Her children are convinced that had circumstances been different – a possible reference to the long hours Eric worked – Barbara had the talents and gifts to further her skills in a number of areas. But she chose to be at home. Her own mother had died when she was eight and her father, Edwin, had decided to move with his children – Emily, George and Barbara – into the Spence family home at Magheralin, joining his sister May and brother Howard. Barbara's decision to be full-time at home for her own family was possibly due to her experience of missing her own mother.

Hospitality to friends and, at times, strangers was a feature of the Gallagher home. Before the outbreak of the Troubles overnight hospitality was sometimes given to people in particular need. Visiting speakers at Mission anniversaries or special services were entertained at the manse and this would mean overnight hospitality if the speaker was from England. From time to time Eric would bring a colleague or friend home for tea, sometimes arriving without advance notice to Barbara.

Dr Colin Morris was a friend the family loved to entertain both when he travelled over from England or when he was living in Northern Ireland. David remembers: 'We had a tremendous affection for Colin Morris; for a while he was almost part of the family. We all sparked remarkably with him.'

This friendship with Colin Morris really developed from three successive visits in 1973 when he stayed in the Gallagher manse. Wesley's Chapel in City Road, London, where Morris was minister, had been declared unsafe for congregational worship and its whole future was under review. Consequently Morris felt himself at a loose end until a decision was reached. He had phoned Eric with the offer that he might be able to come over to Belfast with small teams of ministers who would work alongside their Irish colleagues for a week or two. Eric found that Belfast ministers welcomed the suggestion and the scheme was soon up and running. Morris came over with each of the teams.

Eric recalls an evening during one of these visits:

> One night will remain in my memory. He was always difficult to get to bed. If he could not be persuaded to go

upstairs before midnight he was certain to stay down for a long time afterwards. On this particular small-hours morning he and Barbara got into an animated argument about the distance from the manse to Dr Stanley Worrall's house in Adelaide Park. Barbara argued quite correctly that it was two or three hundred yards. Colin would have nothing of it: it was for him at least half a mile away. They argued the toss until at length Barbara, I think, said that the only way to settle the argument was for them to pace it out. They put their coats on and out they went into the cold air of the early morning.

Barbara took a great interest in the congregations with which Eric served, attending women's meetings and other organisations. Activities in the Belfast Central Mission often provided opportunities when she could don her apron and share in the work. During the various refugee crises of 1969 and the early 1970s she took control of the situation and made sure that people were as comfortable as possible and that meals were provided for everyone. Helen is unstinting in appreciation for her mother's work when the refugees were given shelter in the Grosvenor Hall: 'Mum was fantastic; she just got in and washed the loos and worked alongside everybody. She was wonderful with the families. She had a real empathy with them, especially the women.'

After Eric became Superintendent of Belfast Central Mission the Gallagher family Christmas was one which, for the most part, they shared with others. On Christmas Eve the family was involved in the annual street collection for the Mission: Eric collected; Barbara was busy catering; and the children helped in whatever way possible. On the evening of Christmas Eve the family opened some of their presents because they knew that the next day would be spent mostly at the Hall.

On Christmas morning they went to the service in the Hall and then back to the manse where they opened the remaining presents. They then returned to the Hall to help prepare and serve the men's Christmas dinner. It, in turn, was followed by entertainment provided by members of the Male Voice Choir and others. The afternoon's festivities were hardly over before it was time to be in the Large Hall for the Christmas Night concert. One of Eric's Christmas memories of the early years at the Hall is of the children playing in the classrooms and of their being looked after by relatives: 'In those years the Greenwood [his colleague at the Mission] and Gallagher children did not know what it was to spend Christmas Day in their own homes.'

Holidays in the month of August were definitely a time for fun and family bonding. There were a number of holidays in Kerry and one in Donegal. Crossing the Irish Sea, they had holidays in Wales or in Devon and Cornwall. France was another favourite. Sometimes they went camping; on other occasions they may have swapped houses, rented a caravan or holiday house, or taken bed and breakfast. They always went away for a month. Eric had a clear conscience about this: 'At least I had no hesitation in most years in taking what holidays we could manage with integrity. They gave me the chance of spending long hours and days of companying and playing with them and, I would hope, of leaving some influence on them.'

In the summer of 1961 they had a memorable camping holiday in Oslo. Eric had been chosen as a delegate to the World Methodist Conference and he carefully planned things so that Barbara and the family could travel with him. Each delegate had been offered £50 to cover all the travelling expenses. He bought a six-feet-long tent and set off for Oslo via Stranraer, Dover, Calais, Belgium, Holland, West Germany, Denmark and Sweden and got there safely. Harold Sloan, using his experience in military service and holidaying in Europe, had assured Eric that they would be able each morning to wash dirty clothes before breakfast, hang them on the tent ropes and pack them dry after they had eaten. It didn't quite turn out as Sloan had suggested: 'In the event we reached Oslo with a car load of wet clothes. It rained practically all the way.'

On their first night camping in Europe, Helen got lost: 'I went off to get water in the Dutch campsite and I got lost. I think I was wondering around the woods for about an hour, absolutely distraught. I wouldn't talk to anybody although many people were trying to help me. Then suddenly I heard my name being called and I realised Dad was looking for me.' The sense of comfort and security she received on being found by her father was important for her: 'Funnily enough, many of my memories from holidays are actually of Dad lifting you up, just protecting you if there was any kind of danger or fright or worry.'

They camped in Oslo for a week prior to the World Methodist Conference and then moved into a Bible College for the week of the Conference. Eric was proud of the fact that the total travelling costs for the family exceeded the £50 allowance by only £6!

Even on holidays Eric could not stop working! He made sure that the family got a portion of his time each day but then he would turn to his work. After 1969, he found it difficult to absent himself from Belfast. Holidays were not always possible. He had bought a caravan and kept it at the Juniper Hill Caravan Park, near Portstewart. It was on holiday in Portstewart that he frequently jotted down thoughts relating to the violence and the political situation. One summer he wrote A Testament of Faith and Hope for Ulster. On another holiday he wrote Creed and Deed in Northern Ireland. Neither document was ever published.

Family prayers were a feature of the Gallagher home when the children were younger. Before going out to school in the morning the family would gather round the breakfast table and Eric would read a story from a Children's Story Book; this would be followed by prayers. When there was not time for prayers at the table, they would have short prayers at the front door before going out to school. As the children got older they rebelled a little at the practice and, rather than impose family prayers, Eric stopped them. Ruth, Helen and David respected their father for his sensitivity to their feelings.

Both parents did their best to protect the family from the occasional abusive phone call. Sometimes the measures they took succeeded, sometimes not. However, bomb scares could not be hidden! One bomb scare occurred when Eric was confined to bed. Ruth relates what happened:

That particular night Dad was really unwell. He normally wasn't unwell but, from time to time, he would get a slipped disc in his back. At times when he was absolutely exhausted this disc would move and he would be confined to bed. He really couldn't move.

In the middle of the night the doorbell rang and it was the army to say that, if they were right, they thought that what they saw outside our house was a device. We would have to get out. They came up to see Dad in his bed and said he would have to get out. He said he was prepared to move to the back of the house, and the family would go. They said, 'No, you must go too.' So several soldiers came in and they assisted him out. They put him flat on his back in a Landrover which they had driven up to the kitchen door. We all piled in and were taken to the Ulster Defence Regiment's Headquarters at Windsor Park. Our neighbours on either side were told they had to get out too, so we all ended up in our dressing-gowns in the middle of the night.

The post-Feakle period was a particularly difficult time which had repercussions for the family, though it was some time before Eric realized the extent to which his own children suffered because of their father's involvement in talking to the IRA. He writes: 'Ruth and Helen, the former working in Social Services and the latter temporarily in the Civil Service, quickly found out what ostracism meant and yet they never breathed a word about the hostility they encountered. David was at university and had, I believe, an easier time.'

Eric and Barbara were proud of their children and valued the continuing links with them after they married and set up their own homes. Ruth, David and Miriam Twyble live in Lisburn. Helen graduated with a Modern Languages degree from Trinity College, Dublin, her father's *alma mater*, but eventually decided on a nursing career. In the early summer of 1979 she married Alan Shiel, a personnel officer. They live in Dublin and have three children: Sarah, Michael and Eoin. David graduated in politics from the Queen's University of

Belfast, and decided on a teaching career. In 1987 he married another teacher, Norma Wilson. They now live in Lisburn with their two sons, Jonathan and Neil. Both David and Norma teach at the Methodist College, Belfast, where David is Vice-Principal.

Barbara and Eric were very fond of their grandchildren and enjoyed the time spent with them. They particularly enjoyed family gatherings, their birthdays and holidays. Helen speaks of the special way in which her father related to each one of them: 'He adored them and each one individually, recognising their strengths and needs. He enjoyed their company immensely and was greatly amused by them as well. He often wrote poems and nonsense verses for them.'

After 'RH' died in 1965 Eric's siblings looked up to him as the head of the wider Gallagher family circle. They are all now retired but pay tribute to the interest he always took in their families.

Evelyn and her husband, Joe Pope, have had an interesting life. Joe finished up as Vice-Chancellor of the University of Aston while Evelyn kept her eye on the successful Technical Equipment company they jointly founded many years ago. They live in Nottingham.[5] After serving in the army during the Second World War, Herbert was for many years senior surgeon in Ards hospital. On retirement in 1977 he and Dorothy took up residence at Quinton Bay, near Portaferry but moved a year later to Comber. Mabel and John Frost continue to live in Holywood where so much of their married life was spent and where John was Principal of Sullivan Upper School. Helen married James (Jimmy) Todd and went with him to Kenya where he worked for some years in veterinary and tea research before returning to Northern Ireland. The remainder of his working life was spent in the service of the Department of Agriculture in the Queen's University of Belfast from which he retired in 1984, having been Professor of Agriculture, Chemistry and Food Science. They live in the Todd family home in Boardmills.

16

Retirement

A prophet Church will analyse the issues of the day, the small ones as well as big ones, in the light of the gospel. Its judgments will be based on Biblical truth and insights. It is no part of the Church's task to tell politicians and economists how to do their work. Its obligation is to state clearly the Christian principles for a just society. When those principles are ignored, the Church, if it is true to its Lord, will say clearly that the laws of God are flouted.

Eric Gallagher, author of the Pastoral Address
to the Methodist Church in Ireland,
Reports and Agenda, 1990

In the early 1970s Eric and Barbara had wisely begun to consider the purchase of a bungalow for their retirement. They decided they would like to settle in Portstewart on the north coast. It had a number of attractions: they both liked the area; there had been suggestions of some kind of connection with the New University in Coleraine;[1] they felt it would be wise to get away from the Belfast Central Mission; they thought their family were likely to be in Britain; and some members of their respective family circles had hinted at the possibility of retiring to the Coleraine/Portstewart area.

These considerations seemed compelling at the time, so after some extensive house-searching they purchased Number Six, Sunset Park in Portstewart. It was a beautiful new bungalow with all the accommodation they required and it was reasonably priced. Every window at the back overlooked the bay; there were magnificent views of Castlerock and the cliffs above Downhill as well as the mountains away beyond Lough Foyle in County Donegal. At the front there were also glimpses of the sea above the roof tops in the town below.

They enjoyed the initial experience of retirement: 'At long last we had the thrill of living in our own house, of closing the door each evening in the near certainty of not being disturbed and being free from the phone calls that had dominated our lives for so many years.' They spent time exploring the north coast and found pleasure in being able to do the shopping together. Eric comments: 'We were ecstatically happy.'

Yet within a few years, Eric and Barbara began to reassess their original plan to live in Portstewart. Perhaps this was brought about by his continued involvement with Belfast Central Mission projects, perhaps by his editorship of *The Methodist Newsletter*, perhaps by his voluntary work with various management boards. The fact is that Eric's workload had not, in reality, reduced significantly. His acceptance of various responsibilities – many of which necessitated regular journeys to Belfast, Newcastle and Dublin – soon brought his work commitment to something approaching his pre-retirement level.

In September 1983 they moved to Lisburn, ten miles south of Belfast. The change of location brought with it a change in lifestyle. More demands and requests were made on both of them. Barbara was pleased to become a regular helper at Christian Aid's weekly luncheons in Lisburn. They were able to sign up each year for Adult Education courses in the Queen's University of Belfast and, of course, they were much nearer to their family and brothers and sisters. But they missed Portstewart: 'We missed the quiet and the scenery and the breath-taking walks we had so much enjoyed in the North.'

More significantly there was another change. Eric began to notice little differences in Barbara:

> As the 1980s passed the mid-way mark, life for each of us began to change imperceptibly. In normal circumstances in former days Barbara would have been anxious to entertain our friends. She always would have been determined to return any hospitality we received. The wish to do so seemed to disappear. She seemed to lose her keen interest in people and affairs. She became

less energetic and was content to sit down after a meal in her armchair. She might activate the television set but took no keen interest in any programme. It was all so much out of character. Forgetfulness and general slowing up were increasingly evident.

Barbara saw various consultants during 1991 and 1992. She was seen on a number of occasions by a cardiologist. She was cleared of any heart problem. Then in the summer of 1992 Professor Robert Stout confirmed Eric's fears by diagnosing Alzheimer's disease.

These family circumstances provide the context in which Eric spent his retirement in the 1980s and early 1990s. What then of the voluntary work – with a few exceptions it was all voluntary – which he undertook during this period?

Belfast Central Mission

Dr Norman Taggart, Eric's successor at Belfast Central Mission, asked him to be responsible for the running of Castle Rocklands and the homes at Millisle, both time-consuming jobs. He also asked him to be available for consultation on the business and financial side of the Mission's work. Taggart was grateful for his help, but these were all jobs which required him to travel to Belfast from Portstewart where he lived during the early years of his retirement.

Eric also agreed to take quarterly appointments on the BCM preaching plan. In addition to this commitment he records that he 'found himself' preaching regularly on the Lisburn, Ballynahinch and Coleraine Circuits.

The Blackburn Trust

Another socially-related activity was his work as a Trustee of the Blackburn Trust. Soon after Eric's appointment as Superintendent of Belfast Central Mission in 1957 he had been asked to join the management committee of Blackburn House, a residential hostel for unmarried mothers in Annadale Avenue (South Belfast). When these premises were sold he was invited to become a Governing Trustee – and, for a period, Chairman – of what became known as the Blackburn Trust, which now concentrated for the most part on assisting organisations dealing with women's needs and those of young children.

Eric appears to have enjoyed this work and felt the demands of the Trust to be light.

Publications and the media

Christians in Ulster 1968-1980, published by Oxford University Press in 1982, edited jointly by Eric and Dr Stanley Worrall, ranks as one of the major publications to have been written about the Troubles. Both men, but especially Eric, were significant figures in the late 1960s and 70s, and were well placed to record the history of the contribution – or lack of it – made by Christian people and Churches during this period.

Stanley Worrall had received the initial request from Oxford University Press to write the book. Faced with various pressures on his time – including the chairmanship of the Northern Ireland Arts Council and the restoration of the Grand Opera House after major bomb damage – he asked Eric to share the task with him. Working closely with Worrall enabled Eric to get to know him better: 'Prior to this Stanley Worrall, though a good friend and, until his retirement, a near neighbour, seemed somewhat aloof and hard to know. To work with him, however, became a pleasure and privilege.'

They carefully mapped out 'a plan of campaign'. Each of them would be responsible for certain sections of the proposed book with some chapters to be, as it were, a joint effort. When each of them concluded a draft section, it was submitted to the other for comment or correction with regard to fact or style. Then they met together in Portstewart or Belfast to discuss their findings and corrections. Following this pattern the final draft was eventually completed on time.

Eric's son, David, helped in some of the research.[2] They found the interviews they had with various people particularly interesting. Eric recalls a joint interview they had with Dr William Philbin, the Roman Catholic Bishop of Connor:

Bishop Philbin invited us to have afternoon tea with him in his home at Lisbreen, Somerton Road, Belfast. The interview went well and we spent a couple of hours with him in easy conversation. Coming away, I remarked to Stanley that in my opinion we had learned more than the Bishop really intended to tell us. I thought we should be careful about the use we should make of all the information. Stanley did not see it that way and was convinced that we were free to make use of anything he had said to us. Thirty-six hours later I had a letter from the Bishop. He confessed that in frank conversation with two friends he had temporarily forgotten that they were on business bent. He would be grateful if we were circumspect in our use of what he had talked about and would be appreciative to see anything we might put on paper about the interview before going to print. He assured us that there would be no arbitrary censorship. We respected his wishes.

Another task for which Eric was admirably suited was the writing of *At Points of Need. The story of the Belfast Central Mission 1889-1989.* As the centenary of the Mission approached Dr Taggart and the Mission Committee asked him to write the story of the Mission since its foundation in 1889.[3] It was an important task. BCM had been the first of the city missions initiated by Methodism and had served the city magnificently during this period. There was a good story to tell and Eric told it well. Dr Stanley Worrall, who was asked to write the foreword, comments: 'It is a fascinating story of Christian enterprise and of devotion often bordering on the heroic. It is a significant piece of social history. It is a gallery of portraits. It is a mine of anecdotes, some humorous, some deeply moving.'

Perhaps the heaviest responsibility which Eric undertook during his retirement was his editorship of the *The Methodist Newsletter*, the unofficial monthly publication of the Methodist Church in Ireland. From 1979-95 he was the sole editor – a task which is currently shared by three editors! References to his editorship in his Autobiographical Notes suggest it may have been at times more of a burden than a privilege: 'Thus began sixteen years of absorbing interest but also of allowing nothing, absolutely nothing, to interfere with certain days in each month. It was a difficult discipline. On occasions other commitments had to go by the board.'

Eric had a routine which he followed each month. It was necessary to collect copy as and when it was available in Aldersgate House, bring it home for editorial preparation (to Portstewart until after the summer of 1983), and have it, along with his own contributions, ready for arrival in Newcastle – *The Methodist Newsletter* was printed by *The Mourne Observer* – on a given Tuesday each month. Proofs came back a couple of days later to be corrected and sent back with additional material in good time for all to be ready for him to go to Newcastle to 'put the paper to bed'. Apparently, even when he was living in Portstewart, he never missed a deadline!

When Eric and Barbara moved to Lisburn, both Aldersgate House and *The Mourne Observer* were much more accessible. As Barbara's illness developed, it became inadvisable for her to be left alone and so until she was cared for in a Day Centre, she invariably travelled with Eric to Newcastle. He deeply appreciated the kindness shown by *The Mourne Observer* staff:

> *The Mourne Observer* staff were most considerate to her, made space and a chair available for her to sit, supplied her with magazines which sadly latterly she could hardly read or understand. They made hairdressing appointments for her. At the appropriate time I would bring her to the hairdresser, who phoned the printers when she was ready and I would slip out to collect her and bring her back. Frequently, and almost right up to the end, we would have lunch in Newcastle on *The*

Mourne Observer day. That was something Barbara greatly looked forward to as she did the car run back to Lisburn over the mountains and through Dromara.

In undertaking the editorship of the *The Methodist Newsletter* Eric was making a useful contribution to Methodism but the responsibility also provided him with a means by which he could share his ideas with a wider public. It meant that in retirement he still had a channel through which he could influence others. In his editorials he had the freedom to express his opinion on current topics. He was also free to decide who should be the regular contributors. In essence, although he was answerable to an editorial committee, he was responsible for determining the character of the newspaper.

Under the title 'Sons of this world' his editorial in May 1981 first applauded the fact that the Lord Mayors of Belfast and Dublin had travelled together to the United States to represent their case to the American public: 'Together they have projected a positive image to the American people. Together they have warned the Americans about the corruption of violence and about the danger of giving money that can be used for the furtherance of violence.' He went on to contrast this with the lack of a united front on the part of the Churches who were proclaiming their unity of purpose but failing to put it into practice:

> The Churches do it differently. For ten years and more the Irish Churches have been proclaiming to high heaven that they have much in common; that there is more to unite them than to divide them. They have proclaimed – hands on hearts – that there is no religious war in Ireland. To prove it the Church of Ireland has sent its delegation to the American corridors of power and influence. The Presbyterians are now in full flight and in greater strength on a similar mission. The Methodists, we understand, are to send a one-man team later. Already the comments and questions are coming back from America: If you are all so united, why could you not have sent a united team? Was it not possible to send a joint

Protestant-Roman Catholic team or at least a joint Protestant team?

One can sense Eric's disappointment at what he increasingly felt was evidence of a diminishing enthusiasm for ecumenism. On this occasion he appealed for a sense of integrity on the part of the Churches:

> If it was possible, it should have been done. If it was not possible, the sooner we admit the fact to ourselves and the Americans the better. There are no medals for lack of courage or self-deception. The journey of the Lord Mayors is an uncomfortable judgment on the Churches.

Eric knew that the tide of opinion within the Protestant Churches, and especially within Presbyterianism, had turned against closer ecumenical relationships during the 1970s. In 1978 the Presbyterian Church in Ireland had suspended its membership of the World Council of Churches and two years later had voted to confirm its withdrawal. The public argument used by those who had led the move to withdraw membership centred on the existence of the Special Fund of the Programme to Combat Racism and, in particular, a grant of £43,000 which it had given to the Patriotic Fund in Rhodesia (later renamed Zimbabwe). Such grants, it was alleged, were being given to support terrorism at the very time when the existence of Northern Ireland was being threatened by terrorism. Many of those who wanted to retain membership of the WCC saw this argument as a pretext concealing an increasing anti-ecumenical trend within Presbyterianism.[5]

The issue of the hunger strikes in the Maze Prison – headline news in 1980 and 1981 – also attracted Eric's attention in *The Methodist Newsletter* editorials. In March 1976 the British Government had denied special category status for those convicted of terrorist offences after that date and in March 1980 it had announced the phasing out of special category status to those convicted of terrorist offences irrespective of when the crime was committed. Republican prisoners particularly saw themselves as political prisoners and interpreted the new legislation as a criminalising of their campaign. They protested by refusing to wear prison issue clothes and then extended this by refusing to wash or use toilet facilities, often smearing the cell walls with their own excrement.

The situation was further exacerbated when some of the prisoners decided to go on hunger strike. Seven republican prisoners went on hunger strike on 27 October 1980 and soon these were joined by others. The situation appeared to be in deadlock: Mrs Margaret Thatcher, the British Prime Minister, indicated that it was not an issue on which she was prepared to compromise: 'Let me make one point clear about the hunger strike in the Maze Prison. I want this to be utterly clear. There can be no political justification for murder or any other crime. The government will never concede political status to the hunger-strikers, or to any others convicted of criminal offences in the province.'[6]

On 18 December 1980 this first hunger strike was called off following an appeal from Cardinal Tomás Ó Fiaich who hinted that there might be some movement to grant political status. When this did not materialize another hunger strike commenced on 1 March 1981, led by Mr Bobby Sands, the IRA leader in the Maze Prison.

World attention was further drawn to the issue on 26 March when Sinn Fein nominated Sands as a candidate for the vacant Fermanagh/South Tyrone Westminster seat, following the death of its sitting MP, Mr Frank Maguire. The election, held on 9 April when Sands was 40 days into his hunger strike, gave Sands a narrow victory over Mr Harry West, the Ulster Unionist Party candidate.

Sands died in prison on 5 May and between this and 20 August another nine republican prisoners on hunger strike died. By 3 October the remaining hunger strikers had called off their protest.

Throughout the protest Eric backed the policy of the Methodist Council on Social Welfare and the Irish Methodist Conference – a policy he had helped to shape – which urged the British Government to seek a resolution to the problem but supported its unwillingness to compromise on the question of political status. In the November issue of *The Methodist Newsletter* he welcomed the end of the hunger strike:

> Today, thank God, the Hunger Strike Mark Two is part of history. Before it ended, more young men of their own volition, and still more who had no choice outside the Maze, had been killed as well. It would perhaps be too much to think that the appeal of the Conference had much weight, but honour to the parents and those inside the Roman Catholic Church who, at long last, were able to persuade the strikers to call off their fast.

Before concluding his editorial Eric gave his own succinct analysis of the consequences of the hunger strike and appealed – as he often did – for a leader to emerge who would break the political deadlock:

> Ireland, North and South, whether we like it or not, will never be quite the same again for the strike has polarised the community as nothing else has ever done. Northern Ireland needs someone to break the mould and jump the political rut. If Islam could produce the vision and courage of a President Sadat, why cannot so-called Christian Ulster do the same?

Membership of the Press Council was less demanding but very interesting. Eric had been approached in 1978 to join the Council and he accepted on the understanding that he could not fully participate until he retired the following year. He was the first member of the Council to come from Ireland.

Eric was particularly attracted by the offer because he learned that the internationally famous lawyer, Lord Shawcross of Nuremberg Trial fame, was the Chairman. To his great disappointment when he attended his first meeting of the Council, Shawcross announced that he was presiding at his last meeting!

The membership of the Council was composed of a number of representatives of the national and provincial press and of other members appointed by the Independent Membership Commission. The latter category was drawn from the ranks of retired civil servants, solicitors, social workers, business magnates, academics, educationalists, the National Union of Journalists – and individuals such as the Bishop of Peterborough, a retired admiral and Eric himself.

The Council met monthly and he was impressed that it took its work seriously. Eric was appointed to one of the scrutiny committees. Although the Council had no sanctions beyond insisting that its judgments should be printed in any offending paper it was clear that no paper of repute relished an adverse judgment. Some of the cases they dealt with were petty: others far from it. On occasions he was horrified and appalled at the limit to which cheque-book journalism could and did descend. During his time the Jeremy Thorpe, the Yorkshire Ripper and other notorious cases were considered by the Council.

Eric explains what the work involved:

> Every case, serious or otherwise, called for detailed consideration of lengthy documents, summaries, as well as the original articles complained of, and, to boot, an eventual draft judgment before the case went to the full Council itself. There were also protracted oral hearings during which complainant and complained against faced searching questions from the committee in question. Each member was free and indeed expected to ask his or her quota of questions. It was a rare experience, for instance, for me to put direct questions and supplementaries to Arthur Scargill among the many who appeared before our committee.

When he had completed his term of service on the Religious Advisers' Panel of Independent Television, Eric thought that would be the end of this kind of activity. Not so. In 1980 he was invited by Dr Brum Henderson, Managing Director of Ulster Television, to become a member of what was designed to be a revamped Religious Advisers' Panel for UTV.

For the next five years he sat under Henderson's chairmanship with three other members of the panel: Archbishop Robin Eames, Dr Jack Withers and Monsignor Joseph Maguire, the parish priest of Downpatrick. They were joined in their meetings by senior executives of the company.

Eric is cautious in his assessment of how much they achieved: 'As with the IBA panel in London I always had the feeling that our tacit approval, as distinct from our opinion, was what was required. I may be wrong.' The generous luncheons which always followed their business meetings may have been the carrot to secure their goodwill!

Education

Service on various school and education boards had always taken up a lot of Eric's time. He continued to serve on these boards in his retirement.

Membership of the Belfast Education and Library Board continued until 1985. The 1980s were years of what Eric describes as the 'management of contraction' brought about by the community unrest and consequent demographic changes. It was an unpleasant task for the members of the Board as they had to consider the falling enrolments and, in some instances, the closures of schools, many of which were contested. Accusations of sectarian bias were common. Demonstrations and deputations, public access to Board meetings and at times embarrassing press coverage were the order of the day.

Meetings at times could be quite explosive. Especially memorable for Eric was the shock and uncertain silence at one meeting when an irate loyalist member advocated the incineration of Catholics. He recalls the incident:

> Members just did not know how to react. The incident had occurred during the morning session of an all-day meeting. During the luncheon interval I intimated to the chairman that I would wish to dissociate myself from what had been said. Harold Smith [Chairman] had been as shocked as I was but seemed reluctant to have the

matter raised in the afternoon. However, I felt that I had no option and accordingly early in the afternoon session I said my say. I was very pleased that other members associated themselves with what I said. In the event the episode resulted in a police court case.

Each Board member served on a number of School Management Committees (SMCs, later referred to as Boards of Governors). Over the years Eric had served on several SMCs, though – fortunately – not all at one time. They included the Boys' Model Secondary School, Annadale Grammar School, Gort na Mona Secondary School, Orangefield Secondary School, Kelvin Secondary School and Blythefield Primary School. He comments on his appointment as the first Chairman of Annadale: 'Saying that the position should go "round", I served for one year. My example was not followed.'

Eric became closely involved with two of these schools: Gort na Mona and the Boys' Model, especially the latter.

His connection with the Boys' Model commenced in 1953 and he continued as a Governor until the mid-1980s. For about 12 of these years he served as Chairman of the Board. From his Autobiographical Notes it is clear that Eric had a high regard for the work of this school, its staff and pupils. He speaks warmly of the contributions of its headmasters: 'I came to have the highest regard for the professionalism and dedication of the successive Headmasters with whom I worked: Norman McNeilly, Ernest Davis and David Thompson, who took up office just prior to my retirement from the Board.'

In recognition of Eric's long service with this school, it was fitting that the modern technology building was named The Gallagher Building.

The Methodist Church in Ireland also continued to make demands on Eric's time by appointing him to various education boards: The Board of Education, including the Northern Executive of that Board; the Board of Governors of Edgehill Theological College; and the Board of Governors of the two schools which the Church had set up in the nineteenth century: Wesley College, Dublin, and Methodist College, Belfast.

Wesley College, Dublin, was opened by the Methodist Church in 1845. It has maintained its reputation for excellence since its foundation. Eric joined its Board of Governors in 1978 and served until 1989. Attending the Board meetings helped him to learn more about life in the Republic of Ireland. The Church had appointed him to spend his entire ministry in Belfast and he was conscious of his lack of familiarity with the ideas of people in the South. But membership of the Wesley Board had another special bonus as it gave Eric and Barbara an excuse to stay overnight with Helen and Alan.

Eric deemed one responsibility in the field of education to be particularly special: by far the greatest satisfaction for him when it came to committee work was his connection with the Methodist College, Belfast. His father had trained for the ordained ministry at Methodist College when it served the dual purpose of theological hall and school. Eric's teenage schooling had been in 'Methody'. His siblings, and later his own children, had all been pupils at the school. He himself had served as school chaplain for eight years, from 1942-50. And the links continue through his son, David, and daughter-in-law, Norma, both teachers in the school.

He had been appointed a governor in 1950 when he left the school following his time as chaplain. He continued as a governor until 1992, serving on the Board for 42 years, and he was Board Chairman for three of these years, from 1977-80. His length of service adds weight and authority to the tribute he has paid to the manner in which the Board conducted its business:

> In my forty-two years on the Board I rarely, if ever, saw it reach anything but a consensus. Its aim was always what was best for the pupils. Class or creed did not matter. The Board has always been jealous for its reputation as a leader in educational provision. The school has attracted praise, a deserved reputation, criticism, envy and jealousy. It has been open to reason

and change and it would be a mistake to assume that it is only concerned with vested interest.

Eric was not one who wanted to preserve the eleven-plus selection system, so long a yardstick which determined which pupils could attend the school.[7] He firmly believed it had its shortcomings:

> I for one am conscious that the present selection procedure is far from perfect. We cannot be satisfied with a system which, however unintentionally, consigns young people to a future where their true value and potential are not recognised and developed. In the long run the community is also the poorer.

On two occasions the Board acknowledged the immense contribution he had made to the school and to society in general. In 1985 he was the guest of honour at the Senior Prize Distribution. He comments: 'It was an occasion which has since been a source of a great sense of privilege and of the intense pleasure it gave me to see Barbara distribute the prizes in her own graciously inimitable manner.'

The second honour was possibly even more significant than the first: the publication in 1994 of *Esteem. Liber amicorum. Essays in honour of Revd Dr R.D.E. Gallagher*, edited by T.W. Mulryne (Headmaster) and W.J. McAllister (School Chaplain). Nineteen contributors – people with whom Eric had worked or had shared friendship – referred to different aspects of his life and service to the Church and community in general. Many of the writers were themselves well known for their public service: Viscount Tonypandy, Archbishop Robin Eames, David Bleakley, Paddy Devlin, Gerry Fitt, Jim Molyneaux, Merlyn Rees and Cardinal Cahal Daly.

The preparation and actual presentation of the book came as a surprise to Eric. Some time previously he had suggested – and financially sponsored – the inauguration of a special annual College Lecture. He envisaged that the lecture would be given from time to time by a recognized authority in his/her field of excellence, known for Christian commitment, who would be willing to lecture the Sixth Form pupils, *inter alios*, and be ready to face questions on the relevance of his/her faith in that particular field.

Mr Paul Boateng, the Ghana-born Westminster MP, had been invited to give the inaugural lecture in the Christmas term of 1994. Eric recalls the event:

> To my astonishment the lecture hall in McArthur Hall was packed not only with Sixth Formers and staff but also with friends and associates with whom I had worked over the years. At the conclusion of Paul Boateng's stimulating lecture the Chairman, Professor Robert Stout, asked the Headmaster to speak. I expected the Principal to add his tribute to the lecturer. Instead he presented me with the book of essays entitled *Esteem – Liber amicorum Eric Gallagher*.

He deeply appreciated the presentation of *Esteem*. One thing he regretted: Barbara was ill and unable to share the experience with him.

In 1979 Eric had been appointed by the Northern Ireland Office (NIO) to succeed the Very Revd Dr J.H.R. Gibson as Chairman of the Board for the Training Schools at Rathgael and Whiteabbey. He stepped down from this position in 1986. His appointment more or less coincided with the setting up by government of a major committee to enquire into childcare provisions under the chairmanship of Sir Harold Black, former secretary to the Northern Ireland Cabinet. The Board made a written and oral submission to the Black Committee, as it was called. Following the publication of its report the NIO proposed the virtual elimination of the Training Schools from the childcare system. Eric records the Board's response: 'The Board and its officers shared the suspicion of the Catholic schools that the Department of Health and Social Services [DHSS] had its eye on the finances that might be released by the closures.'

It soon became obvious to Eric and the Board that they had 'a fight on our hands'. The Board felt it had a responsibility for the staff it had recruited: jobs were at stake. It was even more convinced that, in spite of all the criticisms, the schools were making a positive contribution and that there was a necessary place for them in the system.

Battle plans were drawn up:

> I was of the opinion, and had little difficulty in persuading my colleagues, that we should establish common cause with the Catholic schools. And so began a period of happy and successful co-operation with St. Patrick's [Boys] and St. Joseph's [Girls] in Middletown, their senior staffs and their governing Boards. It fell to me, at Bishop Philbin's insistence, to chair our joint consultations and lead our deputations to Government. They were happy and successful occasions. Some of them were memorable.

The joint deputations convinced the Government of their case. Eric was delighted when Mr James Prior, Secretary of State for Northern Ireland, accompanied by Sir Ewart Bell, the Head of the Northern Ireland Civil Service (and a former MCB pupil), and top civil servants from the NIO and DHSS, announced at a final meeting with the deputation on 7 December 1983 that the future of the Schools was assured. He recalls: 'It was a famous victory.'

This had been a very busy time for Eric. In addition to visiting the Northern Ireland Office on several occasions he had to attend a committee discussion on the report about the Training Schools in the House of Commons. Mr Gerry Fitt MP had not been able to visit the schools and arranged to meet Eric on the morning of the debate so that he would be fully informed about the business:

> He requested me to meet him on the morning of the committee at Westminster Tube Station. When we met, he brought me to one of the refreshment rooms in the Commons. He asked me to bring him up to date with the current situation. To my discomfort and surprise (and I think also to his) the civil servant advising the Government was seated two tables away with no one in

between. He enquired what brought me to Westminster. My reply was simply that I was doing my homework.

The debate that afternoon was interesting. From time to time various Northern Ireland MPs came over to him to check that their information was correct. Eric felt this had been the turning point in the controversy. He returned to Belfast and gave a positive report to his Board colleagues. His optimism proved to be correct.

Eric's administration of the Benjamin Moore Memorial Trust Fund is further evidence of his involvement in the field of education during his retirement.

His work with the Trust had started during the 1970s but grew significantly from 1983 onwards. The original benefactor was a Mr Ben Belcher, the President of a well-known American business firm, Benjamin Moore and Company. Belcher's mother had grown up in County Cavan and this had prompted his desire to assist, if possible, in the education of children in County Cavan and County Monaghan.[8] Belcher shared his ideas with the Revd Dr Charles Ranson, an Irish Methodist Minister who was then serving as Dean of the Theological School at Drew University in New Jersey.[9] It was Ranson who had put Belcher in contact with Eric.

Eric contacted governors in both Wesley College, Dublin, and Methodist College, Belfast, and was not surprised to learn that both colleges had pupils who came from these two counties. Initially a Trust Fund was not set up but a clear and accountable arrangement was set in place by which monies from the company could be made available to assist the education of pupils from Monaghan and Cavan who were at Wesley and 'Methody'.

In the autumn of 1983 a cheque for $100,000 dollars – at a time when the sterling equivalent was about £100,000 – arrived from the company. After further consultation Eric realized the time had come to set up a Trust Fund with trustees drawn from the two colleges. And in the late 1980s pupils at Wilson's Hospital School in County Westmeath also became beneficiaries of the Trust.

Over the years the Trust has been able to subsidize the education of young people to the sum of £10,000 annually. Eric comments: 'The work of the Trust is eminently worthwhile. How parents, some of whom to our certain knowledge are in very reduced circumstances, meet the costs of boarding education I just do not know. Real sacrifices must be involved even with the substantial grants in the Republic from the Secondary Education Committee.'

In 1995, after some 20 years' service, he decided it was important to appoint a successor who would take over the administration of the Trust. The Revd Dr Edmund Mawhinney, Secretary of the Methodist Church in Ireland 1990-2004, agreed to become a trustee and take over the secretaryship.

Ecumenism and Reconciliation

In various ways Eric continued to encourage ecumenism and reconciliation. He did this through his public addresses; his association with groups committed to these twin aims; and, above all, by his example.

The visit of Pope John Paul II to the Republic of Ireland at the end of September 1979 was a momentous occasion, especially for Irish Catholics. It is estimated that as many as 250,000 were at Drogheda when he made his famous appeal for an end to violence in Ireland. The Pope had said: 'To all of you who are listening I say: do not believe in violence; do not support violence. It is not the Christian way. It is not the way of the Catholic Church. Believe in peace and forgiveness and love; for they are of Christ.'[10]

The Church of Ireland and the Presbyterian and Methodist Churches were invited to appoint delegations to meet him in Dublin. Although he was retired and not holding any official position in Inter-Church affairs, Eric, to his surprise, was invited to be a member of the Methodist delegation.

The meeting with the Pope took place in a convent in Drumcondra. Eric recalls the event:

We were arranged in denominational groupings and each of us was introduced to the Pope by the late Cardinal Tomás Ó Fiaich in his own human and inimitable way. It was moving to meet and be greeted by this most gracious and remarkable man. His private persona seems so much at odds with his reluctance to extend the frontiers of inter-communion relationships. He could have achieved so much more.

Each of the delegations, especially the Presbyterians, had hoped that there would be time to discuss various matters with the Pope. However, their hopes were dashed: they were told that the crowded timetable would not permit it. All the prepared documentation was collected and forwarded to the Pope via the Papal Nuncio. They were told a reply would eventually be made to the points raised in the prepared statements.

In Gallagher and Worrall, *Christians in Ulster 1968-1980*, the authors suggest that it was a mistake to limit so severely the time allocated for the delegations to meet the Pope:

> In retrospect, an opportunity should clearly have been given for a longer and more relaxed meeting. A rushed informal encounter at the end of a long and tiring day is neither dialogue nor adequate preparation for it. The potential significance of this historic meeting was not fully grasped by those who arranged it. In any case, it was, though not on purpose, a unilateral arrangement, and unilateral arrangements are not calculated to make the most of ecumenical occasions, even of a papal visit.[11]

During his active ministry, and then in his retirement, Eric supported two institutions, both known for their promotion of reconciliation and founded by the well-known Jesuit, the Revd Dr Michael Hurley: the Irish School of Ecumenics and the Columbanus Community for Reconciliation.

The Irish School of Ecumenics (ISE) had been founded by Hurley in 1970. It offered postgraduate and certificate studies in the areas of peace and reconciliation. At its commencement it provided the postgraduate classes in Milltown, Dublin, within the premises of the Jesuit seminary. It was a happy arrangement as the Jesuit community gave solid support to the venture. University recognition for the postgraduate work was obtained through the University of Hull.

Most of Eric's support for ISE was given during his retirement. He started to lecture for the School in the Certificate Course and also agreed to be one of its patrons. Michael Hurley explains why Eric did not give more open support to the School in the 1970s:

> He himself was caught between a rock and a hard place. He would have wanted to support ISE as much as possible – he confessed this to me more than once – and eventually on his retirement he did become actively involved: he worked hard to secure official recognition and in consequence some financial support from the main churches. In the early 70s, however, the politico-religious situation was extremely tense and in that situation efforts were being made to forge for the first time official contacts between the churches, in particular the churches of the Irish Council of Churches and the Catholic Church. Eric Gallagher played a prominent part in these efforts and soon found out that Jesuits were not *personae gratae* to the Catholic Church authorities in the North and likewise ISE, especially after the Mixed Marriage Consultation [in 1972]. For the greater good, as he saw it, in order not to jeopardise the emerging official relationship with the Catholic Church and a consequent improvement in community relations, Eric wisely decided to postpone his support for ISE.[12]

He also gave support to the Columbanus Community for Reconciliation, founded by Hurley in 1983. Eric was involved from the early days of the venture, including the process which eventually led to the purchase of premises at 683 Antrim Road in North Belfast. His duties as a patron – a position which he held from 1984-94 – were not as demanding as at ISE: 'They involved regular visits to 683, meetings of Patrons at least annually, and in rota doing the inspection of the property and holding interviews with each community member.'

At the beginning of June 1984 Eric shared in leading a three-day inter-church pilgrimage to the island of Iona where the missionary monk St Columba had established himself in 563. He shared the leadership of the party with Cardinal Tomás Ó Fiaich and the Revd Dr Ray Davey, the founder of the Corrymeela Community for Reconciliation, based near Ballycastle on the North Antrim coast. Ó Fiaich, a former professor at St Patrick's College, Maynooth, County Kildare, and an expert on Celtic Studies, was in his element. The *Irish Times* reported: 'For several hours, noteless, he did spiritual courier – on the way to Oban on the Friday night, over the rocky roads of Mull next morning – preparing the way for Iona with a history of Columba, or more frequently Colmcille [the Irish name], rich in quotations in Irish from the saint's poems.'[13] The paper also reported Eric's comment: 'It was worth it as an exercise in doing something together.'

Eric's advocacy of ecumenism and reconciliation continued in many of his public addresses and lectures. His material was always good, his lectures carefully prepared. Frequently his topic was an analysis of the situation in the country, an attempt to spell out what the churches should be doing and possibly what they had failed to do. To say that the themes and material were often similar from one talk to the next does not diminish in any way the quality of what he said. References to some of these talks provide an insight into how he continued to interpret the situation in Northern Ireland and, indeed, how he himself was responding to events.

On 8 March 1983 he gave the London Lecture of the Irish School of Ecumenics entitled 'The Irish Churches in a Divided Society – 1968-1983. Facts and Lessons.'[14] Towards the end of the talk he returned to the theme of the accountability of the Churches:

> The Northern Ireland problem puts the credibility of the Churches to the test: the credibility of all of us. You will recall the Biblical judgment not on what we have

done but rather on what we have left undone. And the question is 'Have we done enough? To save lives? To stop deaths? To build the good and just society?' We have been long on words and short on actions.

At this point in his talk he appears to reveal his own personal sense of exasperation with the lack of action on the part of the Christian community. He explained that he had been to another major inter-church meeting at Ballymascanlon and the experience had disturbed him:

> We had another Ballymascanlon encounter last week: we talked for six long hours and went home without a single resolution to our credit. Nothing was done. Deliberate? Indifferent? Incompetent? I just don't know but it worries me.

On 21 September 1983 Eric was in Clones, County Monaghan, lecturing on 'The Contribution of the Churches to Reconciliation – Plus or Minus'. Earlier that year Dr Cahal Daly had acknowledged that there was a religious dimension to the conflict in the country. Eric quoted the Bishop: 'There is a religious aspect to our conflict. The Churches do bear some blame for our tragic divisions and do have responsibility for pointing a way forward. The nature of our blameworthiness may differ. The content of our responsibilities may vary. Yet the Churches should be providing a model to the wider community in that which is an essential defining characteristic of the Christian gospel, namely, that it is a gospel of reconciliation.'

Eric developed Dr Daly's statement, suggesting ways in which Christians can put reconciliation into practice: Catholics and Protestants should become more conscious of the presence of Christ in each other; quoting prayers from the Methodist Covenant Service he said they should be more willing to forgive one another; they should be more sensitive to feelings of hurt identified by others; referring to John Wesley's *Letter to a Roman Catholic* he encouraged folk actively to support one another in all that they held in common.

These were themes he had spent a lifetime articulating in his sermons and public addresses. But he never tired of repeating them.

The Board of Inter-Church Affairs of the Irish Council of Churches requested Eric to prepare a paper, 'Irish Ecumenical Hurdles', in 1990. After his customary historical overview of developments and problems in the ecumenical field this paper majored mainly on relationships between the Protestant Churches and the Roman Catholic Church. It was possibly one of the most outspoken of Eric's critiques regarding the obstacles he saw being thrown up by representatives of the Roman Catholic Church.

Eric focused on the Irish Roman Catholic attitude to ecumenical development as set out in their 1978 Directory. Acknowledging their expressed desire for 'Christians to come together in one flock' he was critical of the terms which the Directory specified on which co-operation and developing relationships could take place in the interim period before the flock became 'one'. He declared:

> Those terms allowed for no discussion on a number of issues which were non-negotiable, notwithstanding the fact that there is controversy about some of them inside Roman Catholicism itself. The ultimate authority lies in Rome and since 1976 there would seem to be grounds for thinking that less emphasis is being placed there on developing meaningful relationships with the Reformed and Anglican traditions.

Even allowing for these restrictive constraints which emanated from Rome, Eric went on to suggest that there was a high degree of apathy towards ecumenism within the Roman Catholic Church in Ireland. He complained that there was little awareness of the secular and materialist challenges facing every Church and wondered if this accounted for the absence of any ecumenical imperative. The Irish Roman Catholic Hierarchy, with few exceptions, were reluctant to enter into serious dialogue with Protestantism:

Occasions when the Hierarchy consider any issue sufficiently serious or compelling as to warrant consultation with other Churches are few. Understandably, but regrettably, with notable exceptions, diocesan Bishops and Maynooth act unilaterally.

This was possibly Eric's most forthright criticism of what he saw as negativity within the Roman Catholic Church and specifically Irish Roman Catholicism. I am not aware of his uttering such strong criticisms in the 1970s or 80s. Did the conservatism of Pope John Paul II and the inevitable consequences of this conservatism in Ireland account for Eric's outspoken comments? Or did he feel that his seniority and experience gave him the authority to be so forthright? His paper was written for circulation within the Irish Council of Churches but he was not the kind of man who reserved his criticism of others for occasions when the criticized were absent. In one way or another these comments would have been passed on to members of the Irish Roman Catholic hierarchy.

Having commented on problems within Irish Roman Catholicism, Eric proceeded to focus on obstacles to ecumenism created by the Protestant Churches. He suggested there was a failure within Protestantism to take seriously the biblical teaching on the nature of the Church. He believed that an overemphasis on the spiritual experience of the individual Christian, in particular her/his vertical relationship with God, tended to obliterate a deep concern for relationships inside the whole Body of Christ.

He was also critical of 'an indifference born of denominational strength'. Protestants needed to be on their guard against a sense of denominational triumphalism:

> There can be a Presbyterian or Anglican triumphalism as well as a Catholic triumphalism and there could be a Methodist one also, if there were enough Methodists around. There is a sturdy Protestant individualism in all our Churches which encourages us to 'go it alone' if we are strong or numerous enough. There is no need to

bother about the others if we can do it ourselves, whatever it may be. Denominational one-upmanship is the enemy of 'belonging together'. The history of cooperation out of weakness and rarely out of strength tells its own story.

At the Greenhills Annual Day Conference on 21 January 1991 Eric had been asked to speak on 'A Future for Ecumenism in Ireland'. He was much more optimistic on this occasion compared with his analysis presented to the Irish Council of Churches a year earlier.

He felt that over the past quarter of a century ecclesiastical attitudes and relationships had changed dramatically. Eric qualified the statement slightly by adding 'at certain levels and places'. He was not prepared to say that the picture was uniform. 'Nonetheless', he declared, 'from what might be called a zero or zero-minus position, relationships have moved through an almost unbelievable progression.' Not always given to illustrating his points by reference to his own personal experience, on this occasion he made no apology for referring to the change in restraints which he felt had sometimes influenced the degree of openness in his own ecumenical practice:

Let me illustrate with a personal experience. On his appointment as Bishop of Ardagh and Clonmacnois, Bishop Daly graciously invited the late Principal James Haire and myself to his consecration in Longford Cathedral. I wished to accept but, as I was then in high office [President] in our Methodist Church, my advisers counselled me that my attendance would be inopportune and likely to be divisive. Reluctantly, I was constrained to decline the invitation. Principal Haire accepted on condition that he could wear collar and tie and sit incognito in the body of the congregation. When Bishop Daly was translated to Down and Connor [1982], he again invited us to be present accompanied by our wives. This time we accepted without reserve or qualification. We were seated in the front row of the congregation in St

Peter's Cathedral in Belfast and during the service the Bishop came down to greet us. A month ago I was honoured to be one of several Protestants in the clerical procession at his memorable installation as Archbishop of Armagh and Primate of All-Ireland.

In January 1993 Eric gave a lecture for the Irish School of Ecumenics entitled 'My Ecumenical Vision'. He summarized that vision in three points.

Firstly, his vision included the entwining of evangelism and ecumenism. 'A world that needs reconciliation,' he declared, 'will not listen to a Church that has not experienced it.' He emphasized that John 17 was every bit as important as John chapter 3.16. He punched his message home by saying: 'The search for unity is not an optional extra.'

Secondly, he wanted to see integrity, humility and spirituality. Integrity he understood, in this context, as the search for, and experiencing of, greater truth, rather than the surrendering of truth. Humility meant a recognition that none of us has a monopoly of truth. And the spirituality that he wanted to see in Irish ecumenism was a spirituality that holds each of us close to Christ, the crucified and risen head of the Church. Such a spirituality meant: 'The nearer we come to Him the closer we will be to each other.'

Thirdly, he wanted Christians to be more conscious that they belonged to the UNA SANCTA [the one, holy, catholic and apostolic church] rather than the denomination serving as their primary allegiance. In moving words Eric declared: 'The UNA SANCTA was the womb that bore me. In it I live and move and have my being. It is the final goal towards which we stumble and struggle – one Church above, beneath.'

Eric's final words in relating his ecumenical vision were really words for himself but they must have had an impact on his audience: 'The ecumenical vision is an ecumenical imperative. How I would like to start the pilgrimage all over again so as to be more satisfied that I have not been disobedient to the vision.'

Politics

In 1983 Eric was approached by Professor Desmond Rea, at that time Professor of Economics at the University of Ulster, who suggested that he might consider taking charge of a new project, 'Working Together', about to be launched by Co-operation North.[15] The organization, started in Dublin, had already been in existence for five years. As the name suggests it aimed at encouraging friendship between the people of Ireland, North and South.

The project Rea had in mind was really an essay competition, designed to elicit suggestions for cross-border co-operation in any field of activity. Financially the proposition looked attractive as the organization indicated there would be a generous emolument for his services. On this occasion, Eric realized he did not have the time to manage the project: 'The more I considered their proposition the more convinced I was that I had neither the time nor the facilities to accept.' But he indicated he was ready to serve in a voluntary capacity, if they so wished. He was prepared to chair a supervisory committee which might recruit and pay someone to organize the competition under the guidance of the committee.

In the event, with help from others, he was able to form a committee but was unable to appoint someone to organize the competition. The 'nuts and bolts' of the project were seen to by Co-operation North staff in Dublin under the watchful eye of Mr Hugh Quigley, the organization's Chief Executive. The competition was run in three age groups with the Northern and Southern winners of each group being rewarded by a trip to the United States.

Judges were appointed to assess the submissions. Eric felt that overall the number and quality of the entries were disappointing, although some were of real merit. One of them, the suggestion of a North/South Maracycle, became an annual event attracting hundreds of participants each year.

On the completion of the competition Eric and a co-leader, Mrs Brigid Wilkinson, led the party of prize winners to the United States. In Washington they were given red-carpet treatment by the Irish and British ambassadors and made a number of interesting visits, including one to meet the Speaker of Congress, Mr Tip O'Neill. In New York they visited the United Nations building.

Another interesting invitation came Eric's way in 1983. He was invited to become a founder member of a body to be known as Anglo-Irish Encounter. It was the brainchild of the British and Irish Governments led by Mrs Margaret Thatcher and Dr Garrett Fitzgerald. They had decided at their last summit meeting to set up a Board of some 18 persons, half of whom would be from the Irish Republic and half representing the United Kingdom, including some from Northern Ireland. The Board would hold conferences and seminars, bringing together personnel from the different parts of the two jurisdictions with a common interest in a given subject. It would report yearly to the two Foreign Ministers.

The concept intrigued Eric and he accepted the invitation. They arranged conferences on various topics: the Press; Broadcasting; the Churches; the Health Services; Youth Employment; Drug Abuse and Alcoholism; and political affairs.

The experience of working with Anglo-Irish Encounter – later renamed British-Irish Studies – was one that Eric enjoyed. He felt it was time well spent: 'I look back on my years with Encounter with considerable pleasure. After a lifetime of living and working to a considerable extent in restricted ecclesiastical circles, it was refreshing to meet with folk from secular bodies and wider vocational backgrounds: it was likewise challenging to have the opportunity of attempting in some way to present a Christian viewpoint.'

In September 1984 Eric took part in a residential conference of academics and political scientists in the College of William and Mary in Williamsburg, Virginia. The overall title of the conference was 'Northern Ireland – Living with the Crisis' and Eric's subject was 'The Faith and its forms in a time of crisis'.

One of the tragedies of the Northern Ireland crisis, he suggested, was the fact that people were becoming so accustomed to violence that they were no longer horrified by it:

Perhaps we have become so inured to violence, so accustomed to it that we have become de-sensitized. One sometimes wants to ask how much more killing, how many more bombs will it take before the pressures force people to meaningful and purposeful negotiation. Violence has become acceptable: that is the ultimate obscenity.

The most significant thing about this conference for Eric was the chance meeting he had in Washington, prior to going to Williamsburg, with Father Sean McManus, a leading light in the Irish National Caucus. Eric had been staying in Quaker House, East Capitol Street, which was just a few doors away from the Irish National Caucus offices. McManus had taken exception to something Eric had said the previous autumn at a conference in Corrymeela. The speech had been reported in some American newspapers and caught McManus' attention.

As he walked along East Capitol Street Eric noticed the Irish National Caucus offices and on the spur of the moment decided to call and endeavour to talk with Father McManus. He was greeted by McManus' secretary who recognized him. The secretary was a former nurse in the Royal Victoria Hospital, Belfast, where Eric had been Methodist Chaplain while Superintendent of the Belfast Central Mission. Her father had been assassinated by loyalists. She told Eric that Father McManus was unwell that day and was spending the day in bed at home. However, she insisted on phoning him and he in turn insisted on coming to the office to see Eric. Eric recalls that meeting:

> We had a long conversation together in which I endeavoured to convince him that changes were in fact taking place in Northern Ireland employment practices. I told him that we had to live together and pleaded with him that he should try to understand the Protestant people and to love them rather than continually finding fault with them. Altogether we had a very civilised, though frank, conversation.

They had lunch together and later McManus left Eric to the airport en route for Williamsburg.

Eric was not sure what effect, if any, he had had on McManus. However, some years later, he was pleased to hear him emphasizing the need to understand and have the goodwill of the Protestant people.

In July 1985 Eric was one of the speakers at a conference on 'Church and Society' in Oxford. He had been asked to speak on 'The Politics of Reconciliation'.

Much of his address was focused on what might happen when the violence came to an end in Northern Ireland. By 1985 the province had experienced violence for 16 years. People had never thought that that kind of situation would linger on for so long. However, few had ever turned their attention to consider the measures needed to 'keep the peace' when violence ended.

Eric pressed the case for advance thinking on what would be required to keep the peace and avoid a return to violence:

> In this company I need not stress that unless, when peace does come, attempts are made to win the peace, that peace will rapidly become less than peace. It will degenerate rapidly into something much less than toleration and from that to latent or open hostility. There must be a process of normalisation, actively promoted, not only by Government, but also by other responsible opinion formers.
>
> Peace, reconciliation, forgiveness – call it what you will – does not come by accident. It must be planned: it must have structures. Otherwise the pressure of unforeseen and traumatic events could destroy overnight any emerging goodwill.

The Churches, he suggested, as well as the Government, had a part to play in preparing to keep the peace. In reaching a just solution to the conflict the Churches had to help people recognize that some degree of compromise would be required:

> The issues are such that no side can get what it wants without depriving the other side of what it wants. The

aspirations of each side may be legitimate as long as they are sought legitimately. But equally the aspirations of each side are mutually exclusive. At the end of the day if there is to be any politics of forgiveness and reconciliation in Northern Ireland the price will inevitably mean compromise on all sides. That honesty and courage are needed from political leaders but not only from political leaders. The Churches so far have been long on well-intentioned statements that call for goodwill in the most general of terms. They have been remarkably short in suggesting, let alone spelling out, some of the surrenders that may well have to be made if the just and acceptable society is to come.

When David Bleakley became Secretary of the Irish Council of Churches in 1979 he had contacted Eric and persuaded him to take on the secretaryship of the Board of Inter-Church Affairs, a task formerly undertaken by the Secretary himself. It was a position which Eric welcomed in that it brought him into direct contact with the Irish ecumenical situation.

One of the fruits of his time in this office was his membership of a small sub-group, Faith and Politics, which sought to relate their faith to the Irish situation. Membership of the group included both Catholics and Protestants. Over the years it published a number of thought-provoking articles. One of its most significant actions was its publication of *A Declaration of Faith and Commitment* in 1986.

Eric was closely involved in its preparation, being responsible for the first draft of the document. Some extracts from the *Declaration* conveys its value:

We believe
We believe that all our land belongs to God: not to Unionists or Nationalists. All of us have to live in it and share it together.

We seek
We seek justice for everybody in our society. Therefore we claim no rights or privileges for ourselves which we

are not prepared to share with our fellow-citizens of other traditions.

We reject
We reject that justice can be achieved by the use of violence. We are inter-dependent and we must accommodate each other. Bigotry, discrimination, intimidation and distortion of the truth should have no place in our relationships.

We declare
We declare that government must respect the rights of both communities and the police must impartially serve both traditions.

We pledge
We pledge ourselves to obey God's will and word rather than give unqualified support to any political leader or manifesto, whether Nationalist or Unionist.

The *Declaration* included a section 'Scriptural Basis and Underlying Reasons for this Declaration' so that the public would be aware of the biblical principles underlying the document. About 50 lay and clergy from both Protestant and Catholic traditions had signed the *Declaration* and an invitation was issued that others might join with them in this declaration and commitment.

In the early winter of 1991 the daily press reported that an initiative was about to be launched, designed to consult as wide a spectrum as possible of Northern Ireland people about the current state of society in the region and to elicit their suggestions for the future. It was stated that a reasonable number of patrons for the project would be appointed. Some days later Eric received an invitation to become one of the patrons. All that was involved was to allow his name to appear on the list of patrons and to attend the launch of the project – to be known as Initiative '92 – in the Europa Hotel.

Eric was pleased to see such an initiative get off the ground and agreed to be one of the patrons. He attended the launch and later discussed with his son, David, the possibility of the two of them making a written submission to the Commission which was envisaged.

At the turn of the year Professor Simon Lee, Professor of Jurisprudence at the Queen's University of Belfast, one of the project's initiators, wrote to Eric with the suggestion that he might become 'more closely involved with the project'. This, Eric learned, was Simon Lee's way of asking him to become a Commissioner! Again, he accepted.

The team of Commissioners appointed was impressive. Professor Torkel Opsahl, Professor of Law at the University of Oslo, was Chairman. In addition to Eric there were five others: Lady Faulkner of Downpatrick, former BBC Governor for Northern Ireland and widow of the late Brian Faulkner, last Stormont Prime Minister and Head of the 1974 Power-Sharing Executive; Mr Padraig O'Malley, political scientist and Senior Fellow at the John W. McCormack Institute of Public Affairs at the University of Massachusetts in Boston; Professor Ruth Lister, Professor of Applied Social Studies at the University of Bradford; Mr Eamonn Gallagher, former EC Director-General of Fisheries; and Professor Marianne Elliott, Professor of History at the University of Liverpool. Mr Andy Pollak, the well-known *Irish Times* journalist, served as Co-ordinator.

Eric found the work of the Commission exciting but very demanding. Barbara's illness, however, gave him some concern: 'Had I known in January 1992 how Barbara's illness would develop, I don't think I would or could have contemplated taking part. As it was she was still mobile, though lethargic and increasingly seeming to "switch off".'

Submissions began to arrive early in January 1993. Altogether they received 554 written submissions involving some 3,000 persons. All had to be read and each Commissioner was expected to prepare a written summary of each submission. In the months of January and February they held oral presentations and question sessions in Belfast, Derry, Enniskillen, Dungannon, Coleraine and Newtownards. Two school assemblies were held in the Queen's University of Belfast and the Guildhall in Derry. Visits were made to the

Royal Ulster Constabulary (RUC), Government ministers and civil servants in Belfast, London and Dublin.

Each Commissioner was responsible for a draft of at least one section of the eventual report. Eric was asked to write two sections of the report. The drafts were circulated to members of the Commission and eventually, over a long weekend in April 1993, they examined and finalized the drafts line by line. These became the official report of the Commission, accompanied by a first-rate summary of the totality of submissions from the pen of Andy Pollak.

The report was launched at a major press conference in June. Presentations were made to Government ministers in Belfast, Dublin and London and also to Mrs Mary Robinson, the Irish President. Professor Opsahl and Eric made a visit to Meghaberry Prison to see the leaders of IRA women and male loyalist prisoners but due to some misunderstanding they saw only the former group.

Chapter Six, 'Sinn Fein and the Paramilitaries: Coming in from the Cold?', was possibly the most significant section of the report. As the title of the chapter suggests the Commission recommended that informal channels of communication should be opened with Sinn Fein. The full text read:

> We recommend accordingly, that informal channels of communication should be opened with Sinn Fein with a view to persuading the IRA first to move towards a de-escalation in the level of violence and eventually to a ceasefire that would lead to a drastic reduction in the number of security forces deployed in Northern Ireland, and/or their return to barracks. Though we respect the refusal of the current political parties to have Sinn Fein officially at talks on the future of Northern Ireland until it shows signs that it is willing to work within an agreed constitutional structure, the party nevertheless should be given help and encouragement to join the constitutional process, if that is what it desires.[16]

The diagnosis in 1992 that Barbara had Alzheimer's disease was naturally a heavy blow for Eric and the family. The deterioration in her condition continued and by the summer of 1994 things were quite difficult. By then Barbara was attending a day centre from Monday to Friday. She had begun to wander off and was lost one day for two hours. Movement was increasingly unsteady. Word recall and comprehension had all but gone. Other faculties were fast disappearing.

On the Sunday morning before Christmas Barbara had an accident. Eric recalls what happened: 'She fell out of my arms in the bathroom and hit her head heavily against a radiator. We called a doctor: there were no bones broken but she never was the same again.'

Barbara was admitted to the Lagan Valley Hospital on 10 January. The remaining days of her life are described by her husband:

> By mid-February after further rapid deterioration she was confined totally to bed. Ruth and David at some time each day shared the vigil with me. Helen came from Dublin as frequently as she could, accompanied when it was possible by Alan and the family. Her sister and brother, my siblings, some others, among them a few close friends, silently by their presence spoke their last fond farewells. On the morning of 27 February, with Ruth, Helen and David with me at her bedside, David read some Scripture passages and I commended her to the God and Father of us all. Very shortly afterwards, in the presence of the four of us, she slept quietly and peacefully away. The graciousness and loving smile that were so typical of her down the years stayed with her to the end. She died as she had lived, with dignity.

The funeral service was held in the University Road Church where Eric had served from 1954-57. The Revd David Houston, in the absence in America of the Revd David Kerr, Superintendent of Belfast Central Mission, made the arrangements. Various ministers took part, including the Revds Harold Good and Edmund Mawhinney, President of the

Methodist Church in Ireland. The Revd Ted Lindsay, a lifelong friend of both Eric and Barbara, paid an inspiring tribute.

In his Autobiographical Notes Eric expresses what Barbara meant to him:

> So ended fifty years, all but a few months, of unclouded married life. Life, and the pressures of our appointments, and, of course, the years of communal strife, gave us far too little leisure and time together. Like everyone else we had our problems but we faced them together. From the beginning she gave of herself without reserve. Where there was a need or difficulty she did not know what it was to hold back. Other people's concerns, those of the family and especially mine, were her concerns. Nothing was allowed to stand in the way of her love and support for the children and for me.
>
> With her passing a light went out of my life. Sometimes I think that a light has died inside me. But I am grateful for the memories. They still shine bright and clear. I thank God for all she meant to me and to our children.

17

Glory

I have fought the good fight, I have finished the race, I have kept the faith.

2 Timothy 4.7

Barbara's death affected Eric deeply. They had had a strong love for each other, had shared so much together, so it is understandable that he found life without her very difficult. One of the ways he tried to cope was to edit an updated version of her poems, *Embers and Echoes*, and this was published in December 1995. Like Barbara, he occasionally wrote poetry and shortly after her death he penned these words about his wife:

Barbara

Now that I'm old, bereft and prone to tears,
And putting in my days, I take your book
Embers and Echoes, where I try to look
For recollections of the happy years,
Years when you were young and full of life,
When love and beauty filled your eyes
When you beyond all others were the prize
I sought and won and you became my wife.

But though you've dealt with death and those who kill,
I find in what you write remembered grace
And love which never left your smiling face.
At peace I rest content. I love you still.

In the latter half of 1995 Eric felt unwell and underwent several hospital checks which revealed that he had both thyroid and heart problems. Then in May 1996 he became seriously ill and was admitted to the Lagan Valley Hospital in Lisburn. Initially, the family and Eric were told he had not long to live. Some time later, when chronic renal failure was diagnosed, he was placed initially on a twice-weekly – to be increased to a thrice weekly – routine of dialysis treatment. These two-hourly sessions were immensely tiring for him.

Illness brought with it further radical changes. As a circuit minister he had visited and cared for the sick in his congregations. For the 22 years he was Superintendent of the Belfast Central Mission he was also Chaplain at the Royal Victoria Hospital, Belfast, so a large part of his busy ministry had included ministering to the sick. Then he had been Barbara's main companion and chief nurse throughout her illness. Now he found himself in need of other people's love and care.

Eric wanted to retain his independence in his own home for as long as possible and with the help of many people he was enabled to do this. His immediate family, as well as his wider family circle, rallied round and supported him. For them all it was a precious time as they ministered to each other. Ruth and David were living nearby and kept in constant contact with him. Helen travelled up from Dublin and frequently stayed with him in the days she was not working. Neighbours, too, offered support and the Social Services and District Nursing Service provided wonderful help.

Then in October 1999 Eric asked the family to begin looking for a suitable nursing home. They found that a room was available at the El Shaddai Nursing Home in Lisburn and he moved there at the end of the Hallowe'en holiday. The home was run by a caring management team and had a lovely atmosphere. He took a great interest in the staff and became familiar with the circumstances of each of the nurses.

As fate would have it, he was in El Shaddai only a matter of weeks. He was soon transferred to the Belfast City Hospital to be cared for so well by Dr Billy Nelson and the staff of Ward 11. It was here that Eric died on 30 December.

A Service of Remembrance and Thanksgiving for Eric's life and work was held in University Road Methodist Church on Wednesday, 5 January 2000. Various clergy and laity representing the Methodist Church, the Roman Catholic Church in the person of Cardinal Cahal Daly and the Irish

Council of Churches took part. The address was given by the Revd Edmund T.I. Mawhinney, whose ministry had been much appreciated and admired by both Barbara and Eric. In a very sensitive address Mawhinney reminded everyone of the great breadth and extent of Eric's ministry. His final comments suitably summarized the points he had made in his address:

> Eric Gallagher – one of Mr Wesley's preachers, able administrator, who walked at times the lonely path of the prophet, ecumenist, peacemaker and bridge-builder, opponent of disadvantage, who consistently related Christian principles and gospel values to the social and political affairs of the community; Eric Gallagher – father, grandfather, brother – we give thanks to God.[1]

Eric had hoped to live long enough to see the dawn of the new millennium. He did not quite manage this but his legacy will surely influence for good the opening decades of the third millennium.

What, then, was his legacy? Readers will come to their own conclusions on this. The purpose of writing this book is to ensure that his legacy – whatever conclusions are reached – is not forgotten or overlooked. In a sense the telling of the story communicates the legacy. That certainly is my hope. However, I suggest that there are three main areas – clearly interrelated – in which Eric made an enormous contribution and which together form the substance of his legacy in Ireland.

His ecumenical vision provided the foundation for most of his developing ideas. From an early age he caught the vision and hope of the emerging ecumenical movement. Its leaders were the men who inspired him. His 1961 sermon on 'Church Unity', already quoted at the beginning of chapter 9, partly summarizes his thinking and teaching on ecumenism: 'Whether I like it or not I am driven inexorably to the firm conclusion that God's will for the Church is that it should be one.'

The fact that many of the leaders of the other Protestant Churches at that time shared this vision created a situation in which joint church schemes were proposed and initiated. Some, but not all, of these joint arrangements – Methodist/Presbyterian and Methodist/Church of Ireland – are still in existence.

Eric's approach to the mission of the Church was influenced by his conviction that disunity was a scandal and, more than that, a hindrance to the divine commission to mission.

This ecumenical vision was one which brought him into contact with Roman Catholic clergy and laity. The group brought together by Canon Robert Murphy in the late 1950s and 60s must have been influential in developing his ecumenical understanding. It laid the foundation for his future involvement in numerous Catholic and Protestant joint ventures. He became a key figure in creating the structures which matured into the Irish Inter-Church Meeting ('Ballymascanlon'). His persistent personal support for inter-church action was a witness and inspiration to all within the wider Christian community and those outside it. This part of his legacy is immense.

His concern for social justice was not unrelated to his ecumenical vision. Ecumenism is basically a concern for the whole inhabited world. For Eric, concern for social justice was biblical and central to Christian teaching. He frequently referred to the emphasis on social justice found in the teaching of the Old Testament prophets and in the work and teaching of Christ himself.

However, his concern for social justice was not limited to his preaching. He was convinced it had to be given practical expression in the structures of society: social, religious, economic and political. While purposely avoiding membership of any party political group, he made it his business to challenge political leaders to initiate changes which would provide justice and human rights for everyone in the community. To this end he was concerned about unemployment, bad housing conditions, and anything which tended to hinder people achieving their God-intended potential in society.

He was aware that concern for human rights could lead to radical changes in the political structures of Northern Ireland but he was fearless in encouraging an openness to whatever changes might be required. Attention has already been drawn to the fact that he was the first publicly to suggest that a political solution to the Northern Ireland problem might include consideration of structures which would allow for representatives of various political persuasions to share together in Executive Government – a concept later attempted in the 1974 Power-Sharing Executive and advocated in the 1998 Good Friday Agreement. His sharing of this vision on 13 November 1971 when addressing the Scottish Assembly of the Royal Institute for International Affairs in Edinburgh is surely historic.

People knew that he was an advocate for social justice and many respected him for his stand on human rights issues. In fact that respect was often strongest among people not known for their church connections.

The various honours Eric received were essentially tokens of recognition for his contribution to the wider community in these areas of ecumenism and social justice. In 1971 the Queen's University of Belfast had awarded him an honorary Doctor of Divinity. In 1972 he had received an OBE from the Queen and this was upgraded in 1987 to a CBE, not least for his contribution to Rathgael Training School as he chaired it through difficult days.

The third area in which his legacy is evident is in the influence he had within Methodism. To a considerable degree he was successful in communicating his ecumenical vision and concern for social justice to the Methodist people, both clergy and lay. Yes, there were those who rejected his stand on these issues but they were a minority within Methodism. Eric was acutely conscious of this sense of rejection in some quarters. In more private conversation there were times when he expressed his disappointment that certain circuits in Irish Methodism no longer invited him to preach.

Many younger Methodist ministers – that is, the generation of ministers which followed him – were particularly influenced by him. Edmund Mawhinney has explained the nature of this influence:

> He was a model of ministry for many of us. When there was an opportunity to express that to him in recent months, he was genuinely surprised. As a student, I worked for a couple of years in the Belfast Central Mission during holiday periods. I learned then of his commitment to, and volume of, work, and his management of time. Yet he always seemed to have time. Later, a few of us as students approached him with an idea for publicising the Edgehill College magazine, in which we were hoping for his involvement. I know now how unrealistic the request was. But he listened and came up with another suggestion. Some hours later we received a telephone message from him to say that he had arranged that the Lord Mayor would be willing to be presented with the first copy, and some press coverage had been arranged. All done in the midst of what I now realise was a very busy schedule.[2]

Eric was an ecumenist but this did not prevent him being proud of his Methodist heritage. He saw no conflict between cherishing his Methodist roots and also encouraging the search for Christian unity. He inherited from his father an interest in Methodist history, particularly the life and work of the Wesleys. His congregations were soon made aware of this interest. His encouragement in the production of a play on the life of John Wesley while he was minister of Cregagh Methodist Church is still remembered by those who took part.

Eric's lifelong interest in Methodist history was nurtured by his involvement in the Wesley Historical Society (Irish Branch). From 1993-96 he was President of the Society, having served as Vice-President for many years prior to this.

What then of Eric's weaknesses? Different readers will draw different conclusions. In encouraging his disciples to seek perfection Jesus acknowledged their weaknesses. Eric was aware of his own weaknesses and faults but his sermons testify to the fact that he constantly sought the perfection Jesus taught. And it seems to me that he was well along the road to Christian perfection.

Eric was a good and great man. Slightly shy by nature, he may have been misunderstood by some who thought him a little aloof. He was far from it. He could mix with people from every section of society.

His goal in life was to serve others. He fervently believed that the fullness of life can be found only in Christian discipleship. He has set a good example which will continue to challenge succeeding generations.

Eric Gallagher will be remembered by those who knew him as a man of searing integrity, a man of unflinching courage, a man of wit and wisdom, a man unafraid to offer radical leadership and accept the consequences, a pastor, a friend and a Christian gentleman.

Notes

Chapter 1

1. 'The Ulster I want to see' was not one of Eric's many public addresses. While on holiday in Portstewart in the 1970s he occasionally made 'Jottings' containing his thoughts on the issues of the day. This was one of those jottings.

2. Interview with Sandy Scott, 18.4.2000.

3. Michael Hurley, 'Eric Gallagher, Peacemaker', *Doctrine and Life*, February 2000.

4. Interview with Cahal Daly, 28.6.2000.

5. Correspondence with Ken Wilson, 8.3.2000.

6. Gerry Fitt, Sense, tolerance and fairness, *Esteem* ed. T.W. Mulryne and W.J. McAllister, p. 22.

7. Paddy Devlin, Breaking down barriers, *Esteem*, p. 15.

8. Jim Molyneaux, Beneficial objectives, *Esteem,* p. 20.

Chapter 2

1. Robert H. Gallagher, *My Web of Time*, Nelson and Knox, Belfast, 1959, p. 30.

2. Eric Gallagher's unpublished *Autobiographical Notes*. These were extensive notes covering the whole period of his life. Subsequent quotations from these *Autobiographical Notes* will not be referenced.

3. Robert H. Gallagher, *My Web of Time*, p. 6.

4. *My Web of Time* pp. 6-7.

5. In 1816 Methodists in Ireland had divided over two interrelated issues: Wesleyan Methodists favoured the granting of permission to its preachers to administer the Sacrament of Holy Communion, Primitive Wesleyans withheld it; secondly, Wesleyan Methodists no longer saw themselves as societies within Anglicanism, whereas Primitive Wesleyans preferred to keep the link. In 1878, shortly after the disestablishment of the Church of Ireland, the two bodies came together to form the Methodist Church in Ireland.

6. Each Methodist congregation is known as a 'society' – a term which goes back to the origins of Methodism – and most societies are linked together with other societies into a 'circuit'.

7. Letter from Evelyn Pope, 19.4.2000.

8. Interview with Mabel Frost, 18.4.2000.

9. Interview with Herbert Gallagher, 17.2.2000.

10. J.C. Beckett, *A Short History of Ireland*, Hutchinson, London 1958, p. 177. The period of violence in Northern Ireland, 1968-93, was also known as 'The Troubles'.

11. R.H. Gallagher, *My Web of Time*, Nelson and Knox, Belfast, 1959, pp. 44-45.

12. Jack Gilpin, Letter, May 1999.

13. Robert Gallagher, *John Bredin*, Wesley Historical Society (Irish Branch), Belfast, 1960; Robert Gallagher, *Adam Clarke*, Wesley Historical Society (Irish Branch), 1963; and Robert Gallagher, *Pioneer Preachers of Irish Methodism*, Wesley Historical Society (Irish Branch), 1963.

14. Ronald Marshall, *Methodist College, Belfast. The First 100 Years 1868-1968*, Belfast, date of publication not known, p. 90. See also J.W. Henderson, *Methodist College, Belfast, 1868-1938*, Vols. I and II, published by the Governors of the Methodist College, Belfast, 1939.

15. *Methodist College Belfast*, p. 98.

16. Notes by Fred Jeffrey.

17. Sermon 'You are Rich', preached between 1940 and 1961, but not at M.C.B.

Chapter 3

1. Lay evangelist was the term used for a lay worker who served in various capacities: preaching and leading in worship, visitation, and possibly youth work.

2. The five other candidates included: Alan R. Booth, J. Dawson Cairns, James P. Campbell, Robert J. Storey and Frederick Twinem.

3. 'Dictators and Dictatorship', a paper presented at the TCD Philosophical Society in late 1934.

Chapter 4

1. Martin Wallace, *Belfast Telegraph*, 10.6.60.

2. *Belfast Telegraph*.

3. Interview with Edward R. Lindsay, 22.1.1999.

4. Collegians Rugby Club had been formed by former Methody pupils but both Lindsay and Booth, as former Wesley College pupils, would have been welcome.

Chapter 5

1. 'Duncher' is the Belfast term for a flat cap.

2. The War Services Committee of the Methodist Church in Ireland considered all applications for chaplaincy to the Forces.

3. See Jonathan Bardon, *A History of Ulster,* Blackstaff Press, Belfast, 1992, pp. 552-86; Janet Devlin, 'Bombs Over Belfast', A Series marking the 60th Anniversary of the Blitz, *Belfast Telegraph*, 7 April 2000; Brian Barton, *The Blitz. Belfast in the War Years*, Belfast,1989.

4. James Craig had taken the title Lord Craigavon on his elevation to the peerage.

5. Bardon, *A History of Ulster*, p. 561.

6. *A History of Ulster*, p. 563.

7. Eric Gallagher, 'Through an Eastern Window', *Portadown Times*, 20. 6. 1941.

8. Correspondence with Noel Burnside, 12.10.96.

Chapter 6

1. Correspondence with Donald Hayes, 10.1.2000.

Chapter 7

1. 'Reading of Stations' is the terminology used in the annual Irish Methodist Conference for reading and finalising the Stationing of Ministers in the Methodist Church in Ireland.

2. Alan Buchannan was later appointed Archbishop of Dublin.

3. Martyrs' Memorial Church opened on 3 October 1969 and has been regarded as the 'flagship' for Ian Paisley's Free Presbyterian Church.

4. Interview with Helen Todd, 19.4.2000.

Chapter 9

1. Eric Gallagher *At Points of Need. The story of the BCM 1889-1989*, Blackstaff Press, Belfast, 1989, pp. 8-9.

2. *At Points of Need*, p. 23.

3. The new wing was named in memory of the Revd R.M. Ker, Superintendent from 1905-25.

4. They did not belong to the Wesley Deaconess Order but were the last of the old style 'Mission Sisters'.

5. Robert Bradford resigned from the Methodist Church in 1974 and became MP for South Belfast. He was the first Northern Ireland MP to be assassinated in the Troubles when he was shot dead by a five-man Provisional IRA squad at a community centre in Finaghy, in his constituency, on 14 November 1981.

6. Correspondence with Bill Brown, 3.6.2002.

7. Some who attended these Film Services refer to a sense of acute embarrassment when Eric appealed for a generous offering. For his part Eric was concerned that some attended these Film Services and gave little or nothing in the offering.

8. *Belfast Newsletter*, 13.10.1958.

9. *Revivalist*, November 1958. Both the *Protestant Telegraph*, a newspaper, and the *Revivalist*, a magazine, were under Ian Paisley's editorial control.

10. Eric's article, *The Protestant Churches and Ian Paisley*, published by Abingdon Press in 1969, is possibly the only direct public response he ever made to Ian Paisley. See reference to the article in chapter 11.

11. *Belfast Telegraph*, 4.1.1964.

12. 'Assembly's College' was the Theological College of the Presbyterian Church in Ireland. When the theological department of Magee College, Londonderry, was amalgamated with the Assembly's College in 1980, the new college was named Union Theological College.

13. Canon Anthony Hanson was Professor of Theology at Hull University from 1963-81.

14. *Northern Whig*, 16.1.1961.

15. See Eric Gallagher, Points At Need, pp. 153-158.

16. The authors of the *Wesleyan* were Billy Buchanan, McMillan Carson, Richard Clarke, Ernest O'Neill, Cecil Rice and Donald Williamson. Buchanan, President MCI 1990-1991, was the only one of the six who stayed in Ireland.

17. Correspondence with Donald Williamson, 5.2.2003.

18. *MCI Reports and Agenda*, 1967, p. 161-63.

19. *Presbyterian Herald*, October 1948, p. 186.

20. Soon after Eric was appointed Secretary of the Conference he was given the assistance of the Revd Harold Sloan as Joint Convenor of the Inter-Church Relations Committee.

21. For a brief period the Congregationalists had shared in the Conversations along with the Methodists and Presbyterians.

22. Interview with Robert Murphy, 29.8.2000. The group often met in Jimmy Haire's house and included – along with Murphy, Haire and Eric – the following clergy: Cahal B. Daly, Desmond Wilson, John M. Barkley and Eric Elliot.

23. The location of the new university was a point of contention. Nationalists favoured Londonderry but Unionists preferred Coleraine. The choice of the latter was considered by some as one of the decisions that triggered the outbreak of violence in 1969.

24. The Methodist Church in Ireland, *A Call to the Methodist People and a Statement of what the Methodist Church Believes*, Belfast, 1966.

Chapter 10

1. Quotations in this chapter are taken from a large book containing press cuttings – unfortunately the actual newspaper is never identified – letters and cards.

2. The main points of NICRA's campaign included calls for: a universal franchise for local government elections instead of one based on rate-payers and the ending of the company vote ('one man, one vote'); the redrawing of electoral boundaries to end gerrymandering; the introduction of laws to end discrimination

in local government employment; a compulsory points system for public housing to ensure fair allocation; the repeal of the Special Powers Act; and the disbanding of the wholly Protestant police reserve force, the Ulster Special Constabulary (the B Specials).

3. On a few occasions the PCI Moderator 'on grounds of conscience' has not felt able to publicly identify himself with the Roman Catholic Primate.

4. Gallagher is referring to some criticism in Ireland that the Programme to Combat Racism was funding terrorism in South Africa and Rhodesia (Zimbabwe). This allegation received considerable support among Presbyterians and was possibly the main reason behind the PCI decision to withdraw from the WCC in 1980.

Chapter 11

1. The Ulster Protestant Volunteers (UPV) was a Loyalist paramilitary organisation which regarded itself as a society of Protestant patriots committed to upholding the Constitution of Northern Ireland as an integral part of the United Kingdom. It was under the control of the Ulster Constitution Defence Committee (UCDC) which had been set up in 1966 under the chairmanship of the Revd Ian Paisley.

2. Electoral changes were implemented in 1971.

3. Eric Gallagher and Stanley Worrall, *Christians in Ulster 1968-1980*, OUP, 1982, pp. 41-42.

4. Quoted in Tim Pat Coogan, *The Troubles*, London, Hutchinson, 1995, p. 36.

5. In a complicated election some Unionists stood as pro-O'Neill candidates and some clearly opposed him. The election indicated that 10 'Official' Unionists still opposed the Prime Minister.

6. *Belfast Telegraph*, 10.1 1969.

7. Norman W. Taggart, *Conflict, Controversy and Co-operation. The Irish Council of Churches and 'The Troubles', 1968-1972*, Columba Press, 2004, p. 94.

8. The six signatories were: James McCann, the Church of Ireland Primate; Jack Withers, the Presbyterian Moderator; Gerald Myles, the President of the Methodist Church in Ireland; Albert McElroy, Non-Subscribing Presbyterian Church; Joseph Cooper

of the Moravian Church; Lt.Col. George Snell of the Salvation Army, and Norah Douglas of the Religious Society of Friends.

9. Cardinal Conway's analysis that Loyalists were responsible for the 18 April bombings was later proven to be correct.

10. Probationary ministers served on circuit for two to three years after College training and prior to ordination. The annual 'trial sermon' was the term used to assess a probationer's preaching and conduct of worship during a designated evening service. Local ministers first met to listen to the probationer and following the service they analysed her/his homiletical skills.

11. *Conference Agenda*, 1969.

12. Interview with Sandy Scott, 18.4.2000.

13. *Irish Times*, 30.12.1969.

14. Bew and Gillespie, *Northern Ireland. A Chronology of the Troubles 1968-1993*, Gill and Macmillan, 1993, p. 18.

15. *Protestant Telegraph*, 18.3.1967, pp. 6-7.

16. Taggart, *Conflict, Controversy and Co-operation, The Irish Council of Churches and the Troubles*, 1968-72. p. 99.

17. *Conflict, Controversy and Co-operation*, p. 99.

18. *Conflict, Controversy and Co-operation*, p. 67.

19. Later called the Inter-Church Reconciliation Fund.

20. Quoted in Farrell, *Northern Ireland: The Orange State*, Pluto Press, 1990, p. 270.

21. W.D. Flackes & Sydney Elliott, *Northern Ireland. A Political Directory 1968-1993*, Blackstaff Press, p. 214.

22. *Northern Ireland. A Political Directory 1968-1995*, pp. 249 and 109.

23. Interview with Eric Gallagher, 9.12.1996.

24. W.D. Flackes & Sydney Elliott, *Northern Ireland. A Political Directory 1968-1993*, p. 110.

25. This information has been checked with Professor Richard English, School of Politics and International Studies, the Queen's University of Belfast.

Chapter 12

1. Bew and Gillespie, *Northern Ireland. A Chronology of the Troubles 1968-1993*, p. 46.

2. Barbara Gallagher, *Embers from the Fires of Ulster*, Christian Journals, 1977, p. 39.

3. Bew and Gillespie, *Northern Ireland. A Chronology of the Troubles 1968-1993*, p. 53.

4. *Irish Times*, 26.6.1972.

5. Bew and Gillespie, *Northern Ireland. A Chronology of the Troubles, 1968-1993*, p. 54.

6. *Northern Ireland. A Chronology of the Troubles 1968-1993*, p. 56.

7. Gallagher and Worrall, *Christians in Ulster 1968-1980*, p. 134.

8. *Presbyterian Church in Ireland Annual Reports*, 1974, p. 98.

9. Taggart, *Conflict, Controversy and Co-operation, The Irish Council of Churches and 'The Troubles', 1968-1972*, pp. 111-112.

10. *Irish Times* 27.9.1973.

11. Bew and Gillespie, *Northern Ireland. A Chronology of the Troubles 1968-1993*, p. 60.

12. *Northern Ireland. A Chronology of the Troubles 1968-1993*, p. 61.

13. *Protestant Telegraph* 26.5.1973.

14. Bew and Gillespie, *Northern Ireland. A Chronology of the Troubles 1968-1993*, p. 72-73.

Chapter 13

1. Garrett Fitzgerald, *All in a Life. Garrett Fitzgerald, An Autobiography*. Dublin, Gill and Macmillan, 1991, p. 238.

2. Gallagher and Worrall, *Christians in Ulster 1968-1980*, pp. 90-91.

3. Ken Bloomfield, *Stormont in Crisis. A Memoir*. Belfast, Blackstaff Press, 1994, p. 215.

4. Gallagher and Worrall, *Christians in Ulster 1968-1980*, p. 96.

5. *Belfast Telegraph* 21.12.1974.

6. Gallagher and Worrall, *Christians in Ulster 1968-1980*, p. 96.

7. W.D. Flackes and Sydney Elliott, *Northern Ireland. A Political Directory, 1968-1993*, pp. 157-158.

8. *Belfast Telegraph* 12.12.1974.

9. *Newsletter* 13.12.1974.

10. *Belfast Telegraph* 12.12.1974.

11. *Cork Examiner* 12.12.1974. The appeal was signed by William Cardinal Conway, Roman Catholic Primate; G. Temple Lundie, PCI Moderator; R. Desmond Morris, MCI President; and George O. Simms, COI Primate.

12. Eric Gallagher, *At Points of Need. The Story of the Belfast Central Mission 1889-1989*, p. 114.

13. Bew and Gillespie, *Northern Ireland. A Chronology of the Troubles 1968-1993*. p. 97.

Chapter 14

1. Sandy Row came under the aegis of the Belfast Central Mission in 1982.

2. Interview with Robin Roddie, 4.3. 2004.

3. Bew and Gillespie, *Northern Ireland. A Chronology of the Troubles 1968-1993,* p. 109.

4. *Methodist Recorder* 10.1.1976.

5. Bew and Gillespie, *Northern Ireland. A Chronology of the Troubles 1968-1993*, p. 106.

6. *Northern Ireland. A Chronology of the Troubles 1968-1993*, p. 113.

7. W.D.Flackes and Sydney Elliott, *Northern Ireland. A Political Directory, 1968-1993*, pp. 157-58.

8. *Violence in Ireland. A Report to the Churches*, Christian Journals, Belfast, and Veritas Publications, Dublin, 1976.

9. Interview with Cardinal Cahal Daly, 28.6.2000.

10. *Violence in Ireland. A Report to the Churches*, pp. 50-51.

11. Interview with David Gallagher, 3.7.2000.

12. Barbara Gallagher, *Embers From the Fires of Ulster*, Christian Journals, Belfast, 1977.

13. The Durham 'Big Meeting' was a gathering of Methodists across the north-east of England to which many of Methodism's leading preachers were invited. It was held around the same time as the Durham Miners' Gala.

14. *The Methodist Newsletter*, October 1977.

15. *The Methodist Newsletter*, November 1977.

16. Belfast Central Mission *Inter-Com,* June 1979. *Inter-Com* was the name of the news sheet given to members of the Grosvenor Hall congregation.

Chapter 15

1. Eric Gallagher's unpublished Prayer Notes, 18.12.1976. These were handwritten notes of his daily 'conversations' with God during part of the 1970s.

2. Interview with Helen Shiels, 30.8.2000.

3. This is referred to in chapter 9.

4. Interview with Ruth Twyble, 26.6.2000.

5. A knighthood was conferred on Joe Pope in 1980.

Chapter 16

1. The source and substance of this suggestion are not given in Autobiographical Notes. He describes the idea as 'a pipe dream but persuasive'.

2. David Gallagher's doctoral thesis, 'The failure of attempts to solve the Northern Ireland problem, 1972-1980', made him eminently suitable to assist in this research.

3. This request must have been made before Norman Taggart left the Mission in 1987.

4. *The Methodist Newsletter*, May 1981.

5. PCI's withdrawal of membership is considered fully in Dennis Cooke, 'A failed romance? Irish Presbyterianism and the World Council of Churches' in *Ebb and Flow. Essays in Church History in honour of R. Finlay G. Holmes*, ed. by W. Donald Patton, Presbyterian Historical Society of Ireland, 2002.

6. Bew and Gillespie, *Northern Ireland. A Chronology of the Troubles 1968-1993*, pp. 138-57.

7. The 11+ selection system was introduced in 1948 and has continued, in principle, to the present. Children in their final year of primary school sat a test – usually two one-hour papers, but the precise format has varied. About 30 per cent of the children – those with the highest scores – were offered places in grammar schools, the others attended secondary schools. Among the many criticisms of the system were that selection, based on a couple of short tests, was a very blunt instrument, that those who did not achieve the highest grades suffered a loss of self-esteem, that selection at 11+ was too early as it made no allowance for children who were late developers, and that some children were unfairly advantaged as their parents could pay for extensive coaching.

8. Counties Cavan and Monaghan are two of the nine counties in the Province of Ulster. Both counties are within the jurisdiction of the Republic of Ireland. The border separates them from Counties Armagh, Tyrone and Fermanagh in Northern Ireland.

9. Dr Ranson was MCI President 1961-62.

10. Bew and Gillespie, *Northern Ireland. A Chronology of the Troubles, 1968-1993*, p. 134.

11. Gallagher and Worrall, *Christians in Ulster, 1968-1980*, p. 147.

12. Michael Hurley, *Healing and Hope. Memories of an Irish Ecumenist*, The Columba Press, 2003, pp. 60-61.

13. *Irish Times* 1.6.1984.

14. This was a London-based lecture organised by friends of the ISE in London.

15. Co-operation North was renamed Co-operation Ireland in 1998.

16. *A Citizens' Inquiry. The Opsahl Report on Northern Ireland*, edited by Andy Pollak, The Lilliput Press, 1993, p. 56.

Chapter 17

1. Funeral Address by the Revd E.T.I. Mawhinney.

2. Funeral Address.

Bibliography

Primary Sources

Gallagher, Barbara, *Embers from the Fires of Ulster*, Christian Journals, 1977.
Embers and Echoes, Christian Journals, 1995.

Gallagher, Eric, *At Points of Need. The story of BCM 1889-1989*, Blackstaff Press, Belfast, 1989.
Autobiographical Notes (unpublished).
Jottings (unpublished).
Papers and Speeches (unpublished).
Prayer Notes (unpublished).
Poems (unpublished).
Sermons (unpublished).
The Protestant Churches and Ian Paisley, Abingdon Press, 1969.

Gallagher, Eric and Worrall, Stanley, *Christians in Ulster 1968-1980*, OUP, 1982.

Select Bibliography

Adams, Gerry, *Before the Dawn. An Autobiography*, Brandon, Dingle, 1996.
Free Ireland: Towards a Lasting Peace, Brandon, Dingle, 1986.

Bardon, Jonathan, *A History of Ulster*, Blackstaff Press, Belfast, 1992.

Barritt, Denis P. and Carter, Charles F., *The Northern Ireland Problem*, OUP, London, 1962.

Barton, The Blitz. *Belfast in the War Years*, Belfast, 1989.

Beckett, J.C. *A Short History of Ireland*, Hutchinson, London, 1958.
The Making of Modern Ireland 1603-1923, Faber and Faber, London, 1966.

Bell, J. Bowyer, *The Secret Army. The IRA, 1916-1979*, Poolbeg, Dublin, 1995.

Bew, Paul and Gillespie, Gordon, Northern Ireland, *A Chronology of the Troubles -1993*, Gill and Macmillan, 1993.

Bishop, Patrick, and Mallie, Eamonn, *The Provisional IRA*, Corgi Books, 1992.

Bleakley, David, *Peace in Ulster*, Mowbrays, London, 1972.

Bloomfield, Ken, *Stormont in a Crisis. A Memoir,* Blackstaff Press, Belfast, 1994.

Boyd, Andrew, *Brian Faulkner and the Crisis of Ulster Unionism*, Anvil Books, Tralee, County Kerry, 1972.

Brewer, John D., and Higgins, Gareth I., *Anti-Catholicism in Northern Ireland, 1600-1998. The Mote and the Beam*, Macmillan Press, London, 1998.

Coogan, Tim Pat, *The Troubles. Ireland's Ordeal 1966-1995 and the Search for Peace*, Hutchinson, London, 1995.

Cooke, Dennis, *Persecuting Zeal. A Portrait of Ian Paisley*, Brandon, Dingle, 1996.

Curtis, Edmund, *A History of Ireland*, Methuen, London, 1957.

Cusack, Jim, and McDonald, Henry, *UVF*, Poolbeg, Dublin, 1997.

Daly, Cahal B., *Steps on my Pilgrim Journey. Memoirs and Reflections*, Veritas, Dublin, 1998.

Devlin, Paddy, *Straight Left. An Autobiography*, Blackstaff Press, Belfast, 1993.

Dillon, Martin, *The Shankill Butchers. A Case Study of Mass Murder*, Arrow Books, London, 1990.
  The Dirty War, Arrow Books, London, 1991.
  God and the Gun. The Church and Irish Terrorism, Orion, London, 1998.

Ellis, Ian, *Vision and Reality. A Survey of Twentieth Century Irish Inter-Church Relations*, The Institute of Irish Studies, The Queen's University of Belfast, 1992.

Ellis, Ian, and Hurley, Michael, *The Irish Inter-Church Meeting. Background and Development*, IICM, Belfast, 1998.

Farrell, Michael, *Northern Ireland. The Orange State*. Pluto Press, London, 1990.

Fitzgerald, Garrett, *All in a Life. Garrett Fitzgerald, An Autobiography*, Gill and Macmillan, Dublin, 1991.

Flackes, W.D. and Elliott, Sydney, *Northern Ireland. A Political Directory 1968-1993,* Blackstaff Press, 1994.

Gallagher, Robert H., *My Web of Time*, Nelson and Knox, Belfast, 1959.
  John Bredin, Wesley Historical Society (Irish Branch), Belfast, 1960.
  Adam Clarke, Wesley Historical Society (Irish Branch), 1963.
  Pioneer Preachers of Irish Methodism, Wesley Historical Society [Irish Branch], 1963.

Harris, Mary, *The Catholic Church and the Foundation of the Northern Irish State*, Cork University Press, Cork, 1991.

Hayes, Maurice, *Minority Verdict. Experiences of a Catholic Public Servant*, Blackstaff Press, Belfast, 1995.

Henderson, J.W., *Methodist College, Belfast, 1968-1938*, Vols. I and II, published by the Governors of Methodist College, Belfast, 1939.

Holland, Jack, and McDonald, Henry, *INLA. Deadly Divisions*, Torc, Dublin, 1994.

Hurley, Michael, *Christian Unity: an ecumenical second spring?* Veritas, Dublin, 1998.

    Healing and Hope. Memories of an Irish Ecumenist, Columba Press, Blackrock, County Dublin, 1993.

Liechty, Joseph, and Clegg, Cecilia, *Moving Beyond Sectarianism. Religion, Conflict, Reconciliation in Northern Ireland*, Columba Press, Blackrock, County Dublin, 2001.

Marshall, Ronald, *Methodist College, Belfast. The First 100 Years 1868-1968*, Belfast. Date of publication not known.

Mitchell, George, *Making Peace. The inside story of the making of the Good Friday Agreement*, William Heinemann, London, 1999.

Mulryne, T.W. and McAllister, W.J. (eds.), *Esteem. Liber amicorum. Essays in honour of Revd Dr R.D.E. Gallagher,* Methodist College, Belfast, 1994.

McIvor, Basil, *Hope Deferred. Experiences of an Irish Unionist*, Blackstaff Press, Belfast, 1998.

McKittrick, David, and McVea, David, *Making Sense of the Troubles*, Blackstaff Press, Belfast, 2000.

Pollak, Andy, (ed.), *A Citizens' Inquiry. The Opsahl Report on Northern Ireland*, Lilliput Press, Dublin, 1993.

Patton, Donald W., (ed.), *Ebb and Flow. Essays in honour of R. Finlay G. Holmes.* Presbyterian Historical Society of Ireland, Belfast, 2002.

Purdy, Ann, *Molyneaux: The Long View*, Greystone Books, 1989.

Richardson, Norman, (ed.), *A Tapestry of Beliefs. Christian Traditions in Northern Ireland*, Blackstaff Press, Belfast, 1998.

Stewart, A.T.Q., *The Ulster Crisis. Resistance to Home Rule, 1912-1914*, Faber and Faber, London, 1979.

Taggart, Norman W., *Conflict, Controversy and Co-operation. The Irish Council of Churches and 'The Troubles', 1968-1972*, Columba Press, 2004.

Taylor, Peter, *Loyalists*, Bloomsbury, London, 1999.

    Violence in Ireland. A Report to the Churches, Christian Journals, Belfast, and Veritas Publications, Dublin, 1976.

White, Barry, *John Hume. Statesman of the Troubles*, Blackstaff Press, Belfast, 1984.

Index